EXPLORING THE GERMAN LANGUAGE

SALLY JOHNSON

Lecturer,
Department of Linguistics,
Lancaster University

ARNOLD

A member of the Hodder Headline Group
LONDON • NEW YORK • SYDNEY • AUCKLAND

First published in Great Britain in 1998 by
Arnold, a member of the Hodder Headline Group,
338 Euston Road, London NW1 3BH

http://www.arnoldpublishers.com

Co-published in the United States of America by
Oxford University Press Inc.,
198 Madison Avenue, New York, NY 10016

British Library Cataloguing in Publication Data
A catalogue entry for this book is available from the British Library

Library of Congress Cataloging-in-Publication Data
Johnson, Sally A.
  Exploring the German language / Sally Johnson.
    p.   cm.
  Includes bibliographical references and index.
  ISBN 0–340–66330–8 (hardcover). — ISBN 0–340–66329–4 (pbk.)
  1. German language—Grammar.   2. German language—Textbooks for
foreign speakers—English.   I. Title.
PF3112.J64   1998
438.2´421—dc21   98–18303
                                                                          CIP

ISBN 0 340 66329 4 (pb)
     0 340 66330 8 (hb)

1 2 3 4 5 6 7 8 9 10

Production Editor: Rada Radojicic
Production Controller: Priya Gohil

Composition in 10/12pt Sabon by Phoenix Photosetting, Chatham, Kent
Printed and bound in the United Kingdom by MPG Books Ltd, Bodmin, Cornwall

Contents

Preface

As is often the case with books of this kind, this volume has been written primarily with the needs of my own students in mind. For the past few years, I have been teaching German linguistics and sociolinguistics at Lancaster University. I have used many excellent textbooks but have failed to identify any one volume which fulfilled all our needs simultaneously. These included: a) coverage of the diverse areas which I wanted to introduce to students; b) a style which was accessible, in particular, to first years; and c) the provision of exercises which students could pursue in their own time. I sincerely hope that students other than those at Lancaster will also be able to benefit from it in the future.

Recent developments in British university teaching of foreign languages remain something of an enigma. Students (we are told) are increasingly opting for 'practical' degree schemes with *language* as their primary focus. Yet despite this perceived demand, the kind of structured teaching which can be offered by specialist linguists seems sadly lacking. Too few courses, for example, dedicate sufficient time to formal training in pronunciation. We send students abroad, largely unprepared for the considerable linguistic variation they are certain to encounter (at least in German-speaking countries). And we espouse communicative approaches to grammar teaching using 'real texts' yet, for the most part, fail to pass on to students the enormous insights afforded by discourse analysts into the properties of the very texts we work with. In short, the focus on practical language teaching does not appear to be matched by the provision of linguistic and sociolinguistic approaches which see language as a meaningful and worthwhile object of study in its own right.

Students are requesting 'practical' degree schemes which concentrate on language. *Culture* – which frequently and ironically goes by the name of *content* – is then presented under the separate rubric 'option'. Ongoing disputes about whether these options can be taught in the foreign language are a further illustration of the artificial opposition between language and culture. Moreover, the continuing debate on the state of students' grammatical knowledge fails to take into account that if you all but erase the one area of study which has traditionally bridged the language/culture divide, namely, literature, *and* fail to teach in the foreign language, then it is no surprise that students struggle to absorb the grammatical structures they so desperately need. Where is their extended exposure to the language going to come from?

Like its sister volume, *Exploring the French Language* (Lodge *et al.*, 1997), this book is an attempt to provide an alternative approach – one where language is simultaneously conceived of as *form* and *content*. Though no single text can transform the scenario I have somewhat polemically sketched, it can nonetheless help in a small way to change it, by providing students with a systematic framework for studying both the German language and the German language *as* culture. When writing this book, therefore, it has been my aim to introduce students of German not only to the insights of linguistics and sociolinguistics generally but also to try to dismantle from the outset the notion that language and culture are somehow discrete objects of study. It is my hope that, after reading this book, they too will appreciate, first, that the German language cannot be learned adequately without reference to the culture(s) of the German-speaking countries and, second, that many fascinating cultural insights can be accessed by exploring the language used in those countries.

Sally Johnson
Lancaster, August 1997

Acknowledgements

Even a single-authored book is ultimately a joint venture, and there are many people I would like to thank personally for their help, advice, and support. I am indebted to Martin Durrell without whose recommendation this book might never have happened and also to Katrin Kohl for her advice in the early stages. Lesley Riddle at Edward Arnold was a most supportive editor, who was always available and willing to discuss the project. Many thanks also to Elena Seymenliyska, Rada Radojicic, Bill Houston and Susan Dunsmore at Arnold for their copy-editing and production of the book. Anthony Lodge and his colleagues kindly allowed me to see the unpublished manuscript of their volume *Exploring the French Language*, which was most helpful, and particularly influenced my own Chapters 1 and 10.

I would like to thank my friends and colleagues in the Department of German Studies at Lancaster University: Graham Bartram, Manuela Beck, Allyson Fiddler, Christine Flude, Margaret Ives, Phil Payne, Dankmute Pohl, Birgit Smith, Annik Taylor and Tony Waine. Without the term's sabbatical leave in the summer of 1996, during which they all covered for me in one way or another, I would never have been able to complete the project.

My sabbatical leave was spent at the Institut für deutsche Sprache (IDS) in Mannheim and was generously funded by the Deutscher Akademischer Austauschdienst (DAAD). Many thanks to the head of the IDS, Professor Dr Gerhard Stickel, for making me so welcome, and also to Dr Ricarda Wolf for her great kindness and hospitality.

There are a number of other people whose hospitality I have enjoyed along the way: Hans and Rosa Muhr in Vienna; Rudi, Marie and David Muhr in Graz; Angelika Böll, Hille Schüren, Manuel Schüren and Viktor Böll in Cologne; Karl-Heiner and Janis Busse in Göttingen; Kirsty Cameron and Michael Martin in Münster; Angelika Martin in Berlin; and André Magar, Monique Magar, Ian Sayers and Patricia Magar-Sayers in Haguenau, Alsace.

I would particularly like to thank Patrick Stevenson and Martin Durrell who read the whole of the manuscript and made many excellent suggestions for improvement. Beth Linklater, Margaret Ives and David Nott also read earlier drafts and made many useful comments. Thanks also to all those students at Lancaster between 1993 and 1998 who took my courses, 'German Linguistics' (Germ 212) and 'Language and Society in the German-speaking Countries' (Germ 213). Very special thanks to the following students who read various chapters and also tried out the exercises: Hayley Burgess, Susan Cocker, Helen Edwards, Mathew Epps, Margaret Evans, Steven Garbutt, Karen Hirst, Julie Humpherson, Jemima Looser and Embjörg Sudhof. It goes without saying that any remaining errors are entirely my own.

The artwork was provided by Jonathan Geddes in the Graphics Unit at Lancaster University, the funding for which was kindly made available by my colleagues in the 'Centre for Language in Social Life' in the Department of Linguistics at Lancaster University.

Examples in section 5.1 are taken from Fox (1990). All the examples in section 5.2 (with minor modifications) are taken from Hall (1992). The majority of examples in sections 5.3 and 5.4 are taken from MacCarthy (1975), Fox (1990) and Hall (1992). Examples in section 6.3.1 are from Fox (1990), chapter 3. Exercise 2 in Chapter 6 has been adapted from Kürschner (1993: 83). Most of the German examples in section 8.2.1 are taken from Fox (1990), chapter 6 and Kürschner (1993), chapter 2.

The author and the publisher would like to thank the following for permission to use copyright material:

Bravo for 'Flirting with Disaster – Abgefahrene Komödie', © BRAVO 27/1996; Langen Müller Herbig, Munich, for extracts from Brigitte Schwaiger *Der Mann fürs Leben*, © 1993; dpa Deutsche Presse-Agentur GmbH for 'Gehaltsausbau' from *Frankfurter Rundschau*, 19 June 1996; Deutschland for 'Marion Gräfin Dönhoff – Dame am Puls der Zeit', from *Deutschland*, vol. 2, April 1996, © Zeitschrift 'Deutschland'; Focus Magazin Verlag for 'Sozialdemokraten: Für eine "linke Regierung" mit der PDS' © FOCUS 27/1996; *TV Hören und Sehen* for 'Weniger Drogentote. Grund zur Entwarnung?', © *TV Hören und Sehen*, Ulrike Fach, 27/1996.

Every effort has been made to trace all copyright holders of material. Any rights not acknowledged here will be acknowledged in subsequent printings if sufficient notice is given to the publisher.

Last but certainly not least, thanks to Frank for food, love, endless proof-reading, and even more endless discussions about this book and the nature of language and language teaching. His consistent kindness, enthusiasm, and support were, as always, what kept me going.

1

Introduction

Most people who learn German do so with a practical purpose in mind: to be able to communicate with others in German-speaking countries. In order to achieve this, they dedicate themselves to the practical tasks of reading, writing, speaking and listening to the language. But there comes a time when more advanced learners begin to feel that this practical approach is insufficient. They realise that successful communication does not only depend on *knowing* the German language – they also need to *know about* it. Why is this?

There are many things which people know intuitively about language but can only comment upon in a fairly superficial manner. When listening to their own language, for example, most people can discern different national and regional accents. But how many can actually say something specific about how or why pronunciation varies? Similarly, most people have implicit knowledge about what is grammatically right and wrong in their own language. But how many can really analyse the mistakes made by a non-native speaker in order to explain them clearly and competently? Part of the problem, it seems, is that people tend not to have the necessary *vocabulary* with which to talk about language. This compares to trained linguists who generally know how to describe differences in pronunciation or can account for grammatical errors. This is not least because they have a command of the appropriate **meta-language**, in other words, the language used for describing language.

Linguistics is the academic discipline concerned with the study of language. It deals with many different aspects of language, of which pronunciation and grammar are but two examples. Having said this, it is not the purpose of this book to provide the reader with an introduction to linguistics in general terms (see, for example, Fromkin and Rodman, 1993). Instead, the aim here is to introduce advanced learners of German to the methods and meta-language developed by linguists, and then apply these to the study of German. Among other things, it is hoped that students will thereby discover new ways of talking *about* the German language.

At this stage, the reader would be perfectly justified in asking 'Why spend time and effort talking *about* German, when I could be getting on with the task of actually learning the language?' Perhaps it is easiest if I try to offer a personal explanation here. First of all, I have always found that possessing the vocabulary to describe language has helped me enormously when faced with things I do not understand in German. Rather than having to satisfy myself with explanations such as 'Well, that's the way German is', linguistics offers me a more structured approach. In short, I have found that linguistics has helped me to learn German more easily. The second point is that a knowledge of linguistics has actually increased my enjoyment of learning German. It has enhanced my curiosity about the language, constantly leading me to ask new questions about the way it works and how it compares to English. Third, I have found linguistic knowledge to be an invaluable tool when teaching both German and English as a foreign language. While there are many aspects of both languages which I still have difficulty explaining to students, linguistics has given me the vocabulary I need to discuss language with learners, describing the problems they encounter, and helping to find solutions to those problems.

But the fact that a knowledge of linguistics can function as a useful aid when teaching and learning foreign languages is only part of the story. This is because language is not just the medium we use to *communicate* with others – it is also the tool with which we *think* about ourselves, other people, and the world in which we live. Have you ever wondered how much thinking you can do without language? How can you describe your ideas, friends, or surroundings without resorting to words? Moreover, the particular language with which we do our thinking – whether English, French, or Japanese – is central to our sense of who we are in cultural terms. Indeed, one of the main differences between English-, French-, and Japanese-speaking cultures is not merely the fact the different languages are used; it is that each of those languages permits, sometimes even encourages, different ways of thinking about the world.

It follows, then, that if we want to understand something about the way in which German speakers think about themselves and the world in which *they* live, then a useful place to begin is by looking at the language they use in order to do so. Again, this is because the German language is not simply the medium via which German speakers communicate with one another, it is closely bound up with who they are culturally. In short: the study of language is also the study of culture. With the help of this book, it is therefore hoped that students will find new ways of exploring not only the German *language,* but of talking and thinking about German-speaking *cultures*.

1.1 Outline of the book

Exploring the German Language is divided into three sections: Part I, The history and geography of German; Part II, The structures of German; and Part III, Using German in the real world.

1.1.1 Part I: The history and geography of German

Chapter 2 introduces the reader to the historical development of German. Why study the history of the language? Is it not possible to learn German by concentrating on the way it is used today? On one level, the answer is yes. You can no doubt acquire German without knowing very much about where it comes from. But you can learn so much more if you have a basic understanding of how the language has grown over the years. Why is it, for example, that the English words 'father' and 'mother' are so like the German *Vater* and *Mutter*? In what ways did National Socialism or the division of Germany affect the use of the language in the twentieth century? These are all questions which can only be answered by considering the German language in its historical context. Moreover, the history of German is also the history of the people who speak it. Exploring the development of the language is, therefore, an interesting way of discovering more about the customs and traditions of German-speaking cultures.

Chapter 3 considers German from a slightly different perspective: geography. If you are going to learn a foreign language, then it is helpful to know exactly where it is spoken. Most learners of German are aware that the language they are studying can be used in Germany, Switzerland, and Austria. But it is generally less well known that there are German-speaking individuals and groups in France, Denmark, Belgium, Italy, Poland, Israel, and many other countries around the world. This does not, however, mean that the language enjoys the same status in each of those places. Students need therefore to appreciate how and why the use of German would be likely to provoke very different reactions in parts of Italy or Belgium than in, say, Poland or Israel – reactions which are invariably linked to the historical issues discussed in Chapter 2.

1.1.2 Part II: The structures of German

Chapter 4 and Chapter 5 provide an introduction to pronunciation. For most learners of German, the importance of being able to *speak* – and not just write – the language has increased markedly over the years. Most courses now place considerable emphasis on oral tasks performed in German, such as presentations, summaries, or interpreting. Clearly, therefore, it makes sense to spend time and effort on the acquisition of correct pronunciation. Poor pronunciation can lead to all kinds of misunderstandings, and good pronunciation is one of the main means by which we create an impression upon the people with whom we are conversing. These two chapters are dedicated to helping students understand more about the way in which German is pronounced. They describe the sounds of German in detail and provide practical guidance on the kinds of problems typically experienced by non-native speakers. Moreover, Chapter 5 shows how differences in German and English patterns of intonation can account for the occasional intercultural misunderstandings which may occur between speakers of the two languages. This is because, in some situations, German and English have different ways of using intonation to express such sentiments as politeness and friendliness.

The next two chapters discuss a different aspect of language structure, namely grammar. Chapter 6 concentrates on the structure of German words while Chapter 7 deals with the structure of German sentences. 'Grammar' is a familiar and frequently rather ominous concept where students of foreign languages are concerned. The extent to which it is studied explicitly varies according to trends in language teaching methodology and the preferences of individual teachers and students. But there comes a point at which most learners realise that they need to know more about grammar. Sadly, what many students tell me is that they would like to spend time on the subject, but often have difficulty understanding the terminology used in the grammar books available to them. Once again, the problem would appear to be one of meta-language. As you will see in Chapters 6 and 7, the way in which linguists talk about grammar is not necessarily the same as the approach taken by writers of grammar books, but there is considerable overlap. After reading these two chapters you will therefore hopefully feel more readily equipped with the specialist vocabulary needed to use grammar books and other reference works such as dictionaries.

Having looked at the grammar of words in Chapter 6, Chapter 8 turns to the meaning of German words. It may seem rather strange to spend a whole chapter discussing meaning. Surely words mean what they mean! But consider what it is like translating a passage from German to English. Quite apart from the fact that the grammatical structures of the two languages may differ, there are many situations where the most direct translation of a word is not always appropriate. Chapter 8 takes a look at the relationship between words and the objects, concepts and ideas to which they refer. Importantly, it shows how that relationship need not necessarily be the same across languages. Thus, one of the most challenging aspects of translation stems from the fact that words which appear to have the same meaning are often used in different ways in different languages.

1.1.3   Part III: Using German in the real world

All learners know that, in practice, speaking or writing a foreign language involves using structures such as sounds, words, and sentences simultaneously. Having said this, the study of language does not end with the analysis of sentences. Part III therefore considers the way in which German works 'beyond the level of the sentence'. In other words, it looks at what happens to the language when it is used in real situations in the real world.

Chapter 9 deals with two relatively new areas in linguistics both of which explore meaning in context. Take, for example, the statement *Mir ist kalt*. If you were to translate this literally, you would no doubt come up with something like: 'I am cold'. Yet there are many situations in which this sentence could mean something different. If you are sitting in a friend's house and it is snowing outside, *Mir ist kalt* might be a polite request to close a door or even to switch up the heating. Clearly, therefore, the meaning of a word or sentence can change considerably according to the context in which it is used. The second half of Chapter 9 looks at a further area where the meaning of German very much depends on context, namely, in written texts. This section shows that it is not only sentences which have to be structured in a certain way, but that there is also such a thing as a 'grammar of texts'. The reader will therefore be introduced to the ways in which texts need to be organised if they are going to make sense, something which is a great help when writing essays.

Finally, Chapter 10 explores another important aspect of language in the real world: how and why different people *vary* the kind of German they use. This chapter brings together every other aspect of the language discussed so far. It shows how the use of the many dialects of German is closely related to the historical and geographical factors outlined in Chapters 2 and 3. We also see that, when talking about different styles of German, such as standard/dialect, written/spoken, formal/informal, we need to draw on the technical terminology introduced in Part II of the book. In this way, we can describe the pronunciation, grammar, and meaning of these varieties much more accurately.

Perhaps most significantly, however, Chapter 10 demonstrates how the study of the German language is also the study of German-speaking cultures. Thus, we explore not only the ways in which different styles of German are *used* by different speakers but also how these may be *interpreted* by others. This takes us back to a point which was mentioned earlier – the German language is central to the way in which German speakers think about themselves, others, and the world in which they live. Moreover, we discover that what sometimes distinguishes German- from English-speaking cultures is not just the fact that two different languages are used – but that the two languages may also be used and interpreted *differently* by their respective speakers.

1.2   Using this book

This book can be read by anyone who is interested in finding out more about the German language and/or used as a textbook to accompany an introductory course in German linguistics. Either way, it has been specifically designed for readers who have little or no knowledge of linguistics, in general, or German linguistics, in particular.

I have tried not to use any technical terminology without explaining it first. Whenever a new term is used for the first time, it appears in bold type. If, however, you come across a technical word or phrase which occurred earlier in the text, then you can refer to the index which will guide you to other pages where the same term is used in a different context.

Another feature of the book is the group of exercises at the end of each chapter. In many cases, the exercises specifically request that the reader go back to a particular section of a chapter, or look at a map or table. The reader should not feel obliged to do all the exercises in one sitting. However, I have generally presented them in the same order in which the topics are covered in the chapter, and predominantly in order of difficulty, so it probably makes sense to do them in the order in which they appear. All answers are given at the back of the book. The exercises can therefore be used for the purposes of self-study.

Finally, at the end of each chapter there is a list of sources and recommended reading. Here I have included those texts to which I have referred in detail when writing this book and/or those which I think are particularly useful for readers who may want to explore certain topics in greater depth. All other references are listed in the bibliography.

THE HISTORY AND GEOGRAPHY OF GERMAN

2

The German language past and present

One of the most exciting things about learning a foreign language is the way in which we constantly discover similarities between that language and our mother tongue. Consciously or subconsciously, we use these links to make sense of words and ideas which we have never come across before. It follows, then, that the more we know about the origins of German and its relationship with other languages, the better we will be at understanding any unfamiliar concepts which we might encounter in the future.

Take the English word 'father', for example. It is easy to see that 'father' is somehow related to the German *Vater*. Even though the two words are spelled and pronounced differently, they are obviously still quite similar. Now consider the Spanish word *padre* and the French *père*. Again, there can be no denying that the word for 'father' is somehow related in all four languages, but the extent of that relationship differs. In terms of their similarity, English and German are closer to one another than to Spanish and French. On the other hand, none of these four languages would appear to have very much in common with Japanese where the word for '(my) father' is *chichi*.

This one example shows how the German language does not exist in isolation. It goes without saying that it is not possible to identify a particular day several hundred years ago when a group of people suddenly decided to speak German. Instead, the language has a long history – a history which is intertwined with that of other languages. In this respect, the analogy of the *family* is a useful one. Languages, like people, have parents, as well as sisters and cousins. In many cases, they even produce their own offspring. Some have a relatively short life-span, whilst others grow to be very old. Most important of all, languages are constantly changing – at each stage in their life they look and behave somewhat differently. Thus, in the same way that the 5-year-old girl bears little resemblance to the 65-year-old grandmother she later becomes, so, the German learned by students today does not look very much like the Gothic or Old High German dialects from which it is nonetheless derived.

So where does German really come from? What is its relation to other languages? How and why has German changed over the centuries? In order to answer these questions, we need to take a brief look at the *history* of the language. We will begin by piecing together the biography and family tree which is unique to German, before describing how the language has developed into the variety which is used today.

2.1 The origins of German

Officially speaking, the German language is approximately 1250 years old. This is, of course, only a very rough estimate and is based on the discovery of the first documents in German, which are thought to date from around AD 750. It is important to bear in mind, however, that the development of a written version of any language almost always follows a lengthy period of spoken usage, and it is known that people had been speaking German or closely related dialects for many years before the language was ever recorded in writing. The real origins of German are therefore to be found considerably earlier. Indeed, in order to understand the relationship between German and other languages, it is necessary to go as far back as 4000 BC.

2.1.1 The Indo-European family of languages (4000–2000 BC)

German belongs to what is known as the **Indo-European** family of languages. The relationship between the various Indo-European tongues can be best represented in the form of a family tree (*see* Fig. 2.1).

From Fig. 2.1, it can be seen that the Indo-European family consists of a number of different language groups, for example, Germanic, Celtic, Romance, Slavonic, etc. We can therefore begin to appreciate that even although German, English, Spanish, and French are all part of the same family, the relationships between them are not equi-distant. English and German are **Germanic** languages, while Spanish and French are members of the **Romance** group. This means that whereas German and English might be thought of as cousins, German and Spanish (or French) are more like second cousins. Japanese, on the other hand, does not feature among the Indo-European languages at all: it belongs to a completely different family of languages found in south-east Asia, namely, the Altaic group.

Languages are spoken by people. The history of any language is, therefore, directly tied up with the movements of its speakers. One of the things which has fascinated scholars is the exact geographical origin of the people who first used Indo-European languages. There has been considerable dispute, but it is generally thought that the earliest speakers were a nomadic group known as the Kurgans, who lived in southern Russia

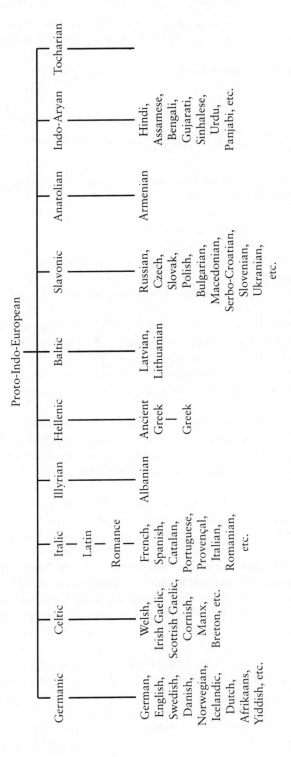

Fig. 2.1 The Indo-European family tree

Source: Adapted from Barbour and Stevenson, 1990: 24/Fromkin and Rodman, 1993: 346

around 4000 BC. Archaeological evidence suggests that the Kurgans then migrated to the Danube area by 3500 BC, arriving in the Adriatic region around 2000 BC.

It was not until the sixteenth century AD that scholars seriously began to piece together the links between the sounds, grammar, and vocabulary of the many different varieties of the Indo-European family. But once the systematic and scientific study of these languages began, linguists concluded that all Indo-European languages probably originated from a single parent form which they called **Proto-Indo-European** (**PIE**). It is, of course, impossible to state with any certainty that anyone ever spoke a discrete language called PIE, in fact, we are probably dealing with a group of related dialects. But whatever the case, there is documented evidence showing that by 2000–1000 BC, PIE had fragmented into a number of other languages such as Greek, Anatolian, and Indo-Iranian.

Even allowing for the fact that PIE may never have existed as a single, discrete variety, there are a number of features which historical linguists and philologists believe were typical of this language or dialect group. Three of these are worth looking at briefly, given their relevance to the study of modern German.

First, it has been possible to say something about the sounds of PIE. For example, there were 22 **vowels** and a large number of **consonants**. Many of these consonants still exist in German such as: 'p', 't', 'k', 'b', 'd', 'g'. It is also probable that the two 'th' sounds in the English words 'the' and 'thing' occurred in PIE, although these were later inherited by English but not German.

Second, it seems that **stress** was able to fall on any syllable of any word (with some limitations), giving the pronunciation of PIE a particularly musical quality. We shall see later how a similar pattern was retained in the Romance languages, but not in Germanic varieties such as English and German.

Third, PIE was a highly **inflected** language. This means that grammatical categories were expressed by changing the structure of words, particularly by adding endings. For example, there was a complex system of noun **declension** and verb **conjugation**. Nouns could be counted in three ways (singular, dual, and plural), there were three genders (masculine, feminine, and neuter), and no less than eight cases (nominative, vocative, accusative, genitive, dative, ablative, locative, and instrumental). Verbs, on the other hand, had three numbers (like nouns), four moods (indicative, imperative, subjunctive, and optative), three voices (active, passive, and middle), and six simple tenses (present, imperfect, aorist, perfect, pluperfect, and future). (Simple tenses are those constructed with one verb only, e.g. *ich ging*, as opposed to compound tenses, which require an extra, auxiliary verb, e.g. *ich bin gegangen*.)

The fact that PIE had such a sophisticated grammatical structure seems to suggest that it had been widely used and had developed over an extremely long period of time. One thing is clear: noun declension and verb conjugation in modern German represent a considerable simplification of the many forms which occurred in PIE!

2.1.2 *The Germanic languages (2000–500 BC)*

Up to 2000 BC, many Indo-European tribes had made their way to the areas around the Baltic Sea which now constitute southern Sweden, Denmark, and northern Germany. This was the beginning of the Bronze Age. Inevitably, this process of mass migration meant that the original Indo-European languages (or dialects) spoken by these groups underwent a number of changes – changes which eventually led to the development of what is known as **Primitive Germanic**. As with PIE, there is no real documented evidence for the existence of Primitive Germanic as a discrete language, but various of its characteristics have subsequently been pieced together by scholars. There are three main differences between PIE and Primitive Germanic.

The first important difference concerns the stress placed on individual words. Whereas PIE had quite free stress patterns, with the emphasis falling on more or less any part of the word, Primitive Germanic underwent a move towards initial stress. This shift, known as *der germanische Akzentwandel*, meant that the emphasis now began to fall on the first syllable of words. This is something which continues to typify modern languages of Germanic origin such as German and English.

The second difference relates to a phenomenon known as **ablaut**. This is a system whereby vowels are modified in order to mark grammatical categories. PIE used ablaut to indicate tense forms, many of which were adopted by Primitive Germanic, and then passed on to English and German. It is for this reason that a number of verbs in the two languages still follow identical patterns, for example:

English	German
eat/ate/eaten (e/a/e)	*essen/aß/gegessen* (e/a/e)
drink/drank/drunk (i/a/u)	*trinken/trank/getrunken* (i/a/u)

Alternatively, some follow a similar, though not identical, pattern of ablaut:

English	German
stand/stood/stood (a/o/o)	*stehen/stand/gestanden* (e/a/a)
sit/sat/sat (i/a/a)	*sitzen/saß/gesessen* (i/a/e)

There are several categories of ablaut used to form tenses in this way, and which give rise to the so-called 'strong' verbs. It is also interesting to note that these are the verbs describing the most basic of human activities, e.g. sleeping (*schlafen*), thinking (*denken*), and the four examples listed above. Having said this, the phenomenon of ablaut only applies to those verbs which *already* existed in PIE, and were then adopted by Primitive Germanic. Any new verbs which entered the Germanic languages from this point onwards followed a different route, using 'd' or 't' in order to mark the past tense. This is the origin of so-called 'weak' verbs and, again, accounts for the similarity between past tense forms in modern-day English and German such as:

English	German
laugheD	*lachTe*
cookeD	*kochTe*

Note how the spelling differs in the two languages, but that the pronunciation of 'd' and 't' is still the same.

The third important development at this time relates to a series of changes affecting the sounds of Primitive Germanic, which are known as the **Germanic (first) sound shift**. These changes were described, along with the system of ablaut and the **High German (second) sound shift** (see 2.1.3), by the German philologist Jacob Grimm in 1822. Jacob Grimm is probably better known as the compiler of Grimm's fairy tales with his brother, Wilhelm. He was, however, first and foremost, a dedicated analyst of the German language. The Germanic and High German sound shifts which he described constitute what is now known in linguistics as **Grimm's Law**. Together, they demonstrate the complex but highly structured way in which a whole series of Indo-European sounds were replaced in Germanic words.

To understand Grimm's Law fully, one would need a detailed appreciation of the way in which the sounds of language are produced, and this is something which will not be attempted until Chapter 4. For the time being, however, two examples of the shifts which occurred will suffice. Table 2.1 shows how the Indo-European sounds 'p', 't', 'k', 'b', 'd', and 'g' remained unaltered in Latin, but changed in the Germanic languages.

From Table 2.1 we can see how Primitive Germanic underwent a series of changes which were then passed on to its many descendants such as German and English. This also means that we are dealing with the point in history where, despite their common Indo-European heritage, the subsequent development of German and English, and Spanish and French was quite different. Thus, the Germanic sound shift did not occur in Latin, and was not passed on to Spanish or French. This accounts for the fact that the modern Spanish and French words for 'father', e.g. *padre* and *père* (Latin = *pater*) still contain the original Indo-European 'p', which shifted to a 'f' sound in the Germanic languages.

Another change which was not inherited by Romance languages was the shift in stress patterns which occurred in Primitive Germanic. This will be

Table 2.1 Examples of the Germanic sound shift

Group A

PIE	'p'	't'	'k'
Latin	*pater*	*tres*	*canis*
GERMANIC	'f'	'th'	'h'
English German	father *Vater*[a]	three (*drei*)[b]	hound *Hund*

Group B

PIE	'b'	'd'	'g'
Latin	*labium*	*duo*	*genu*
GERMANIC	'p'	't'	'k'
English German	lip *Lippe*	two (*zwei*)[b]	knee *Knie*[c]

(Adapted from Barbour and Stevenson, 1990: 26)

Notes: [a]Note that while the spelling may differ from the English, the pronunciation of 'f' and 'v' is the same in 'father' and *Vater*.
[b]Those German words in brackets (e.g. *drei* and *zwei*) differ as a result of the second (High German) sound shift, which will be discussed on p. 18.
[c]Note that the 'k' sound in 'knee' was not always silent.

explored further in Chapter 5, but it is worth noting here how Spanish and French have retained the system of more or less equal stress on syllables, giving them the more musical intonational patterns typical of PIE. The Germanic languages, however, moved to a different pattern of stress, with the primary emphasis falling on the first syllable of each word.

These kinds of changes do not occur overnight, and that no-one can be certain how much time elapsed before they were complete. However, it is generally believed that the first sound shift and the move to initial stress were in place before 500 BC when the Germanic tribes came into contact with the Romans. This is because Germanic words which were later borrowed from Latin retained the original Indo-European sounds and stress patterns. It is for this reason that many English and German words relating to the concept of 'father' still contain the 'p' which occurred in PIE, for example, 'patriarchy' (*Patriarchat*) or 'patriotism' (*Patriotismus*).

2.1.3   *From Primitive Germanic to German (500 BC–AD 750)*

The early Indo-European inhabitants of the Baltic region did not remain settled. On the one hand, this was probably due to the inhospitable geography of the area, which could not supply the necessary food and resources for a growing number of people. On the other hand, there was a general tendency towards military expansionism amongst these groups, which constantly drove them to conquer new territories. With the exception of the **North Germanic** (later the Swedes, Danes, and Norwegians), the majority of the tribes migrated southwards, eventually forming separate groups such as the **East Germanic** (Goths, Vandals, and Burgundians), the **North Sea Germanic** (Ingvaeones, Frisians, Angles, and Saxons), the **Weser-Rhine Germanic** (Franks), and the **Elbe Germanic** (Alemanni, Bavarians, and Lombards). This process of mass migration lasted from 1000 BC until well into the Middle Ages. Indeed, the Germanic world was not really stabilised until the formation of the Frankish empire, culminating in the crowning of Charlemagne in AD 768.

In view of this intense period of migration, it is no surprise to find that Primitive Germanic eventually gave rise to a whole new series of languages. Many of these have since died out, such as Old English, West Norse, and Gothic, but are the direct predecessors of a number of languages still spoken today, for example, English, German, Dutch, Danish, Norwegian, and Swedish. The relationship between the various Germanic languages is outlined in Fig. 2.2.

From Fig. 2.2, we can see that this is the point in history where English and German also begin to go their separate ways. Although both languages are members of the West Germanic group, a number of changes took place around this time which led to the separate development of the two varieties. There are three main differences between English and German forms of West Germanic.

The first feature involves the loss of 'n' (or strictly speaking, loss of the sound represented by the letter 'n'). Thus, in a number of words 'n' was retained in German, but disappeared in English, for example:

uns   → us
Gans   → goose

The second change which took place in early forms of English but not German is **ingvaeonic palatalisation** (after the Ingvaeones, one of the North Sea Germanic tribes). This describes how the sound represented by the letter 'k' in German changed to 'ch' in English. With this in mind, we are then able to see the relationship between words such as *Kapitel* and 'chapter' or *Kirche* and 'church' (note, however, the Scots form 'kirk'). Similarly, 'g' in German shifted to 'y' in English, which accounts for the difference between *gestern* and 'yesterday' or *gelb* and 'yellow'.

Finally, the third, and most significant change is the **(second) High German sound shift**, which occurred in the predecessors of High German,

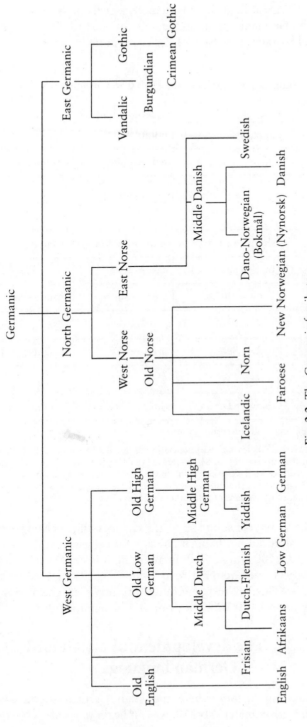

Fig. 2.2 The Germanic family tree
Source: Adapted from Barbour and Stevenson, 1990: 24

but *not* Low German, English or Dutch. This development was described, along with the Germanic (first) sound shift by Jacob Grimm, forming the second part of Grimm's Law (see 2.1.2). The four main changes are outlined in Table 2.2.

Table 2.2 Examples of the High German sound shift

GROUP A

'p' → 'pf'	apple → *Apfel*	pound → *Pfund*	pepper → *Pfeffer*
't' → 'z'	tide → *Zeit*	ten → *zehn*	two → *zwei*
'k' → 'ch'	cow → *Kuh*[a]		

GROUP B

'p' → 'f'/'ff'	sharp → *scharf*	ship → *Schiff*	open → *offen*
't' → 'ss'/'ß'	that → *dass*	eat → *essen*	foot → *Fuß*
'k' → 'ch'	book → *Buch*	seek → *suchen*	make → *machen*

GROUP C

'd' → 't'	bed → *Bett*	deep → *tief*	daughter → *Tochter*

GROUP D[b]

'th' → 'd'	thing → *Ding*	three → *drei*	brother → *Bruder*

(Adapted from Barbour and Stevenson, 1990: 34)

Notes: [a]In most German dialects, the pronunciation of the first sound in the English 'cow' and German *Kuh* is identical. In Swiss German dialects, however, the initial consonant is pronounced not unlike the 'ch' sound in the German word *Loch*, e.g. *Chuh*.
[b]This change is not, technically speaking, part of the second sound shift but is included on account of its similarity to the other developments.

As with the Germanic sound shift, the changes which characterised the High German shift did not happen quickly – it is estimated that they took place between AD 400 and AD 700. In addition, it is important to note that these changes were not adopted to the same extent across the German-speaking areas. This, in turn, accounts for many of the national and regional differences in the pronunciation of German today.

2.2 The development of a standard German language

From the point in history where the High German sound shift was complete, i.e. approximately AD 750, we can begin to speak of 'German' as a language in its own right. However, this still does not mean that there was a single, standardised version of the language, which was the same across all the German-speaking areas. Indeed, a foreigner trying to learn German at this time would have had to choose from a number of different dialects.

The fact there was no standardised variety of German in the eighth century comes as less of a surprise when one considers that there was no unified country in which the language was being used. Although the various German-speaking states were under the aegis of the Holy Roman Empire from 800 until 1806, Germany, as we know it today, has only really existed since its unification by Bismarck in 1871. This means that the rise of a so-called nation–state with one official language took place considerably later in Germany than in other countries such as France and England. This, in turn, is reflected in the relatively late standardisation of German in comparison with French and English. (Both Austria and the German-speaking Swiss cantons have been in existence since the thirteenth century. However, the standardisation of German will be discussed primarily with reference to Germany since this is the largest single German-speaking country.)

2.2.1   The earliest forms of German (750–1050)

In the eighth century, the area which now constitutes the modern German-speaking countries was made up of more or less independent communities ruled by dukes and princes. This is part of the reason why the German language was not a uniform variety, but consisted of a number of dialects. From Fig. 2.3, it can be seen how the names of these different dialects were frequently based on the Germanic tribes which had originally settled in those areas. Note how some of these are still reflected in the names of states in modern Germany, e.g. Lower Saxony, Thuringia, and Bavaria.

The relationship between the various dialects and the subsequent development of standard German must, however, be seen in conjunction with the High German sound shift. To summarise very briefly, the German-speaking regions at this time can be divided into three areas (*see* Fig. 2.3):

- **Low German** dialects were spoken in the area north of the so-called **Benrath Line**, and were not affected by the High German sound shift.

- **Central German** dialects were spoken in the area south of the Benrath Line, but north of the **Germersheim Line**. These dialects underwent most, but not all, of the changes associated with the High German sound shift.

- **Upper German** dialects were spoken to the south of the Germersheim Line in the area which now comprises southern Germany, Switzerland, and Austria. These are the dialects which were most fully affected by the sound shift.

LOW GERMAN

Elbe

Weser

Low
Saxon

Rhine

Ems

Oder

Maas

BENRATH LINE

Saale

Low Franconian

Thuringian

Ripuarian

GERMERSHEIM LINE

Franconian East
Franconian

Moselle

Main

Franconian
Rhenish

Meuse

*S. Rhenish
Franc.*

Danube

CENTRAL
GERMAN

Alemannic

Lech

Bavarian

Rhine

Inn

UPPER
GERMAN

High Alemannic

Rhône

Fig. 2.3 German dialects around AD 800

Furthermore, Central and Upper German can be grouped together as
High German dialects. These are the forms which were affected by the
second sound shift, and therefore provide the basis for the subsequent
development of standard 'High' German.

At this stage in the history of the language, we can therefore see that the
origins of standard German do *not* lie in northern Germany, as is often
assumed. Instead, standard German originates from the areas which now
constitute central and southern Germany, Switzerland and Austria. In
northern Germany, where Low German dialects predominated, the
language initially followed a different route, and this area was not
linguistically unified with the other German-speaking regions until the

seventeenth century. This is shown in Table 2.3 which sketches the so-called 'periodisation' of German, i.e. the main stages in the development of the language.

Table 2.3 The periodisation of German

LOW GERMAN	HIGH GERMAN (= Central/Upper German dialects)
Old Saxon (800–1150) Middle Low German (1150–1650)	Old High German (750–1050) Middle High German (1050–1350) Early New High German (1350–1650)
New High German (1650–)	

Of course, it is not really possible to divide the history of any language in such an orderly fashion, since the transition from one period to the next is never as abrupt as such labels imply. Nonetheless, this kind of categorisation provides a useful overview of the most important phases in the development of German.

So what did the various Central and Upper German dialects – collectively known as **Old High German (OHG)** – actually look like at this time? Here are three extracts from the Lord's Prayer taken from the eighth century:

Alemannic

Fater unseer, thū pist in himile
uuīhi namun dīnan, qhueme rīhhi dīn
uuerde uuillo diin, sō in himile sōsa in erdu.

Bavarian

Fater unsēr, dū pist in himilum
kauuīhit sī namo dīn, piqhueme rīhhi dīn
uuesa dīn uuillo, sama sō in himile est, sama in erdu.

East Franconian

Fater unser, thū thār bist in himile
sī giheilagōt thin namo, queme thīn rīhhi
sī thīn uuillo, so her in himile ist, so sī her in erdu.

Modern English

Our Father who art in heaven
Hallowed be thy name, thy kingdom come
Thine will be done, on earth, as it is in heaven.

(Adapted from Stedje, 1989: 68)

From these examples, it can be seen how the dialects of the Old High German period underwent a significant number of changes in order to evolve into the version of German which is used today.

2.2.2   The development of a written standard (1050–1650)

Prior to 1050, there was considerable variation in the way in which German could be *spoken*. The extracts from the Lord's Prayer also highlight the huge differences between the way in which early forms of German could be *written*. Over the next 800 years or so, the process of standardisation was characterised primarily by the struggle for supremacy between these various written versions of the language.

It is important to remember that in the time of Old High German dialects (750–1050), the majority of texts were not written in German at all. German was perceived by some to be a vulgar, inferior language, spoken by the lower orders of society. For the literate minority, therefore, the language of education and writing was still Latin. However, the development of **Middle High German** (1050–1350) also coincided with the emergence of a lesser nobility who could not necessarily read Latin. This, in turn, led to the demand for texts in German, and saw the rise of Middle High German as a literary language. During this time, some of the finest ever German poetry was written such as the anonymous *Nibelungenlied*.

Literature often functions as an important, unifying force in the development of a language. However, with the growth of an increasing number of towns in the Middle Ages, another need arose: that of a single language with which to administrate the business of the townspeople. One of the most significant influences in the standardisation of written German was therefore the rise of **chanceries** (*Kanzleien*), organisations akin to the modern civil service.

Although it was undoubtedly High German dialects which were the most influential in the development of written German, one of the first unified **chancery languages** (*Kanzleisprachen*) emerged in the Low German-speaking area (*see* Table 2.3). Here, the original **Old Saxon** dialects (800–1150) gave way to an important early standard known as **Middle Low German** (1150–1650). In the fourteenth and fifteenth centuries, this language was widely used by the **Hanseatic League**, a prestigious confederation of North German cities, which included Hamburg, Bremen, Rostock, and Lübeck. During this time, the Hanseatic League enjoyed successful trading links with England, Scandinavia, the Baltic States, Russia, and beyond. Middle Low German continued to play a unifying role in northern areas until the collapse of the League in the sixteenth and seventeenth centuries.

Parallel to the rise of Middle Low German, other important

developments were also taking place. By the middle of the fourteenth
century, the German-speaking area had increased considerably as a result of
the colonisation of eastern Germany (*see* Fig. 2.4). During this time, the
languages of two eastern chanceries, namely Prague and Meissen (Saxony),
were particularly influential.

This is the period when the dialects of the Central and Upper German-
speaking areas are classified as **Early New High German**, that is to say,
1350–1650. During this time, there was one single development which
accelerated the rise of a written German standard more than any other: the
invention of printing from moveable type by Johannes Gutenberg around
1440. Once there was the possibility to print and distribute books, the need
for a unified language became more acute than ever, not least because
typesetters could not readily accommodate wide variations in spelling.

Fig. 2.4 The colonisation of Eastern Germany

Around 1500, printers would use one of approximately ten standardised chancery languages, although this was of little importance in the early days of printing, since most books were still written in Latin.

At the beginning of the sixteenth century, it was not clear which of the many chancery languages used by the printers would eventually provide the basis for a future version of standard German. For a while, it seemed as though the variety known as **Common German** would predominate. This was the written form used in the south around Vienna, Bavaria, Swabia, and Alsace. Ultimately, however, it was the written language of the Saxon chancery, known as **East Middle German**, which would have the greatest influence.

Saxony was not only the centre of the printing industry in the fifteenth and sixteenth centuries, it was also the home of the man who is often referred to as 'the father of the German language': Martin Luther (1483–1546), a theologian, who was anxious to purify the Church from what he perceived to be its corruption by the Catholic bishops. Luther was not primarily a linguist, but through his desire to spread the teachings of Christianity to a wider audience, he embarked upon a series of translations of the Bible from Latin into the language which ordinary people would understand: German. Although there was no unified form of German which Luther could use, nonetheless, it is here that his linguistic talents were employed. His aim was to mould his local East Middle German variety and other High German dialects into a form which could be read and understood by speakers from many different areas.

In order to appreciate the kinds of changes Luther made to the German language at this time, let us look at one or two extracts from the Bible. Here is a brief excerpt from an early translation from Latin into German, published in Fulda around AD 830:

> In themo sehsten manude gisentit uuard engil Gabriel fon gote in thie burg Galileę, thero name ist Nazareth, zi thiornun gimahaltero gommanne, themo namo uuas Joseph, fon huse Dauides, inti name thero thiornun Maria.

The following is taken from the first German translation of the Bible, published by Johann Mentel in Strasbourg in 1466:

> Wann in dem ·vj·moned der engel gabriel wart gesant von gott in die stat galilee der name waz nazareth. zů einer meide gemechelt eim man dez name was ioseph· von dem haus dauids: vnd der nam der meide waz maria.

Luther's own first translation in 1522 looked like this:

> Vnnd ym sechsten mond, ward der Engel Gabriel gesand von Gott, ynn eyne stadt ynn Gallilea, die heyst Nazareth, zu eyner iungfrawen, die vertrawet war eynem man mit namen Joseph, von dem hauße Dauid, vnd der iungfrawen name heyst Maria [. . .]

But by 1546, Luther had modified his translation as follows:

> VND im sechsten mond, ward der Engel Gabriel gesand von Gott, in eine stad
> in Galilea, die heisst Nazareth, zu einer Jungfrawen, die vertrawet war einem
> Manne, mit namen Joseph, vom hause Dauid, und die iungfraw hies Maria.

As a point of comparison, here is the 1611 version of the Bible in English:

> And in the sixth month the angel Gabriel was sent from God unto a city of
> Galilee, named Nazareth. To a virgin espoused to a man whose name was
> Joseph, of the house of David; and the virgin's name was Mary.
>   (All excerpts from Chambers and Wilkie, 1970: 150)

From these extracts, we can see the differences between the Old High
German version of the Bible, the first translation published by Mentel some
600 years later, and Luther's own first translation. In addition, we can
appreciate the way in which Luther modified his own translation, and in
doing so, brought the German language so much closer to the version which
is used today. However, by comparing Luther's 1546 translation and the
English version from 1611, we can also gain an impression of how much
more standardised the English language was by this time. English spelling,
for example, has barely changed since then – something which clearly
cannot be said of German.

Luther's Bible translations had an enormous impact on the
standardisation of German, not least because the Bible was so widely read.
But even though Luther was largely successful in his attempts to develop a
version of German which was understood by speakers of different High
German dialects, the variety he used was still unmistakeably East Middle
German, that is to say, the language of the Saxon chancery. The adoption of
this version of written German by other areas, especially the south, was by
no means straightforward. This was also linked to the fact that after the
Reformation of the Church in 1517 Saxony became Protestant, whereas
many southern areas (with the notable exception of Switzerland) remained
Catholic. Common German was therefore the favoured variety in what
are now southern Germany and Austria, areas which have remained predominantly Catholic to this day.

But despite the various factors impeding the acceptance of East Middle
German, it seems that, at this crucial time in the sixteenth century, the Saxon
chancery was not only the centre of the printing industry, it was also
wealthy and influential. In addition, there were linguistic considerations
which played an important part in the spread of East Middle German rather
than Common German as the new written standard. Thus, although the
language of the Saxon chancery was of High German origin, it belonged to
the Central German group of dialects (*see* Fig. 2.4). This meant that East
Middle German was closer to the Low German dialects used in northern
areas than its southern rival, Common German, which was Upper German

in origin. In a sense, therefore, East Middle German was the logical compromise in the process of unifying the different versions of the language used in the north and the south.

2.2.3   The rise of a spoken standard (1650–1900)

By the middle of the seventeenth century, a standardised written version of German was more or less in place. We are now, therefore, entering the **New High German** period, which began around 1650 and includes the German language in its present form. This means that, generally speaking, anyone studying German today should be able to read texts written from the seventeenth century onwards. Nevertheless, the emergence of a written standard was not paralleled by the standardisation of spoken German. Even though southern areas gradually accepted East Middle German as their written language, they resolutely held on to their local forms of spoken German.

Resistance by the Catholic south to accept East Middle German as the new spoken standard was not the only problem facing those who wished to promote East Middle German at this time. German was still in fierce competition with not only Latin, but also French. Throughout the seventeenth century, Latin remained the language of education, and it was not until the beginning of the eighteenth century that universities slowly began to adopt German as their medium of instruction. However, as many of the important scholarly works at the time had been written in Latin, an ability to read Latin remained crucial well into the nineteenth century.

French, on the other hand, emerged as the most prestigious spoken language in Europe during the late seventeenth century, particularly during and after the reign of Louis XIV (1643–1715). During this time, French was perceived to be the language of 'high' culture, and even the German aristocracy used it as the language of so-called 'polite society', i.e. the ruling élite. This continued to be the case until well into the nineteenth century. So, for example, Frederick the Great, King of Prussia from 1740 to 1786, is reported to have said: *Je ne suis pas fort en allemand.* Similarly, the French writer, Voltaire, referred to German as the language in which one spoke to 'soldiers and horses'. This was the period when a large number of French influences entered the German language, many of which are still in use today such as *Mode, Parfüm, Torte, Hotel, Onkel, Tante.*

Another significant factor which contributed to the changing image of German from the seventeenth century onwards was the formation of **language societies**. These groups were concerned with laying down the rules for correct usage which would then be followed by others. Using literary German as their model, they produced a number of the earliest grammar books and dictionaries. In addition, the language societies were keen to see that the German language remained 'pure', i.e. free from corrupting, foreign influences, especially from Latin and French. Thus, many foreign words were germanicised during this period, for example, *Adresse* → *Anschrift*, *Dialekt* → *Mundart*, and *Autor* → *Verfasser*.

Many members of the language societies believed that the kind of literary German they were promoting was independent of the influences of dialect. Yet most were in fact implicated in the spread of the East Middle German dialect as the new standard. Similarly, by the late eighteenth century, the great writers such as Goethe (1749–1832) and Schiller (1759–1805) were all using this variety of German. However, it was the publication of Johann Christoph Gottsched's *Grundlegung einer deutschen Sprachkunst* in 1748, which finally established East Middle German as the future standard. This was not least because the text was later adopted as the guide to correct usage in Bavarian and Austrian schools (i.e. areas where Common German had traditionally been preferred). On the basis of what he referred to as the language of the 'best writers', i.e. 'high' literature, Gottsched compiled his definitive guide to German grammar and usage. One of his more controversial points was to specify that all German nouns (and not just proper nouns) should be written with capital letters, something over which there has been disagreement ever since.

By the early nineteenth century, German was well established as a literary language. As a result, it was slowly gaining recognition in élite circles as a variety which could also be spoken. Poets and philosophers continued to write in German, and there was lively, scholarly interest in the language. It was during this time, for example, that Jacob Grimm formulated his rules for the Germanic and High German sound shifts. In addition, the Grimm brothers worked on one of the greatest accomplishments in the history of the German language, the *Deutsches Wörterbuch*, although this was not completed until long after their deaths by other linguists in the 1960s.

Much was being done by writers and linguists during this time to secure the future of German as a 'respectable' language. But all of these developments must also be seen against the backdrop of rising nationalist sentiment in nineteenth-century Germany. The unification of the German language cannot be abstracted from efforts to unify Germany politically and economically. This was finally achieved in 1871 when, following France's defeat in the Franco-Prussian wars, Bismarck created the second German empire. The idea that *German* should be the language of *Germany* was crucial.

In addition to the political and economic motives for standardising German, there were important social and cultural developments which meant that, by the end of the nineteenth century, the need for further normification became even more urgent. This was particularly the case regarding German spelling, where there was still considerable variation. Between 1860 and 1900, mandatory education was introduced, and schools all over Germany were supposed to teach standard German. But in order to do so, teachers needed grammar and reference books which laid down the rules of the standard language. Many such texts were therefore written during this time, although a number of disagreements surrounding **orthography** were never really resolved, for example, the spelling of words with 'ss' or 'ß' or the ongoing debate regarding the capitalisation of nouns.

Even by the late nineteenth century, however, standard German still remained a predominantly written language. Strangely perhaps, it was neither politicians nor professional linguists who gave the standardisation of the spoken language its final impulse. Variation in pronunciation was still widespread, and this presented a problem to one particular group of people: actors. Many theatre companies were producing plays which they wished to perform to audiences all over the country. But in order to do so, they needed to be understood by a wide variety of dialect speakers.

This particular issue led to many discussions regarding the establishment of a standard spoken variety of German. A commission of university professors and theatre representatives was formed, eventually leading to the publication of Theodor Siebs' *Deutsche Bühnensprache* in 1898. It is in this work that the pronunciation of standard German is defined as the variety spoken in *northern* Germany. There are many reasons why this was the case, not least the political dominance of Prussia at that time. But either way, the norms for pronunciation laid down at the end of the nineteenth century have persisted to the present day.

However, considering the many different phases in the process of standardisation, we can see the falsity of the common perception that the origins of standard German are to be found exclusively in the north of Germany. *All* of the German-speaking areas have played their part in the development of the standard language at some time or other, and when learning German as a foreign language today, it is useful to have at least a basic understanding of the chequered history of the German language. This is because it is important to appreciate that, despite the general acceptance of a standard written form of German in the various German-speaking areas, the notion of a single, spoken standard is far less persistent than in other countries such as Britain or France, whose languages were standardised much earlier. Thus, although standard German is taught in German schools, and Germans are able to speak it almost without exception, various levels of dialect continue to be used in informal, and sometimes even quite formal, conversation. In addition, Switzerland and Austria have their own norms of standard pronunciation which are somewhat different from the variety which is generally accepted as the standard in Germany.

2.3   German in the twentieth century

German in the twentieth century may not have undergone changes as significant as the Germanic and High German sound shifts, but this does not

mean that it has remained static. Political, social, and economic developments all meant that German had to adapt in order to meet the needs of an
ever-changing world.

As far as the status of German in a European context was concerned,
political events resulted in significant developments. So, following **World
War I** (1914–18) and the 1919 **Treaty of Versailles**, some border areas became
part of Denmark, France, Belgium, and Italy. Similarly, after **World War II**
(1939–45), territories were ceded to Poland, the Soviet Union, and
Czechoslovakia. This not only meant that the local dialects spoken in those
areas experienced decline but that, in many cases, German was completely
replaced by other languages.

In this final section on the history of German, we shall be considering
two specific periods which are closely linked to the two World Wars and
border changes in the German-speaking areas: **National Socialism**
(1933–1945) and the division of Germany (1949–1990). But we shall begin
by looking at some more general trends.

2.3.1   General linguistic trends

The early twentieth century saw the continued promotion of the standard
variety of German which had been forged by the end of the nineteenth
century. This meant that anyone who aspired to social mobility would
generally be expected to conform to standard spoken usage, something
which was particularly promoted in schools. At the same time, the idea of
literary German as the model for the written language was furthered by *der
Allgemeine Deutsche Sprachverein*. This modern equivalent of the old
'language societies', which was particularly active around the time of World
War I, advocated the so-called *Pflege und Hebung* of German. Not for the
first time, such 'cultivation and improvement' implied attempts to see that
German remained free from 'corrupting', foreign influences.

Despite the many efforts to promote standard German as the spoken
norm, traditional dialects continued to be used in rural areas throughout the
twentieth century. Nevertheless, the situation of dialect speakers underwent
a number of changes. This was partly due to the border alterations and mass
migration following the two world wars, but was also the result of further
industrialisation and urbanisation, which meant that more and more people
were moving out of villages and into towns. In addition, the increasing role
played by radio, film, and television in the daily lives of many dialect speakers
led to a blurring of the division between standard German and regional
dialects. All of these factors played a role in the emergence of so-called
regional colloquial languages or *regionale Umgangssprachen*, i.e. varieties
which lie somewhere between the standard language and traditional dialects.

Not only were norms of pronunciation changing, the vocabulary of
German also grew significantly in the twentieth century. It has been

estimated that some 400 000 new words entered the language during this time, one of the main reasons being the need to accommodate rapid developments in science and technology. Frequently, these new terms led to the formation of so-called *Fachsprachen*, i.e. 'specialist languages' in fields such as medicine, engineering, or computing. These highly compartmentalised varieties tend to be employed by a relatively small number of people working in related professions, although the influence of science and technology was also felt by non-specialists. This was particularly so in the case of metaphors which entered everyday usage such as *mit Hochdruck arbeiten* ('to work under high pressure').

Another factor behind the expansion of German vocabulary was the general trend towards internationalisation and global markets, especially following World War II. The increasing economic dominance of the USA led to the incorporation of many Anglo-American terms in German. As a result, words such as *das Leasing* or *der Bestseller* are now common. However, many English loans turn out to be **false friends** from the point of view of the English-speaking learner of German. For example, the German *Drink* is more specific than the English term, and often refers specifically to an alcoholic beverage or cocktail. This means that English speakers cannot be sure that words loaned from English will have exactly the same meaning when used in German.

Grammar was another area where the German language changed during the twentieth century, affecting, in particular, cases, verb forms, and word order. So, for example, the dative 'e' as in *dem Kinde* is now used only in fairly formal situations. Similarly, the genitive case as in *das Buch des Mannes* has been more or less replaced in informal spoken usage by the dative case and *von*, e.g. *das Buch von dem Mann*. None the less, the genitive looks set to survive for some time where the written language and more formal spoken usage are concerned.

As far as conjugation is concerned, German has, over the centuries, gradually moved away from the system of strong verbs formed though ablaut, that is, where tenses are indicated by vowel changes in the middle of verbs (see 2.1.2). The only situation where ablaut looks set to survive in the long term is in those strong verbs which are in constant usage, such as *stehen/stand/gestanden*. This has meant that some of the less commonly used strong verbs such as *wenden* (to turn) are now caught up in a process of shift, with the simple past tense forms wavering between *wandte/wendete* (past participle: *gewandt* or *gewendet*). Significantly, any new verbs which enter the language (e.g. from English) will always be weak forms, e.g. *managen/managte/gemanagt*.

Finally, word order has also undergone a number of changes. Students of German are still taught the traditional patterns of word order where certain verb forms are placed at the end of sentences, e.g. *weil ich keine Lust habe*. While this kind of word order is undoubtedly still correct, German speakers can often be heard using forms such as *weil ich habe keine Lust* in colloquial usage.

2.3.2   The impact of National Socialism

In 1933, the National Socialists came to power in Germany. Then, in 1938, *das dritte Reich* (literally: 'The third empire', the first being the Holy Roman Empire (800–1806), and the second, the unified Germany created by Bismarck in 1871, which ceased to exist after World War I in 1919 when the Weimar Republic was formed), was expanded following the annexation of Austria, known in German as *der Anschluss*. One of the questions which has preoccupied linguists, historians, and writers ever since was the role played by language in this darkest period of European history. To what extent did the German language change as a result of National Socialism? Was there a 'language of National Socialism'? One point which is important to make clear is that German was not transformed beyond all recognition during this time. This was still the same language which was spoken in nineteenth-century Germany, or before and after World War I.

Of course, the emergence of Hitler's Third Reich did mean that the German language acquired new terminology such as *Sturmabteilung (SA)* or *Schutzstaffeln (SS)*. Nevertheless, the introduction of these new terms is probably less important than the way in which existing words were manipulated to political ends. So the anti-Semitic ideology of the National Socialists was reflected in the distortion of ordinary language, which was then used to promote a discourse of race and racism. Jews were described as *Parasiten*, and marriages between Germans and non-Aryans were forbidden and referred to as *Mischehen*. Similarly, the use of foreign words was also discouraged.

This exclusion of all that was non-Germanic went hand in hand with attempts to create – through the use of language – in-group solidarity among the *Herrenrasse* (master race). This frequently implied reference to terms such as *unsere Volksgemeinschaft* (our national community). However, the conscious manipulation of language probably took on its most disturbing form with respect to the Holocaust. Here, for example, **euphemisms** such as *die Endlösung* or *die Judenfrage* were used to downplay the horrific reality of the mass murder of the Jewish people in the concentration camps.

Another area which cannot be overlooked with respect to National Socialism is the crucial role played by language in the **mass media**. This is because the German language did not simply reflect National Socialist ideology through its vocabulary – it was also the main vehicle for the dissemination of Nazi **propaganda**. In this respect, the manipulation of the written language in newspapers was significant, although the role of the spoken word was probably more influential. Thus, the National Socialists were able to convey their emotionally charged rhetoric not only to live audiences at political rallies, but also to the wider population via radio and film.

But in spite of all that can be said about the role of German during this time, it is important to note that 'language' itself was never really central to

National Socialist ideology. The ability to speak German did not guarantee membership of the 'master race' – many Jewish victims of the gas chambers were native German speakers of German nationality. In order to exclude these people, National Socialism emphasised the *biological* dimension of 'race' based on 'blood', as opposed to the *cultural* dimension based, for example, on 'language'.

The question of the impact of National Socialist ideology on the German language did not cease with Germany's defeat. After 1945, the linguistic legacy of National Socialism remained an important issue for many people. Post-war authors often struggled to find adequate forms of expression in German, given that so many ordinary terms could not be rid of their fascist overtones. Heinrich Böll, for example, wrote of: *'die Suche nach einer bewohnbaren Sprache in einem bewohnbaren Land'* (1978: 37). Even today, many words still carry connotations of National Socialism to such a degree that they tend to be avoided in general usage, for example, *der Führer* (leader).

2.3.3   Divided Germany – divided language?

In 1945, Germany was occupied by the four Allied powers: the United States, Britain, France, and the Soviet Union. By 1949, it had become clear that these four countries would not be able to agree on the kind of political system they wished to see in post-war Germany. As a result, the US, British, and French sectors were merged to form the Federal Republic of Germany (FRG) or West Germany. The Soviet sector became the German Democratic Republic (GDR) or East Germany. This division lasted until 1990 when, after a peaceful revolution in the GDR in 1989, the two countries became the new Federal Republic of Germany. So how was the German language affected by political events during this time?

One of the most obvious ways in which German changed is that a new vocabulary was needed in order to describe the political and geographical consequences of division and unification. After the formation of East and West Germany, there were many disagreements on both sides regarding appropriate terms of reference. The GDR, insisting that it be recognised as a separate German state, wished to be referred to at all times as the *Deutsche Demokratische Republik*. But any use of this term in the West would have signalled an acceptance, on the part of the Federal Republic, that there were in fact two German states. This was something which many West Germans refused to acknowledge, even after mutual recognition was formally agreed in the early 1970s. It was for this reason, for example, that the conservative, West German newspaper, *die Bild-Zeitung*, adhered to a rigid policy of printing the name of the GDR in scare quotes, e.g. *'DDR'*, and continued to do so right up until 1989.

The unification of Germany also gave rise to much new terminology. This began with the use of the word *Wende* (literally: turn) to describe the events of 1989. Similarly, after official, political unification in October 1990, new terms were coined to describe the former East and West Germany, the most lasting of which have been *die neuen Bundesländer* and *die alten Bundesländer*, respectively.

Another question which was frequently posed regarding the 40-year division of Germany is whether or not German developed into two separate varieties. From the 1950s onwards, this discussion was complicated by the fact that both countries were keen to blame one another for 'distorting' the German language. At one point there was much debate among both East and West German linguists about the so-called *Vier-Varianten-These*. This **'four varieties thesis'**, originally put forward in the GDR, suggested that there were, in fact, *four* different national versions of German (in West Germany, East Germany, Austria, and Switzerland). But what was effectively being argued was that there were *two* separate varieties of the language, one in the East, and one in the West.

So did German develop into two discrete, national varieties? The answer is 'no'. Despite the separation of the two speech communities, Germans on either side of the border continued to speak the same language. Even the fact that there were two versions of the *Duden* dictionary, one published in Mannheim (West Germany) and one in Leipzig (East Germany) does not seem to have meant that the languages of the two states had become mutually incomprehensible. The grammar and pronunciation of German did not change recognisably.

The main differences related to vocabulary, although even here some of the developments were similar. It is often assumed that the post-1945 influx of English words into German was not experienced in the East. Yet many of these Anglicisms did, in fact, reach the GDR. It is important to remember that Western television programmes were widely received and watched by East Germans (albeit unofficially). English words such as *Jeans, Hit,* and *Disco* were therefore in common usage, especially among young people. At the same time, Russian words were undoubtedly incorporated into East German usage to a greater extent than in the West. This was partly because Russian was the main foreign language learned by pupils in GDR schools, but was also due to the closer political ties with the Soviet Union. Typical Russian words entered the language like *der Subbutnik* (meaning to work 'extra, unpaid hours').

The greatest differences in language use were linked to the starkly contrasting political and economic systems which were established in the two German states. Thus, West Germany followed the US model of a capitalist, free market economy known as *die freie Marktwirtschaft*. East Germany adopted a Soviet-style socialist, planned economy. As a result, West Germany continued to use such terms as *Arbeitgeber* (employer, literally: 'giver of work') and *Arbeiternehmer* (employee, literally: 'taker of work'). However, these were rejected in the GDR on the basis of a Marxist interpretation of labour, which sees the employ*ee* as the 'giver' of work, and the employ*er* as the 'taker'. East German usage tended instead to stress the shared nature of labour through words such as *das Kollektiv* (workers' collective) or *das Kombinat* (big state-run company).

After 1990, it soon became clear that fears surrounding the separate developments of the language were unfounded, and that, on the whole, east and west Germans had little difficulty using German in order to speak to one another. However, this does not mean to say that there have been no communication problems. With the collapse of the GDR system, many east Germans saw themselves having to adapt linguistically to their new situation to a much greater extent than those in the west. Frequently, east Germans have found that words and ideas which were commonly understood in the GDR are no longer meaningful in the new Federal Republic. Alternatively, some words such as *der Broiler* (*das Grillhähnchen*, or 'roast chicken') and *die Plaste* (*die Plastik*) are understood by west Germans but carry specific GDR connotations. Nonetheless, it is still far too early to say whether words such as these will survive the *Wende* in the long term.

Sources and recommended reading

- For a good introduction to the history of the German language see Chambers and Wilkie (1970). For a more detailed account, see Wells (1985).
- Accessible histories in German are Stedje (1989) and von Polenz (1978).
- For more information on the origins of Proto-Indo-European, various language families, and language change, see Section IX, 'The Languages of the World' in Crystal (1997).
- Many books contain specific chapters on the history of German. See, for example, Chapter 2 in Barbour and Stevenson (1990) and Chapter 1 in Russ (1994).
- Stötzel and Wengeler (1995) is a comprehensive collection of essays (in German) on various issues relating to the German language today. See especially Jung on anglicisms, Stötzel on the linguistic legacy of National Socialism, Wengeler on immigration debates, and Hahn on the language of the 'German question'.
- For a fascinating account of the relationship between language, nationalism, and the German nation–state, see Coulmas (1995).
- Glück and Sauer (1995) describes the grammatical changes currently in progress in German.
- Further information on German and National Socialism can be found in Townson (1987).
- See Chapter 3 in Clyne (1995) for a detailed discussion of German in East and West Germany, and linguistic trends since the *Wende*, and Chapter 8 for a survey of recent Anglo-American influence on German vocabulary.

Exercises

1. To which Indo-European family do the following languages belong? Tick the appropriate column in each case.

	GERMANIC	CELTIC	ROMANCE	SLAVONIC	INDO-ARYAN
1. English					
2. German					
3. Italian					
4. Spanish					
5. Russian					
6. Swedish					
7. Hindi					
8. Welsh					
9. Afrikaans					
10. French					

2. To which branch of the Germanic family do the following languages belong? Tick the appropriate column in each case:

	WEST GERMANIC	NORTH GERMANIC
1. Swedish		
2. English		
3. Danish		
4. Icelandic		
5. Yiddish		
6. Dutch		
7. Afrikaans		
8. (High) German		
9. Norwegian		
10. Low German		

3. Select the correct answer.

   1. To which areas did the tribe known as the Kurgans migrate?
      (a) Baltic and Danube
      (b) Danube and Adriatic
      (c) Elbe and Baltic

2. To which Germanic group did the Alemanni, Bavarians, and Lombards belong?
   (a) Elbe Germani
   (b) North Sea Germani
   (c) Weser-Rhine Germani

3. Who formulated the rules which describe the Germanic and High German sound shifts?
   (a) Martin Luther
   (b) Jacob Grimm
   (c) Wilhelm Grimm

4. Which rule accounts for the change from the German *Kirche* to the English 'church'?
   (a) The Germanic sound shift
   (b) The High German sound shift
   (c) Ingvaeonic palatalisation

5. When, approximately, did the High German sound shift occur?
   (a) 700–400 BC
   (b) AD 400–700
   (c) AD 200–500

4. Answer the following questions.

   1. Name the line which divides Low German and Central German dialects.

   2. Which two dialect groups are collectively referred to as High German?

   3. Approximately when were Old High German dialects spoken?

   4. What was the title of the famous, anonymously written poem of the Middle High German era?

   5. What is the German term for 'chancery language'?

   6. Name the four main north German cities of the Hanseatic League.

   7. What was the claim to fame of Johannes Gutenberg?

   8. Who suggested that German was a language for speaking to soldiers and horses?

   9. What was the famous work begun by the Grimm brothers in the nineteenth century, but completed posthumously in the 1960s?

   10. What was the title of Theodor Siebs' 1898 publication, which defined north German pronunciation as the model for standard German?

5. Match the words listed in Column A with the appropriate definitions in Column B.

Column A	Column B
1. *das Kombinat*	(a) The West German newspaper which always wrote the name of the GDR in inverted commas.
2. *die Bild-Zeitung*	(b) A type of language understood by specialists only.
3. *der Allgemeine Deutsche Sprachverein*	(c) A large state-run company in the GDR.
4. *Fachsprache*	(d) Type of language which is neither standard German nor a traditional regional dialect.
5. *der Anschluss*	(e) Economic system set up in West Germany after World War II.
6. *freie Marktwirtschaft*	(f) The theory which suggests that there were two national varieties of German in East and West Germany.
7. *der Broiler*	(g) Term most commonly used to describe the former East Germany after the *Wende*.
8. *die neuen Bundesländer*	(h) The organisation which promoted the *Pflege und Hebung der deutschen Sprache* in the early twentieth century.
9. *regionale Umgangssprache*	(i) German term for the annexation of Austria in 1938.
10. *die Vier-Varianten-These*	(j) The word for 'roast chicken' commonly used in the GDR.

3

The German-speaking areas

Did you know that German is also used in Liechtenstein and Luxembourg, as well as in parts of Belgium, Italy, France, Denmark, the former Soviet Union, Poland, Hungary, Romania, the Czech Republic, Slovakia, the United States, Canada, Latin America, Namibia, South Africa, Israel and Australia? It seems logical to suggest that, when learning a foreign language, it is helpful to know exactly *who* speaks that language and *where*. This chapter gives you an overview of the various countries and regions where German is used.

Let us begin, however, by looking at some general facts and figures about German. How many German speakers are there today? And how does the use of German compare to other languages? It is, in fact, extremely difficult to estimate the exact number of speakers for any language but the total for German would appear to lie somewhere between 90 and 93 million (*see* Table 3.1). This means that, in terms of the various languages spoken world-wide, German ranks about tenth – Chinese, by comparison, has approximately 770 million speakers, English, some 415 million, and Spanish, 285 million. In an international context, therefore, German cannot really be considered amongst the most widely used of modern languages. Moreover, it has definitely lost ground to English over the past hundred years or so, a trend which seems set to continue.

In a European context, however, the significance of German is still indisputable. This is in so far as many countries in mainland Western and Central Europe either have German as their principal language, include a region where German is spoken, and/or are home to a German-speaking minority. German is also used in diplomatic or political negotiations, and is one of the main languages of the European Union. In addition, German functions as a language of trade and industry, often being used as a **lingua franca,** that is to say, a medium of communication between native speakers of other languages. This is a role which is likely to develop in the future, especially in Central and Eastern Europe.

Given the size and range of the German-speaking areas, it will come as no surprise to discover that the status of the language differs considerably from one context to the next. Table 3.1 shows how German variously functions as sole official language, one of several official languages, an official regional variety, or a language with limited or even no formal recognition. In each case, however, the status of German is closely linked not only to geographical, but also historical, factors.

Table 3.1 The status of German and number of speakers

Status	Countries	Number
Sole official language	Germany	78 000 000
	Austria	7 500 000
	Liechtenstein	29 000
One of several official languages	Switzerland	4 000 000
	Luxembourg	370 000
Official regional status	Belgium	100 000–200 000
	Italy	290 000
Limited or no official status	*Western Europe*	
	France	1 200 000
	Denmark	20 000
	Former Eastern Bloc Countries	
	Former Soviet Union (CIS)	1 100 000
	Poland	1 100 000
	Hungary	220 000
	Romania	200 000
	Czech Republic and Slovakia	62 000
	Outside Europe	
	United States and Canada	2 000 000
	Latin America	2 000 000
	Namibia and South Africa	60 000–75 000
	Israel	96 000
	Australia	110 000–175 000

(Figures from Russ, 1994: 8 and Ammon, 1991: 36)

3.1 The status of German in Western and Central Europe

If we are to consider the status of German in Europe, the most obvious place to begin is with those countries where the language has its historical roots: Germany, Austria, Switzerland and Liechtenstein.

3.1.1 Germany

German is the sole official language of the Federal Republic of Germany or *Bundesrepublik Deutschland*. This is the country which came into existence in 1990 following the unification of the former Federal Republic of Germany (West Germany) and the German Democratic Republic (East Germany). It is also the country which contains the largest number of native speakers of German approximately 78 million.

What do we mean when we say that German is the 'sole official language'? Basically, this implies that if you lived in Germany, you would normally expect to hear German on the television and radio, and to be educated at school in that language. German politics will, of course, be conducted in German, and the written form of the language in newspapers or native works of literature will also be German. The same can be said of Austria and Liechtenstein.

Written German has a clearly defined and codified form, which is recorded in dictionaries, grammars, and school textbooks. This is variously referred to as 'standard German' (*Standarddeutsch*), 'High German' (*Hochdeutsch*) or sometimes simply 'written German' (*Schriftdeutsch*). It is this version of the language which is taught in schools and which is normally learned by foreigners.

Despite the existence of a standard form of the written language, however, spoken German is by no means uniform. There is, of course, a standard version of pronunciation based, primarily, on the dialects traditionally used in northern Germany. But German, like all languages, can be spoken with different types of regional pronunciation, vocabulary and grammar. Thus, a north German from Hamburg, for example, will have little difficulty identifying a south German from, say, Munich (*see* Fig. 3.1). This can be compared to the way in which someone from the north of England can discern a southern English speaker.

Although German has sole *official* status, this does not necessarily mean that it is the only language which is spoken there. Many Germans, especially in border areas, will be accustomed to using other languages on certain occasions. Those living close to France or Denmark, for example, might cross the frontier in order to go shopping or even to work in the other country. Germans in such regions are also quite used to watching television programmes in other languages, and perhaps even to being addressed in, say, French or Danish by visitors to their area.

In addition, Germany, Austria, and Switzerland have several million first and second generation migrant workers or *Gastarbeiter* (as they are often euphemistically referred to in German), who were invited from the 1950s onwards to help fill the shortfall in manual labour as a result of the post-war economic boom. This means that there are many people living and working in the German-speaking countries who do not necessarily use German exclusively. Instead, they may speak German outside of the home but converse with their families and friends in Turkish, Greek, Spanish, Serbo-Croatian, or Italian.

From this brief discussion of the German language in Germany, two things should be clear. First of all, even though there is a standardised written version of the language, this does not mean that the type of German

KEY:
1 Nordslesvig
2 Old/New Belgium
3 Alsace and Lorraine
4 South Tyrol
5 Liechtenstein

Fig. 3.1 The Federal Republic of Germany and neighbouring countries

spoken in the different parts of Germany is necessarily the same. Second, just because German has the status of sole official language does not mean that it is the only language which is used.

3.1.2 Austria

The Federal Republic of Austria or *Bundesrepublik Österreich* does not, geographically, belong to Western but to *Central* Europe. Like Germany, however, Austria also has German as its sole official language, with an estimated 7.5 million speakers.

One of the questions frequently asked by foreign learners of German is to what extent the German spoken in Austria differs from so-called *Binnendeutsch*, that is to say, the variety used in Germany. This is a tricky question, not least because many Austrians tire of being likened to Germans, and are often keen to assert their separate identity.

However, if we continue to use the comparison with Germany for the time being, there are a number of observations which can be made. First, it should be noted that the written form of the German language used in Austria is (with a few minor exceptions) the same as the one used in Germany. Advanced foreign students of German will therefore have no more difficulty reading Austrian newspapers or literature than they would have with texts originating from the Federal Republic of Germany.

The greatest difference between the two countries probably relates to the spoken language. So when an Austrian and a German speak to one another, they will generally have few problems of comprehension, given that the language both are speaking is indisputably German. However, there will probably be aspects of the pronunciation, vocabulary, and grammar which mark out each speaker as Austrian or German.

One area where the types of German used in Austria and Germany do differ quite noticeably is in terms of institutional language. Because the two countries have distinct histories and political systems, there are a number of terms which vary. For example, the lower house of parliament in Austria is called *der Nationalrat*, whereas in Germany it is *der Bundestag*. Similarly, 18- or 19-year-old pupils in Austrian schools take an examination known as *die Matura*, whereas the equivalent in Germany is *das Abitur*.

Another area where Austrian German differs from *Binnendeutsch* relates to the kinds of foreign words which have been integrated into the language. It can be seen from Fig. 3.2 that Austria borders not only on Germany,

Fig. 3.2 Austria

Switzerland, and Liechtenstein but also Italy, the Czech Republic, Slovakia, Hungary, and Slovenia in the former Yugoslavia. This inevitably means that different foreign influences have found their way into Austrian German, especially where food is concerned. Thus, green beans are known as *Fisolen* in Austria (*grüne Bohnen* in Germany), and cauliflower is *der Karfiol* (*der Blumenkohl*), both of which are derived from Italian. Similarly, sweetcorn is known as *der Kukuruz* (*der Mais*) and an Austrian speciality is a kind of stuffed pancake referred to as *die Palatschinke*, terms which are probably descended from Czech. Finally, Austrian German contains a number of older words which have disappeared in other German-speaking areas. The first two months of the year are referred to as *Jänner* and *Feber*, for example, not *Januar* and *Februar* as in Germany.

It must be stressed that these differences are fairly minimal from the point of view of anyone learning German as a foreign language. From Fig. 3.2, it can be seen that Austria shares a long border with the south-east of Germany. It is to be expected, therefore, that the forms of German used in this part of Germany have much in common with those used in Austria. This is not least due to the fact that south Germany and Austria both use varieties which are historically of Upper German origin (see 2.2.1).

Another reason why it can be misleading to describe Austrian German solely in terms of its difference from *Binnendeutsch* is because there is also considerable linguistic variation within Austria itself. So, for example, inhabitants of the Austrian capital Vienna, in the east, will normally be able to discern the west Austrian speech of someone from the state of *Voralberg* near Switzerland, or *Tirol* on the Italian border.

Finally, it should be noted that the type of situation in which an Austrian is speaking will also have a noticeable influence on the kind of German used. Most Austrians and Germans have a variety of different ways of speaking German at their disposal. These will depend upon the level of formality, for example, and the person with whom they are conversing. Although all speakers of all languages frequently modify their speech to some extent, it is probably true to say that the range is much broader for Austrians than for the average English speaker. Having said this, most Austrians are also able to use a standardised form of Austrian German. This **Austrian Standard German**, which is used on television or radio news, for example, is not quite the same as the standard variety used in Germany but it is perfectly comprehensible to foreign learners of German who have learned *Binnendeutsch*.

3.1.3   Switzerland

The German language in Switzerland provides a fascinating contrast with Germany and Austria. This is partly because German is officially only one of several Swiss languages, and also because the varieties of German which are used differ in many respects from those in the other two countries. In this section, we shall begin with a general discussion of **multilingualism** in Switzerland, before looking at the specific status of German.

MULTILINGUALISM IN SWITZERLAND

Switzerland has four official languages: German, French, Italian, and Romansch. Defining clearly who speaks which language is not an easy undertaking. This is partly because most Swiss citizens speak at least one of the other three languages. In other words, they are, to a greater or lesser extent, bilingual, trilingual or even multilingual. Moreover, many German, French and Italian people also live and work in Switzerland.

Overall, German is the most widely spoken of the four Swiss languages. It is the mother tongue of approximately 73 per cent of the population, which amounts to some 4 million speakers (though some sources estimate up to 6.5 million). It is also the official language of several Swiss cantons (states) in the central and northern regions of the country, including, as one would expect, the area bordering on Germany (*see* Fig. 3.3). French is the first language learned by some 20 per cent of the Swiss population, and is spoken in the western cantons adjacent to France. (The long interior border which divides the German- and French-speaking cantons is known as *der Röstigraben* – *Rösti*, after a popular potato dish served in German-speaking Switzerland, and *Graben* in the sense of 'trench'!)

Italian is the mother tongue of around 5 per cent of the population in the south of Switzerland close to the Italian border. Finally, Romansch, is

Fig. 3.3 Switzerland

one of the official languages in Grisons (*Graubünden*), a canton in the east of Switzerland, and is spoken by approximately 1 per cent of the Swiss population. Having said this, it is probably misleading to refer to Romansch as a discrete 'language', since we are in fact dealing with a group of five different dialects, although there have been attempts to create a single standard variety called *Rumantsch Grischun*. The remaining 1 per cent of Swiss people speak a language other than German, French, Italian or Romansch.

Although it is not easy to define exactly *who* speaks which language in Switzerland, it is nonetheless fairly clear *where* the different languages are used. According to the Swiss constitution, every canton has the right to specify German, French, Italian, or Romansch as its official language (a small number of cantons are bilingual). This, in turn, means that anyone who lives in, or travels through, Switzerland, knows more or less which language is spoken and where. The way in which the use of different languages within a particular country is divided according to geographical region is known as the **territorial principle**. In Switzerland, this *Territorialprinzip* is considered to be one of the main reasons why there is relative linguistic stability despite the number of different languages spoken, and the potential for conflict between their speakers.

THE GERMAN LANGUAGE IN SWITZERLAND

German is the most widely spoken of the four languages in Switzerland, and is the official language of several cantons in the northern and central regions of the country. But even within this relatively clearly defined territory, the kinds of German which are used vary considerably.

Switzerland, like Germany and Austria, has its own standardised version of German. This is known as **Swiss Standard German** (or Swiss High German) and is the variety of German heard on television and radio in Switzerland, and learnt at German-speaking schools. Its written form is more or less the same as the one used in Germany and Austria, although one important difference is the complete absence of 'ß' ('ss' is used in its place). However, the spoken version of the standard language is very much identifiable as 'Swiss' rather than German or Austrian. This is because some aspects of the pronunciation differ quite noticeably, although a German or Austrian would have little difficulty holding a conversation with a Swiss person speaking Swiss Standard German.

Another area which marks out Swiss Standard German from the standard varieties in Germany or Austria is the vocabulary. Switzerland has its own distinct historical and cultural tradition with the result that certain words differ from those used in Germany or Austria, particularly in the domain of politics and administration. The Federal states of Switzerland are referred to as cantons or *Kantone* whereas in Germany and Austria they are called *Bundesländer*. Similarly, the lower house of parliament is known as *der Nationalrat* (as in Austria) compared to *der Bundestag* in Germany.

If there is one single feature which most distinguishes Swiss Standard German vocabulary, then it is probably the kind of foreign words which have been integrated into the language. The German used in Switzerland is, and always has been, in very close contact with other languages, especially French. Anyone travelling through Switzerland will immediately be struck by the many French words used there. If you wished to travel by train, for example, you would ask for a *Billet* as opposed to a *Fahrkarte*. The person to check your ticket would be called *der Kondukteur* rather than *der Schaffner*.

Swiss Standard German is, however, only one of the many varieties of German which are spoken in Switzerland. It is *not* the version which Swiss people generally use in order to communicate with one another. At home or in shops, for example, a rather different kind of German is heard. There, Swiss speakers use one of several regional dialects, which are collectively referred to as **Swiss German** or *Schwyzertütsch*. These dialects are unmistakably German, but the pronunciation, grammar, and vocabulary differ markedly from those of the standard language.

In many cases, Swiss German dialects are not only spoken, they are also written. The following is an extract from a story written in *Züritüütsch*, the variety of Swiss German used around Zurich.

Zurich Swiss German

De morge
Es isch morge. D wält isch nanig verwachet. De wald isch stile. D tier schlaafed na. En chüele wind strycht über s land und bewegt daa und deet es Gresli.

High German

Der Morgen
Es ist morgen. Die Welt ist noch nicht erwacht. Der Wald ist still. Die Tiere schlafen noch. Ein kühler Wind streicht über das Land und bewegt da und dort ein Gräslein.

English translation

The morning
It is morning. The world has not yet awakened. The forest is quiet. The animals are sleeping. A chilly wind brushes over the countryside and moves blades of grass here and there.

(From Russ, 1990b: 380–1)

We can see then that the status of the German language in Switzerland is both fascinating and complex. On the one hand, German is only one of four official languages spoken. On the other hand, the kind of German used depends on the situation in which Swiss speakers find themselves. In formal settings and with non-Swiss German speakers, they will tend to use Swiss Standard German. In more familiar situations and with other Swiss German speakers, they will use the variety of *Schwyzertütsch* which is spoken in their region of Switzerland. Having said this, there would appear to be an ongoing shift in the domains in which the two types of German occur. Thus, there is increasing demand on the part of Swiss German speakers for *Schwyzertütsch* to be used in areas formerly reserved for Swiss Standard German, e.g. television and radio, especially where regional programmes are concerned.

This situation where two different versions of the same language exist, and where each is used in different situations, is known in linguistics as **diglossia**. Of the two varieties, one is considered to be the **High (H) variety** (e.g. Swiss Standard/High German), whilst the other is deemed to be the **Low (L) variety** (e.g. *Schwyzertütsch*). Other languages whose usage is characterised by this phenomenon include Haitian French, Greek, and Arabic. Moreover, Switzerland, as we shall see later, is not the only German-speaking area which displays diglossia.

It is important to emphasise to non-native learners of German that they should not be disturbed if they do not at first understand *Schwyzertütsch*. Indeed, with the exception of those who live close to the Swiss border, there are many Germans and Austrians who do not readily comprehend the various Swiss German dialects. This is why many television programmes containing Swiss German actually appear with High German sub-titles when shown in Germany or Austria. However, it must also be stressed that the existence of these dialects does not mean that non-native learners of German cannot communicate with the Swiss – it is simply that, when speaking with foreigners (including Germans and Austrians), Swiss people will tend to use Swiss Standard German. Similarly, there is no reason why non-native speakers of German cannot learn *Schwyzertütsch* like any other language. Indeed, there are a number of course books written specifically for this purpose such as Müller and Wertenschlag's *'Los emol.' Schweizerdeutsch verstehen* (1994).

3.1.4   Liechtenstein

Liechtenstein is the tiny principality wedged between Switzerland and Austria (*see* Fig. 3.1). It is the fourth smallest country in the world, with an area of only 160 sq km and has approximately 29 000 inhabitants. Apart from Germany and Austria, Liechtenstein is the only other country which has German as its sole official language. Having said this, the use of German is probably more akin to the Swiss situation in so far as it is characterised by diglossia. Although very little is known about the diglossic situation in Liechtenstein, it has been suggested that the use of a standardised version of

German is more widespread than in Switzerland. This may be related to the fact that some 3000 Austrians and Swiss also live in Liechtenstein, many of whom are themselves speakers of standard German and work for foreign companies in the capital, Vaduz.

In informal situations, inhabitants of Liechtenstein tend to speak so-called Liechtenstein dialect, which is similar to the variety of Swiss German used across the border in Switzerland, and to the German spoken in the neighbouring state of *Voralberg* in Austria. In schools, however, the use of dialect is discouraged. Similarly, the language of parliament, the courts, the church, and administration is clearly defined as standard German.

3.1.5 Luxembourg

Luxembourg, like Liechtenstein, is a landlocked country, this time bordering on France, Belgium, and Germany (*see* Fig. 3.1). The population of approximately 29 000 uses one or more of three languages: **Luxembourgish** (*Lëtzebuergesch*), French, and standard German.

The first language normally learned by Luxembourgians in the home is Luxembourgish. This is a variety of German belonging to the Franconian group of dialects (*Fränkisch*), which are historically of Central German origin (see 2.2.1). Luxembourgish is therefore closely related to other Central German varieties which are used in those parts of Germany immediately to the east of Luxembourg, as well as in south-east Belgium. Yet many Luxembourgians deny that Luxembourgish is a form of German. Moreover, non-native speakers who have only learned standard German might find it rather unfamiliar. Consider, for example, the following passage:

Luxembourgish

Vernünftiges Lëtzebuergesch
Mir hun e sëlléchen Aarbecht vrun eis, an et
gët kee Mënsch, deen se fir eis mécht. Mir
musse selwer kucke, wéi mer eens gin.
Allerdéngs heescht et fir d'éischt ze kucke,
wou mer d'Suen, déi mer bruachen, hirhuelen.

Standard German

Vernünftiges Luxemburgisch
Wir haben eine solche Arbeit vor uns, und es
gibt niemanden, der sie für uns macht. Wir
müssen selber sehen, wie wir uns einigen können.
Allerdings heißt es zuerst zu sehen,
wo wir das Geld, das wir brauchen, herholen können.

English translation

Reasonable Luxembourgish
We have a lot of work in front of us, and
there is no-one who will do it for us. We'll
have to look for ourselves how we can agree.
First of all of course it's a question of where
we can get the money from that we need.

(Adapted from Newton, 1990: 200–1.
Author's own translation of Standard German)

Having acquired Luxembourgish as their first language, Luxembourgians enter school where they learn standard German – a process which is relatively easy, given the close relationship between the two varieties. After this, they learn French, thus eventually becoming trilingual.

The language choices made by Luxembourgians are quite complex. On the one hand, French tends to be the language of the street, appearing on shop and road signs. On the other hand, French and standard German are used in education, whereas French and Luxembourgish are used in parliament. All three languages have written forms, and are employed in the writing of fictional literature. However, which language is chosen by individual authors would appear to depend on social class or education, with intellectuals preferring to write in Luxembourgish, the middle classes in French, and the working classes in standard German.

The status of standard German in Luxembourg is extremely interesting. After World War II, its usage declined in popularity, though not to the extent that French became totally dominant. In schools, pupils are taught to view standard German as the norm – at least where the written language is concerned – but they nonetheless tend to speak Luxembourgish with one another. On the whole, standard German is rarely spoken within Luxembourg except as a means of communicating with Germans and other foreigners. When Luxembourgians do speak standard German, however, it is with a melodic kind of intonation reminiscent of French. As in Switzerland, French has had a noticeable influence on the vocabulary, for example, in words such as *die Tëlëvisioun* (*der Fernseher*).

The way in which Luxembourgians are able to speak three languages is fascinating in itself, but it would also appear to be an integral part of their sense of national identity. On the one hand, this trilingualism means that Luxembourgians are not linguistically isolated from their immediate neighbours. Living in a relatively small, landlocked country, it is clearly useful to have a knowledge of French and standard German for political, economic, and cultural reasons. It also makes sense in view of the fact that many major bodies of the European Union are located in Luxembourg. On the other hand, the ability to speak three languages also seems to function as a way in which Luxembourgians can distance themselves from their neighbours, and thus establish their own unique identity. In other words,

Luxembourgians are Luxembourgians precisely because they speak three languages – although the fact that one of those languages is only spoken in Luxembourg cannot, of course, be overlooked.

3.1.6   Belgium

Three languages are spoken in Belgium: French, Dutch, and German. As in Switzerland, the use of these different languages is divided primarily on geographical or territorial lines. French is spoken in the southern region bordering on France, known as Wallonia, whereas Dutch is the main language of the northern region, Flanders, which borders on the Netherlands. The capital, Brussels, is officially bilingual (French/Dutch). German, on the other hand, is used in a much smaller area. It is spoken along the eastern border with Germany and in the southern region adjacent to Luxembourg around Arlon (*see* Fig. 3.1).

Most discussions of language use in Belgium centre on the highly politicised conflict between French and Dutch. This means that Belgium compares markedly to Luxembourg and Switzerland in the way in which it comes to terms with its inherent multilingualism. Inevitably, the position of German is very much caught up in the controversies surrounding the other two languages, although many would argue that the language has indirectly benefited, as opposed to suffered, from the conflict.

The situation in Belgium is further complicated by the fact that the status of German is not identical throughout the different German-speaking regions of the country. In any discussion of German, therefore, it is necessary to distinguish between two areas: **Old Belgium**, on the one hand, and New Belgium, on the other. The areas collectively referred to as Old Belgium have been part of the country since 1830, whereas **New Belgium** was ceded by Germany in 1920 as part of the Treaty of Versailles following World War I.

Old Belgium consists of Old Belgium North, Old Belgium Central and Old Belgium South, and the status of German differs in each. In Old Belgium North, French is the official language, although German and Dutch are also permitted in some areas of administration. Old Belgium Central and South are considered part of Wallonia, and are therefore officially French-speaking, even though many German speakers live there. The situation in *New Belgium* (Eupen, St Vith, Malmédy) is somewhat clearer. In Eupen, St Vith and the eastern part of Malmédy, German has official status, although French may also be used. In the rest of Malmédy, the situation is reversed: French is the official language but German is also permissible.

Given the differing status of German in the various regions of Belgium, it is not easy to calculate the exact number of speakers. The most recent estimates date from a census carried out in 1947, so the number can probably be considered anywhere between 100 000 and 200 000. The kind of German used by Belgians also varies, with slightly different dialects spoken in the various regions. The written language, however, which is used in the media, is more or less the same as in Germany. German is also taught in some schools in New Belgium, though this, too, is a complex issue. Caught up in the wider conflict between French and Dutch, many parents are keen for these to be the languages of the classroom, a situation which is complicated further by the lack of staff qualified to teach in German.

So what will be the future of the German language in Belgium? Again, this depends upon the region in question. In Old Belgium, French is already dominant. Although German is used at home by some families, French is the main language in public domains (business/church/schools) and semi-public domains (work/media). In New Belgium, the situation is somewhat more ambivalent, depending, to a certain extent, on the political views of individual speakers. Those who see New Belgium as part of Wallonia clearly favour French, frequently arguing that the use of German constitutes a symbol of disloyalty. On the other hand, those who would prefer the establishment of an autonomous region would like to see the preservation of the German language within a multilingual Belgian state. What will be the outcome of these tensions is not clear. At the present time, however, it seems that Belgium contains an interesting combination of German-speaking regions and groups, some of which look set to die out, whilst others are thriving.

3.1.7   Italy

South Tyrol is an autonomous province which lies within the region of Trentino-Alto Adige in the north of Italy (*see* Fig. 3.1). It is home to some 290 000 native German speakers, that is to say, approximately 0.05 per cent of the total population of Italy. South Tyroleans speak a variety of German similar to the Upper German dialects found in Bavaria and Austria, but they often use a variety close to Austrian Standard German in more formal situations.

South Tyrol borders on the Federal State of *Tirol* in Austria. As their names suggest, the two areas originally comprised one state. Prior to 1919, the whole of Tyrol belonged to Austria and was part of the **Austro-Hungarian empire**. Like the German-speaking regions of Belgium and France, South Tyrol was then ceded to Italy in line with the Treaty of Versailles following World War I. However, the population of the province had no say in their change of nationality, and it is generally agreed that, had a referendum been held, the South Tyroleans would probably have chosen to stay with Austria.

The fact that South Tyroleans were initially unwilling Italians had a considerable impact on the language policies which were implemented by successive Italian central governments. In 1922, when the Italian fascists seized power, the use of German was banned in public domains in an attempt to assimilate the German-speaking population. However, their efforts were unsuccessful in so far as German speakers continued to use the language in those places where the authorities had no control: at home and in church. From the mid-1930s onwards, this official ban was coupled with a new industrialisation programme, one of the aims of which was to bring more Italian speakers to the region in order to weaken the status of German and consolidate that of Italian. The proportion of German speakers in South Tyrol then declined further when, as a result of a treaty between Hitler and Mussolini in 1939, German speakers were given a choice between leaving the country, or remaining in Italy and renouncing their claim to minority status. Although the policies of industrialisation and re-settlement were never fully implemented as a result of World War II, there was nonetheless a dramatic reduction in the number of German speakers in South Tyrol during this time.

The relationship between German and Italian speakers from 1945 onwards was never a comfortable one. However, a significant political step was taken when Italy granted regional autonomy to South Tyrol in 1972 and German was given co-official status alongside Italian. This meant that German speakers could now use German when dealing with local government authorities, and German-speaking schools were also introduced. Although this was a positive move in terms of the survival of German, it has led to other, as yet unresolved, tensions with Italian speakers in the region.

In South Tyrol today, the German language enjoys a relatively prestigious status. As a minority language, it is thriving, primarily because it continues to be used. But as shown in discussions of other regions where German is spoken, there are two factors which tend to promote stable forms of bilingualism and both of these are potentially lacking in South Tyrol.

The first problem is that there is no territorial division of German and Italian. In Switzerland, for example, the use of the different languages is clearly demarcated along geographical lines. In South Tyrol, this is not the case. For example, in the capital, Bolzano, German- and Italian-speaking communities live side by side, with children attending either German or Italian schools and learning the other language as a second language. Thus, German is by no means completely dominant within South Tyrol, and will always be, to a greater or lesser extent, in competition with the national language, Italian.

The second factor relates to the domains of usage for German and Italian. In bilingual communities, there is often some form of tacit agreement regarding which language is spoken in which situation. This, in turn, normally helps to stabilise the use of both languages. In South Tyrol, however, it seems that both German and Italian are acceptable in more or less all domains. The use of one language or the other tends therefore to depend on the individual speaker. If Italian is your mother tongue, then you are likely to speak Italian at home, go to an Italian school, and use Italian in your dealings with the regional authorities. Similarly, if German is your first language, then you will probably use German in such situations.

Where the use of a minority language is neither clearly defined along territorial lines nor according to domains of usage, there is always the possibility that the dominant language – in this case Italian – will eventually gain the upper hand. At present, German speakers living in South Tyrol are more likely to be bilingual than Italian speakers. So it could be that the future of German depends on the willingness of Italian speakers living in the region to learn German. However, there are positive trends from the point of view of those who would advocate the continued use of German in South Tyrol. It seems that Italian speakers are recognising the need for a knowledge of German, if only for more general economic reasons – the number of Germans and Austrians visiting the area for tourism (especially skiing) is undoubtedly one factor.

3.1.8   France

Alsace is a region in the north-east of France and is home to an estimated 1.2 million speakers of **Alsatian**. Although Alsatian is often talked of as though it were an independent language, it really consists of a number of dialects. These, in turn, are closely related to the different varieties of German which are spoken across the border in Luxembourg, Germany, and Switzerland (*see* Fig. 3.1). Despite the relatively high number of speakers, Alsatian has no official recognition within France. The reasons for this are to be found in the complex history of the region.

Alsace has had a chequered past, having changed hands six times in the last 350 years, and no less than three times during the twentieth century. Until 1648, the region was part of the (German) Holy Roman Empire. Between 1648 and 1870, it belonged to France. Then, following France's defeat in the Franco-Prussian wars, the area was re-claimed by Germany, and remained in German hands until 1919. However, it was given back to France in accordance with the Treaty of Versailles after Germany's defeat in World War I. During World War II, the region was occupied by the National Socialists from 1940 to 1945. Finally, following Germany's capitulation, Alsace was returned to France, where it looks set to remain. Since that time, a gradual process of Frenchification has occurred, such that French is now indisputably the dominant language. This is due, in no small measure, to the refusal of the French government to grant any form of official minority status to Alsatian.

As far as the spoken language is concerned, Alsatian consists of four dialects, which are used in the different regions of Alsace and Lorraine.

These are:

- Moselle Franconian/*Moselfränkisch*
  (spoken near the border with Luxembourg)
- Rhenish Franconian/*Rheinfränkisch*
  (spoken in Lorraine)
- Low Alemannic/*Niederalemannisch*
  (spoken in the greater part of Alsace)
- High Alemannic/*Hochalemannisch*
  (spoken near the Swiss border)

Although the various Alsatian dialects can be found in written form, the written language is normally standard German. This means that Alsace is characterised by diglossia. Alsatian is the Low (L) variety, used in familiar situations such as conversations with family and friends. Technically therefore, the H variety is standard German – at least where the written language is concerned. However, in those situations where one would normally expect the H variety to be employed, e.g. work, administration, education, etc., it is not standard German which is generally used but French. Thus, the diglossic situation is more complex than in Switzerland. To sum up: the L variety is Alsatian but the H variety is French.

Not only are High and Low forms of language used in Alsace, one often encounters so-called **code switching** between Alsatian and French, i.e. where speakers mix the two varieties in the same conversation. The following is an extract from a play performed in Strasbourg:

Alsatian

T: Ja. Monsieur, sie müehn exküsiere.
C: Vous êtes toute excusée.
T: Waje was kumme Sie eijentlich?
C: Je viens en affaires. Ich moecht im Monsieur Argan e Läwesversicherung proposiere, wo 'ne geje jedi Eventualität deckt. Ich bin, wie sie allewäj schun wisse, Inspecteur vun dr Compagnie 'La Flamme'. Wotte Sie jetzt eso ardlich sin, un mich bim Monsieur Argan aanmelde.

English

T: Yes. Sir, you must excuse me. (i.e. 'please excuse me')
C: You're already excused. (i.e. 'of course')
T: Why have you come? (i.e. 'how can I help you?')
C: I am here on business. I would like to propose a life insurance policy to Monsieur Argan, one which covers all kinds of liability. I am, as you know, head of the company 'La Flamme'. Would you be so kind as to tell Monsieur Argan that I am here.

(From Philipp and Bothorel-Witz, 1990: 314–15. Author's own translation)

So what does the future look like for Alsatian? Most linguists agree that Alsatian is in fact under severe threat of extinction, and there are probably two main reasons for this. The first is that there is no unified variety of Alsatian. It is important to note that whereas Moselle Franconian and Rhenish Franconian belong to the Central German dialect group, Low and High Alemannic are of Upper German origin (see 2.2.1). This makes it very difficult to promote the use of Alsatian in schools or the media since there is no one standard version, which is acceptable to, and understood by, all speakers. However, given the conflict-ridden history of Alsace, the teaching of Alsatian in schools has never really been on the agenda since 1945. This brings us to the second point: unlike in other regions where there are German-speaking minorities (e.g. Belgium and Italy), there are no vociferous political movements in Alsace which see the preservation of Alsatian – not least, through education – as their aim.

Nowadays most Alsatians, and certainly all of the younger generation, consider themselves to be French, albeit *French citizens of Alsace*. Many, it would appear, are keen to avoid the use of Alsatian in order to distance themselves from Germany and the Germans – an attitude which must be seen in its historical context. Parents are no longer particularly anxious for their children to learn Alsatian at home, generally preferring them to speak French. Thus a situation is emerging where the remaining speakers of Alsatian belong primarily to the older generations. As an Alsatian friend of mine in her twenties pointed out: 'When my grandparents did not want my parents to understand what they were saying, they spoke French. But when *my* parents did not want me and my brothers to understand what they were talking about, they spoke Alsatian.'

This is, of course, the most obvious way for any language to die out. If parents no longer teach Alsatian to their children, then it could take as little as two generations for the language to disappear completely. But in spite of this apparent antipathy towards Alsatian, many young people in Alsace still recognise the importance of learning standard German. They may, for example, need to use the language as part of their job or even wish to commute across the border in order to work in Germany. Thus, there appears to be a shift in attitudes, with German increasingly being perceived as a foreign language – the language of Germany.

Whether or not Alsatian is really on the verge of extinction is difficult to say. But it does seem that Alsace is the one where the position of German is the least stable. In fact, some linguists now use the term 'Alsace syndrome' (*die Verelsässerung*) to refer to any situation where the future of a minority language is under serious threat.

3.1.9 Denmark

The last of the nine countries to be considered in this section is quite different from those we have looked at so far. This is because, for the first time, we are dealing with a border area of Germany where there are minority groups on both sides (*see* Fig. 3.1).

The ethnic make-up of the region formally known as the Duchy of Schleswig is highly complex. Many different minority groups settled here in the nineteenth century, and a number of languages and dialects are still spoken today. The Duchy had long been a disputed territory as far as Prussia and Denmark were concerned, culminating in the Prussian–Danish war in 1863 and the subsequent annexation of Schleswig by the Prussians in 1866. Following World War I, the Treaty of Versailles stipulated that the future of the region should be decided by referendum. In 1920, the population was therefore asked whether it wished to belong to Germany or Denmark, and different minority groups came to different decisions. In the northern province, *Nordslesvig*, 75 per cent of the population voted to stay with Denmark. In the south, the majority opted for Germany and the region became part of the German state of Schleswig-Holstein. Border disputes continued well into the 1950s, with both countries hoping for some kind of realignment although this was not to be the case.

One consequence of the 1920 referendum was that both countries were left with linguistic minorities: a German-speaking minority in *Nordslesvig* and a Danish-speaking minority in Schleswig-Holstein. Today, it is estimated that there are some 20 000 German speakers in Denmark and 50 000 Danish speakers in Germany. However, it is difficult to assess the accuracy of these figures, not least since several other languages and dialects are also spoken in these regions. Thus, there are varying numbers of speakers of standard Danish and standard German, South Jutlandish (a dialect of Danish), North Frisian (an umbrella term for some nine different dialects) and Low German. Moreover, the use of these different varieties is not clearly divided according to any kind of territorial principle. In *Nordslesvig* the ethnic German population lives side by side with other Danes, who speak South Jutlandish and standard Danish. These Germans are also likely to speak South Jutlandish (or Low German) at home, restricting their usage of standard German to schools, churches and social clubs.

Probably the single most important reason why Danish and German have survived in the two host countries has been due to the provision of bilingual education. In *Nordslesvig* there are now some 18 schools and 24 kindergartens, which are run according to the German model and where German is the language of instruction. These are attended by approximately 1800 children. Similarly, in Schleswig-Holstein, there are some 53 schools and 62 kindergartens, which are run on Danish lines and attended by approximately 7000 children. Although the establishment of such schools has not been without its problems, there appears to have been considerable success in providing the two minority groups with an alternative to mainstream education.

In conclusion, it would seem that German and Danish are fairly well established in their respective host countries – it is the other varieties which are under threat of extinction: South Jutlandish, North Frisian, and Low German.

3.2   German-speaking minorities in former Eastern bloc countries

With the fall of the Berlin Wall in 1989 and the subsequent political upheavals in the former Warsaw Pact countries, the status of the German language looks set to change rapidly in the twenty-first century. Indeed, given the relative economic strength of Germany and Austria, and the central geographic position which they occupy within Europe, the significance of German is already shifting. For many Eastern Europeans, the learning of German (though, to a greater extent, English) is perceived as a means of improving cultural, political, and economic communications with countries which had very different systems of government to their own during the larger part of the twentieth century. It has been estimated that, of the 19 million learners of German world-wide, 12 million are to be found in Eastern Europe.

However, this would appear to imply that the influence of German is something new to this part of the world when, in fact, nothing could be further from the truth. German has a long history in Eastern Europe, and although the prestige and usage of the language undoubtedly declined in the twentieth century, it is estimated that there are still up to 4 million minority speakers of German scattered across a number of former Eastern bloc countries today. We shall be looking here at the status of German in five such countries: the former Soviet Union, Poland, Hungary, Romania and Czechoslovakia (now: the Czech Republic and Slovakia) (*see* Fig. 3.4).

3.2.1   *Former Soviet Union*

Between 1917 and 1991, the Soviet Union was the world's largest sovereign state, consisting of 15 Soviet Socialist Republics. Following its dissolution in December 1991, 10 of those republics formed a new body known as the 'Commonwealth of Independent States' (CIS). In the old Soviet Union, Russia was the largest of the Socialist Republics, and Russians comprised the main ethnic group (52 per cent of the population), hence the dominance of the Russian language. There were, however, over 100 other ethnic groups and many different languages were spoken. One of these was German.

In the eighteenth and nineteenth centuries, when Russia was under Tsarist rule, there were several waves of German immigration to various parts of the country. Under Catherine the Great, Russian Empress from

Fig. 3.4 Central and Eastern Europe

1762–96 and herself a German, many Germans were invited to settle in the region around the Volga river in order to strengthen the area economically, preparing the way for Russian expansionism in the east. Many such immigrants sailed from Rostock and Lübeck across the Baltic Sea (*Ostsee*) to the Russian port of St Petersburg. They then continued their journey southwards to Saratov and, together with other German speakers from East Prussia and from the Baltic area around Riga, established German communities, which were to become active in many areas of administration, trade, and industry. By the middle of the nineteenth century, there were some 3000 German colonies in Russia and, by the end of the century, several more in Siberia, Kazakhstan, Central Asia, and the Altai region (near China and Mongolia). In 1897, there were some 1.8 million Germans living in Russia, with approximately 400 000 having settled in the Volga region.

The fate of these ethnic Germans in the twentieth century was subject to considerable instability. After the Russian Revolution in 1917, workers communes were formed in the Volga area. These were granted autonomy in 1918 by Lenin and, in 1924, were elevated to the status of 'Autonomous Soviet Socialist Republic of **Volga Germans**', with their own German-speaking administration and schools. In the late 1920s and early 1930s, however, many Soviet Germans were persecuted under Stalin and from 1938 onwards, following the non-aggression pact between Hitler and Stalin, many were deported. Then, in 1941, when the Soviet Union entered World War II in order to fight with the Allies against Germany, many Volga Germans were accused of espionage and their autonomous republic was dissolved. On the basis of emergency laws, many ethnic Germans were interned during the war or forced to engage in hard labour, building railways, for example. As these emergency laws, along with the accusation of collaboration with the German National Socialists, were not formally retracted until the 1960s, it took many years before normal life was resumed for ethnic Germans living in the Soviet Union.

One of the main uncertainties regarding the status of German in the former Soviet Union was whether or not the Volga Republic would ever be reformed – a question which attracted considerable interest outside the country, not least in Germany. This was partly due to the fact that, during the 1970s and 1980s, many ethnic Germans tried to leave the Soviet Union, applying for the right to re-settle in Germany on the basis of their German origin. Such applicants, along with ethnic Germans from other Eastern European countries (mainly Romania and Poland), were collectively known as *Aussiedler*. Until entry was limited by the German government in 1993, many such applications were accepted and, in 1991 and 1992 alone, some 340 000 ethnic Germans left the former Soviet Union for the Federal Republic.

Although there was brief talk in the early 1990s of reviving the Volga Republic, the Russian authorities eventually decided against the idea – not least in view of the high proportion of Russians who have settled in that region over the years. As a result, many ethnic Germans now feel that the future of their language and cultural identity is in severe doubt.

3.2.2   Poland

Of all the German-speaking groups in Eastern Europe, the question of the Polish minority is probably, politically, the most sensitive. Indeed, as far as the German language is concerned, the histories of Poland and Germany in the nineteenth and twentieth centuries are so closely linked that it is virtually impossible to separate the two.

Given that Poland is wedged between Germany and the former Soviet Union, its history was always characterised by a struggle for independence. For many years, it suffered attacks from neighbouring states, being divided up, for example, between Prussia, Russia, and Austria in the late eighteenth century. In 1815, Poland was then granted semi-independent status but was later incorporated into the Russian empire. The first autonomous Polish state was founded after World War I in 1919. In accordance with the Treaty of Versailles, the border with Germany was shifted westward and a number of German-speaking areas thus became Polish. These included the Free City of Danzig (*Gdánsk*), parts of West Prussia (*Westpreußen*) and East Upper Silesia (*Ost-Oberschlesien*). In this way, Poland was given access to the Baltic Sea via the so-called 'Polish Corridor'. Two areas remained in German hands, however: first, East Prussia (*Ostpreußen*) and second, the region between Upper Silesia and West Prussia. In 1939, Poland was secretly partitioned by Germany and the Soviet Union, and then invaded by Hitler's troops.

After World War II, the Polish–German border was significantly redrawn. Germany was divided, and the Oder and Neisse rivers formed the new border between the German Democratic Republic and Poland. Thus, all the former German-speaking territories immediately to the east of the so-called *Oder-Neiße-Linie* became Polish, along with the southern half of East Prussia (the northern half of East Prussia went to Russia). In the aftermath of the war, some 10 million refugees fled these areas for Germany although it is estimated that around 2 million did not complete the journey. In the 1950s, the Poles formally allowed many more Germans to leave. This migration was part of the reason why the existence of a German-speaking minority was always denied by the Polish government and, without such formal recognition, there was no perceived need to grant special rights to German speakers.

Tensions between the Federal Republic of Germany and Poland were exacerbated by the fact that it was some 40 years before the Federal Republic formally recognised the 'new' Polish–German border (although the border was always acknowledged by the German Democratic Republic). It was not until 1990, in the aftermath of German unification, that the new Federal Republic of Germany finally accepted the *Oder-Neiße-Linie* as the border between the two countries, thereby confirming Poland's right to exist in its present form.

It is difficult to calculate the exact number of German speakers in Poland today. In 1957, there were said to be some 1.1 million Poles of former German nationality. However, many of these so-called autochthones have since left Poland and resettled in the Federal Republic of Germany. In 1991 and 1992, for example, some 58 000 Polish *Aussiedler* arrived in Germany.

The precise extent of their German is not really known although initial estimates suggested that around 30 per cent had some knowledge of the language.

3.2.3 *Hungary*

There are presumed to be some 220 000 ethnic Germans living in Hungary today. As in the case of Poland, the history of Hungary is closely linked to that of its German-speaking neighbour. That neighbour is not Germany but Austria (*see* Fig. 3.4).

Although it was an independent kingdom from the eleventh century, the fate of Hungary was always closely connected to that of Austria. From the seventeenth century, Hungary was ruled by the Hapsburgs and, under Emperor Joseph II, German was introduced as the official state language in 1784. Later, in the years between 1867 and 1918, Hungary formed part of the Austro-Hungarian empire, which consisted of a Dual Monarchy covering the twin kingdoms of Austria and Hungary. By the late nineteenth century, only half of the population of Hungary were in fact Magyars, or ethnic Hungarians. Of the remaining 50 per cent, the largest single group was comprised of Germans. During this time, the capital, Budapest, was virtually bilingual.

In the twentieth century, German continued to be widely spoken in Hungary. During the 40 years of Communist rule (1949–1989), it was given some recognition as a minority language, especially after 1968 when there was special provision for German speakers in schools. The language was also used more generally by Hungarians, partly as a means of communicating with East Germans but also being seen as a metaphorical bridge to the West. In this sense, it would seem that German persisted as a lingua franca despite pressure to use Russian. Many Hungarian intellectuals, for example, continued to speak German in their dealings with Czechs, Slovaks, Serbs, Croats, and Slovenians.

Today ethnic Germans are divided throughout several regions of Hungary although there are concentrations in the west of the country around Sopron (*Ödenburg*), Györ (*Raab*), and in the area between the Danube river and Lake Balaton (*der Plattensee*). There are also ethnic Germans in the south of Hungary around Pécs (*Fünfkirchen*), Tolna and Békés. Estimating the total population of these Hungarian Germans is not easy, partly because many are so fully assimilated that they no longer speak German. One survey from 1980 suggested the number who still have German as their mother tongue may be as low as 31 000.

It is difficult to predict what the future holds for German as a minority language in Hungary. But where German as a foreign language is concerned, there appears to be an upsurge of interest. The prestige of German has increased rapidly since German unification although it is in severe

competition with English. The uptake on German language courses is high
and these programmes have received considerable financial support from
the Federal government via the *Goethe Institut*, the cultural body which
represents Germany abroad. German-language newspapers are readily
available, and satellite technology means that many Hungarian households
now receive German-language television programmes. Another important
consideration behind the increased status of German relates to the fact that
some 70 per cent of Hungary's tourists now originate from Austria,
Germany and Switzerland. In 1990, there were an estimated 1.6 million
visitors from Germany alone.

3.2.4   Romania

Of all the German-speaking minority groups in Eastern Europe, Romania
almost certainly has the oldest. The German language was first taken to
Romania by the so-called **Transylvanian Saxons** or *Siebenbürger Sachsen* in
the twelfth century. The descendants of these early settlers have been living
in Romania ever since. Their future, however, is somewhat uncertain in the
light of more recent political developments.

Despite their name, the Transylvanian Saxons were not, in fact, Saxons –
they would appear to have originated from the area around Cologne. They
did not migrate by choice but were called upon by the Hungarians, under
King Géza II (1141–1162), to colonise the region around Transylvania,
which was under Hungarian rule at the time. In the following centuries, a
thriving Protestant community developed, with German-speaking churches
and schools. In 1557, the region also became the first in Europe to make a
formal declaration of religious tolerance. This meant that, in subsequent
years, many persecuted groups settled in the area, including Protestant
farmers from Austria wishing to flee their Catholic rulers.

The two other main groups of ethnic Germans to be found in Romania
today are the **Banat Swabians** and the **Satu Mare Swabians**, both of whom
settled in Romania in the early eighteenth century. The Banat Swabians are
of Hungarian origin, whereas the Satu Mare Swabians originate from
Württemberg, Franconia, and the Rhineland.

However, the population of Romanian Germans is already in severe
decline. According to one estimate, there were some 360 000 ethnic
Germans living in Romania in 1977. By 1990, the number had dwindled to
200 000. The main reason for this huge reduction was migration to
Germany. Despite relatively liberal laws regarding the treatment of
minorities in Romania, including access to German-speaking schools,
media, and cultural activities, many Romanian *Aussiedler* considered the
reality to fall short of expectations. Political dissatisfaction with Communist
rule (1947–1989), particularly under Communist Party leader Nicolae
Ceaucescu, was almost certainly a contributory factor. However, migration

did not subside even after Ceaucescu's overthrow and subsequent execution in 1989, with some 48 000 Germans leaving Romania in 1991 and 1992, probably as a result of the continuing general instability of the country.

3.2.5   The Czech Republic and Slovakia

The history of the former Czechoslovakia is closely linked to that of Germany and Austria due, not least, to its geographical location between the two German-speaking countries. Until 1918, the countries now calling themselves the Czech Republic and Slovakia were ruled by the Austrian Hapsburgs, latterly constituting part of the Austro-Hungarian empire. They united in the aftermath of World War I to form Czechoslovakia but parted company again in 1993. Between 1948 and 1989, the country was ruled by the Communist Party of Czechoslovakia.

The Czech Republic is comprised of the former provinces of Bohemia, Moravia and southern Silesia, with Prague as its capital. Its borders with Germany coincide with the Bohemian Forest in the south-west, the Ore Mountains in the north-west, and the Sudeten Highlands in the north. Slovakia, on the other hand, with its capital Bratislava, lies to the east of the Czech Republic. Parts of its natural borders with Poland, the Ukraine, Austria, and Hungary are formed by the Danube river, and the West Beskids and Tatra mountain ranges, which are part of the Carpathians.

Historically, the German spoken around Prague was extremely influential. The language used by the Prague chancery in the fourteenth century constituted one of the most prestigious varieties of standard German (see 2.2.2). During that time, some of the earliest works of German literature were also written. In terms of writers, however, Prague is probably best known as the birthplace of Franz Kafka (1883–1924), almost certainly one of the greatest literary exponents of the German language in the twentieth century.

In the 1930s, German was estimated to be the first language of some 3.3 million people living Czechoslovakia, who were mainly concentrated in the border regions of Bohemia and Moravia, known as the **Sudetenland**. These provinces were part of Germany until they were ceded to the newly formed Czechoslovakia after World War I. In 1938, they were then annexed by the Germans, paving the way for the subsequent occupation of the rest of Czechoslovakia. Following the restoration of the Sudetenland to Czechoslovakia after World War II, some 3 million Germans were expelled from the region, and became part of the wider process of mass migration which took place across Central and Eastern Europe at that time.

In 1980, the number of ethnic Germans living in Czechoslovakia was thought to be around 62 000, a third of whom were still concentrated in Bohemia. Of these, it would appear that most still have German as their mother tongue, and speak a dialect similar to those heard in Saxony and

Thuringia across the border in Germany. Under Communist rule, German speakers in Czechoslovakia were guaranteed certain minority rights, particularly after 1968. However, some of these would appear to have been implemented only very recently. The first German-speaking school, for example, was not established until 1991.

As in Poland, the issue of the German-speaking minority in Czechoslovakia is extremely sensitive. Indeed, it is only really since German unification that relations between Germany and Czechoslovakia have begun to be normalised. Given the central geographical position of what are now the Czech Republic and Slovakia, it seems probable that the use of German as a foreign language will increase in the near future. As with Hungary, the arrival of several thousand German-speaking tourists per year is likely to play a significant part.

3.3   German-speaking minorities outside Europe

German, is a language which has its historical roots and most of its speakers in Europe. For a variety of reasons, however, minority groups across the centuries have left the traditional German speech area, taking with them various forms of the language. Today it is estimated that there are some 4 million speakers outside Europe. We shall consider briefly the origins of these minorities and the status of the German language in five locations: the United States and Canada, Latin America, Namibia and South Africa, Israel, and Australia.

3.3.1   *United States and Canada*

According to the 1980 census, there are some 1.6 million speakers of German in the United States. These are spread across many different areas although there are larger groupings in California, New York, Illinois, Texas, Ohio, Pennsylvania, Wisconsin, New Jersey, Florida, Michigan, and Minnesota. Canada, on the other hand, has an estimated 440 000 German speakers throughout the provinces of Ontario, British Columbia, Alberta, Manitoba, Saskatchewan, and Quebec. Most of these people use German as the language of the home although there are potentially a further 6 million in the United States, who have acquired a passive understanding of German from older family members.

Many of the German speakers who now live in the United States and Canada left Europe for a variety of political, economic, cultural and religious reasons. Some, however, are descendants of a much older wave of immigration which goes back to the seventeenth and eighteenth centuries. These are members of Anabaptist groups, mainly Old Order Amish and Old Order Mennonite sects, who began to settle in the United States and southern Canada in the 1720s. They took with them Middle High German and Early New High German dialects, mainly from the Palatinate region of Germany (*Pfälzisch*) but also from Switzerland, Württemberg, Alsace, Westphalia, and Hesse (see 2.2.1).

The variety of German which has since evolved, and which is still spoken by some 200 000–300 000 people, is now known as **Pennsylvania German**. It is not uncommon to hear Pennsylvania German referred to in English as 'Pennsylvania Dutch', and therefore classified as a descendant of Dutch rather than German. But this is a misunderstanding since the term does not in fact originate from the English word *Dutch* but from the German *Deitsch*. Today, although all speakers of Pennsylvania German are bilingual in English, Amish and Mennonite groups tend to restrict communication with outsiders as far as possible. Consequently, their archaic form of German has stayed reasonably intact despite some inevitable borrowings from English. Owing to the relatively high birth rate amongst these groups, there is no perceived threat to the continued existence of the language at the present time.

For most other minority speakers of German in the United States and Canada, use of the language has declined considerably, and is gradually being replaced by English. Although there are obvious pressures to use English anyway, this erosion of German can be related at least partly to anti-German sentiment following the two world wars. Thus, Canada, for example, has had an official policy since 1971 aiming to promote the use of minority languages but this has not generally thought to have benefited German greatly. Both the United States and Canada have a small number of German-speaking kindergartens and schools although exclusive use of the language would appear to be restricted to Amish and Mennonite institutions. Finally, in both countries, there is access to German-language newspapers and magazines as well as radio and television programmes although this would not appear to be particularly widespread.

3.3.2   Latin America

There are approximately 2 million speakers of German distributed across almost all parts of Latin America. Although it is, of course, extremely difficult to calculate the exact numbers of speakers in such a large area, the following estimates have been made: Brazil (1.5 million), Argentina (300 000), Paraguay (125 000), Mexico (50 000), Chile (20 000–35 000), Venezuela (25 000), Colombia (10 000–12 000), Bolivia (11 000), Uruguay (8000–9000), Peru (4500), Belize (3000) and Ecuador (1500–3000).

Apart from those who have settled for personal or professional reasons, there are two principal groups of German speakers. The first, as in the United States and Canada, is that of Old Order religious sects, primarily Mennonites. These Latin American Mennonites are descendants of seventeenth and eighteenth century colonists from the Netherlands and Switzerland. They took with them a number of regional dialects, collectively referred to as **Mennonite Low German** *(Mennonitenplatt)* although many speakers also use archaic standard varieties of German on formal occasions. There are Mennonite communities especially in Argentina, Paraguay, Mexico, Bolivia, Uruguay, and Belize.

Another religious group who left Europe for Latin America are the Jews. Many arrived in the 1930s and 1940s in order to flee the National Socialist regime, and have since formed closely knit communities, particularly in Buenos Aires, Santiago and Montevideo. In these three capital cities, there are well-established networks of German-language schools, where it is sometimes possible to take examinations formally recognised in Germany.

The availability of German-language newspapers and radio programmes in Latin America is varied (there is very little access to German television although this will probably change in view of satellite technology). Argentina has a daily German newspaper (which is also available in Uruguay), and Brazil, Chile, and Paraguay have weekly or fortnightly papers. Most of these countries also have some access to radio programmes but, again, the extent of these varies considerably.

3.3.3   *Namibia and South Africa*

The situation of German in Namibia is particularly interesting given that this is the only area outside Europe where the language was granted official status for a prolonged period. Following the settlement of British and Dutch missionaries in the late nineteenth century, the country later became one of a handful of German colonies. Known at the time as **German South-West Africa** *(Deutsch Süd-West Afrika)*, Namibia was a German protectorate from 1884 onwards. Then, after World War I, it was mandated to South Africa by the League of Nations. In 1966, the United Nations assumed direct responsibility for the country, changing its name to Namibia, and recognising the Southwest Africa People's Organisation (SWAPO) as representative of the Namibian population. In 1990, Namibia formally declared its independence.

German, along with English and Afrikaans, was one of three official languages in Namibia's so-called 'white areas'. Until recently, these were separated from 'black areas' according to a system of apartheid akin to that of South Africa. In the black areas, there were a number of indigenous African languages with official status, such as Ndonga, Kwanyame, and Herero. Most white Namibians were either bilingual or trilingual, and a small number of black Namibians belonging to the Herero group also spoke German. It is estimated that there are between 20 000 and 35 000 speakers of German living in Namibia today. With the end of apartheid in the 1990s, a number of changes were made with respect to the status of the different languages. German and Afrikaans, perceived as symbols of black oppression under colonialism and apartheid, have given way – somewhat ironically perhaps – to English, which has been declared the new national language.

There are currently six state schools in Namibia where German is one of the languages of instruction: two in the capital, Windhoek, and one each in Tsumeb, Otjiwarongo, Swakopmund, and Walvis Bay. There are a small number of state schools where German is used alongside Afrikaans in Otavi, Lüderitz, Grootfontein, Omaruru, and Okahandja. In addition, Windhoek has a private school supported by the German government, where German examinations can be taken, allowing pupils access to German universities. There is a German daily newspaper called *Die Allgemeine Zeitung*, and a number of other weekly newspapers and magazines, some of which are characterised, however, by extreme right-wing bias. Approximately 100 hours of radio air-time per week and occasional television programmes are given over to the German language.

According to a census carried out in 1980, there are an estimated 41 000 people in South Africa, who claim to use German as their main language. These speakers live mainly in urban districts of the Cape, Natal, and Transvaal provinces. They use a predominantly standardised form of German, which none the less contains borrowings from English and Afrikaans. There is a strong network of private schools where German is the language of instruction and which, as in Namibia, are supported by the German government. A German newspaper is also available but there would not appear to be access to German-language radio or television.

3.3.4   Israel

There are an estimated 96 000 German speakers living in Israel today. These are almost entirely made up of some of the few German and Austrian Jews who managed to survive the National Socialist regime of the 1930s and 1940s. They would appear to have settled primarily in Haifa, Nahariza, Natana, and Tel Aviv, and a number live on kibbutzim.

Given the very sensitive histories of those German-speaking Jews who have emigrated to Israel, relatively little is known about their current knowledge of the language. Many Jews refuse to speak German and are deeply disturbed by any use of, or reference to, the language. However, having visited Israel in 1985, I can confirm that many older Jews were remarkably keen to speak German with myself and a group of German friends, not least in order to relate their experiences of life under the National Socialists and in the concentration camps. Similarly, there are still German-language newspapers available, and it would appear that a number of Jewish authors still write in German. Nonetheless, it can be reasonably assumed that German will not be passed on to younger generations of Jews, whose first language is now indisputably Hebrew. Consequently, the use of German in Israel will almost certainly diminish in the twenty-first century.

3.3.5 Australia

Estimates of the number of German speakers now living in Australia vary from approximately 110 000 to 175 000. These people are distributed across all parts of Australia although mainly in those areas which are more densely populated in general: New South Wales, Victoria, South Australia, and Queensland. Melbourne is the town with the highest single number of German speakers.

As in the United States and Canada, there has been some antipathy towards German and during the two world wars there were reprisals against German speakers. The use of German has also declined in the light of the more general tendency in Australia to assimilate speakers of languages other than English.

Since the 1970s there has been a more liberal policy on multilingualism in Australia, and attempts have been made, where appropriate, to allow schools to use languages other than English for teaching. Although there are no German-speaking state schools in Australia, there are two German-language weekly newspapers and a small number of radio programmes.

Sources and recommended reading

- The most comprehensive surveys of the status of German in different countries (including non-European areas) are to be found in the German texts Born and Dickgießer (1989), Ammon (1991) and Eichinger (1992).
- The following English texts cover the European context thoroughly: Barbour and Stevenson (1990), Clyne (1995) and Russ (1994).
- Ammon (1995a) looks at German as a national variety in Germany, Switzerland and Austria (in German), while Ammon (1995b) provides a useful overview of the position of German as an international language (in English).

For more information on specific countries, see the following:

- Austria – Muhr (1993), Muhr *et al.* (1995) and Ebner (1992).
- Switzerland – Russ (1987), Sieber (1992), Stevenson (1997) and Hauck (1993).
- Luxembourg – Newton (1987, 1990 and 1996) and Stevenson (1997).
- Denmark – Walker (1987), Byram (1993) and Baetens Beardsmore (1993).
- Italy – Rowley (1987) and Saxalber and Lanthaler (1992).
- France – Hoffmann (1991), Vassberg (1993), Gardner-Chloros (1991), Phillipp and Bothorel-Witz (1990).

- Soviet Union – Domaschnew (1993) and Frank (1995).
- Hungary – Földes (1993).
- Pennsylvania – Van Ness (1994).

Exercises

1. Select the correct answer.

    1. Where is the variety of German known as *Züritüüsch* spoken?
        - (a) Switzerland
        - (b) Luxembourg
        - (c) Alsace

    2. Name the two main languages which are spoken alongside *Lëtzebuergesch* in Luxembourg.
        - (a) Dutch and French
        - (b) French and standard German
        - (c) Standard German and Low German

    3. In which region of which country are the following German dialects spoken: *Moselfränkisch, Rheinfränkisch, Niederalemannisch* and *Hochalemannisch*?
        - (a) South Tyrol, Italy
        - (b) New Belgium, Belgium
        - (c) Alsace Lorraine, France

    4. To which national variety of German is the German spoken in South Tyrol closest?
        - (a) Swiss German
        - (b) Austrian German
        - (c) Liechtenstein German

    5. In which European city was one of the most prestigious varieties of German spoken in the fourteenth century?
        - (a) Prague
        - (b) Frankfurt
        - (c) Budapest

    6. From which language does Pennsylvania Dutch originate?
        - (a) Dutch
        - (b) German
        - (c) English

    7. From which group of German dialects are the languages of the present-day Amish and Mennonite groups descended?
        - (a) *Niederalemannisch*
        - (b) *Schwäbisch*
        - (c) *Pfälzisch*

8. In which region of which country are North Frisian and South Jutlandish spoken?
   (a) Nordslesvig, Denmark
   (b) New Belgium, Belgium
   (c) North-Rhine Westphalia, Germany

9. Name the variety of German which is characterised by diglossia, i.e. has a High and a Low form.
   (a) Austrian German
   (b) Pennsylvania German
   (c) Swiss German

10. What is the collective German term for Low German dialects?
    (a) *Mennonitenplatt*
    (b) *Plattdeutsch*
    (c) *Alemannisch*

2. Answer the following questions.

   1. What is the German name for the German-speaking minority groups in Romania known as the 'Transylvanian Saxons'?

   2. Which of the following former Eastern bloc countries are estimated to have more than 1 million German speakers today: CIS, Poland, Hungary, Romania, Czech Republic, and Slovakia?

   3. In which country does German share its official status with French and Dutch?

   4. In what year following World War I was a referendum held determining the future of German-speaking South Tyrol?

   5. Name the two most significant groups of German speakers in Latin America.

   6. Which is the smallest of those countries where German has the status of sole official language?

   7. Which three languages are officially spoken in Switzerland besides German?

   8. By what name is the former German colony *Deutsch Süd-West Afrika* now known?

   9. In which country is there a minority group of German speakers known as the 'Volga Germans'?

   10. In which city was the writer Franz Kafka born?

3. Match the words listed in Column A with their appropriate definitions in Column B.

Column A	Column B
1. *Danzig*	(a) Austrian word for 'January'
2. *der Kanton*	(b) Austrian or Swiss parliament
3. *Jänner*	(c) French/German language border in Switzerland
4. *die Palatschinke*	(d) Swiss word for 'ticket'
5. *der Nationalrat*	(e) German name for Polish town Gdansk
6. *die Maturität*	(f) Austrian pancake dish
7. *der Röstigraben*	(g) Known in Germany as *der Blumenkohl*
8. *das Billet*	(h) Hungarian town, Pécs
9. *Fünfkirchen*	(i) Swiss equivalent of German examination known as *das Abitur*
10. *der Karfiol*	(j) Swiss state

4. Read the following poem in Swiss German and then provide two translations, one in standard German and one in English:

> Uf em Bärgli bin i gsässe
> hab de Vögel zue gschaut.
> Si händ gsunge, si händ gschprunge,
> schöne Näschtli händ si baut.

(From Stedje, 1989: 192)

5. The following is a birth announcement in Luxembourgish, which appeared in a Luxembourg newspaper. Read it through carefully and then answer the questions below.

> Den Olivier, de Frédéric an d'Esther si frou, d'Gebuert vun hirem Bridderchen
>
> DOMINIQUE
>
> e Samschdag, de 16. Mee 1992, matzudelen.
>   Wien ons grouss Freed dele wëllt, kann dat maachen duurch d'Iwwerweisung vun engem Don op den CCP 65–65 vum 'Mierscher Kannerduerf' mat dem Vermierk 'Don Dominique (XXX).'

(From Hoffmann, 1996: 222)

1. How many brothers and sisters does the newly-born Dominique have, and what are their names?

2. How do they feel about Dominique's birth?

3. When was Dominique born?

4. What are friends and relatives asked to do?

5. Translate the text into English.

THE STRUCTURES OF GERMAN

4

The sounds of German

Which of the world's languages we acquire as our mother tongue is purely an accident of birth. If we grow up in an English-speaking country, then we will probably learn English. Alternatively, if we are born in Germany, Austria, Liechtenstein or the German-speaking part of Switzerland, then our first language is likely to be German. All children have the natural ability to learn any of the world's languages. Thus, a child has no more difficulty learning English or German than Mandarin Chinese. This is particularly true in terms of pronunciation – the sounds of one language are not inherently more difficult to produce than the sounds of another.

One of the things which happens as we grow older is that we lose the capacity to learn other languages with quite the same ease with which we acquired our mother tongue. In particular, this affects pronunciation. This is why it is often difficult to sound exactly like a native speaker, in other words, why we have a **foreign accent**. It is estimated that this innate capacity to learn another language begins to decline around the age of 12, although there is considerable variation from one individual to another. Clearly, some adults with 'a good ear' for languages do manage to achieve pronunciation which is very close to that of a native speaker, especially if they are living in a country where the language concerned is spoken on a daily basis.

The fact that most people are older than 12 when they begin to study foreign languages at school or university does not, of course, mean that they cannot learn the sounds of a new language. Indeed, most adults are quite capable of doing so. But when learners try to imitate the pronunciation of a native speaker, they may need a little extra help. This is where the careful study of sounds can be especially useful. For example, the English-speaking learner of German needs to become aware of those German sounds which do not occur in English. It is also helpful to realise that some sounds which might *appear* to be the same in the two languages are actually pronounced differently. In order to achieve this kind of awareness, however, it is necessary to have a basic understanding of how sounds are produced in more general terms.

Two branches of linguistics are specifically concerned with the sounds of language: **phonetics** and **phonology**. Phonetics is the study of the physical or physiological aspects of sounds, and is normally divided into three areas.

- **Articulatory phonetics** deals with the way in which sounds are made or *articulated*, that is, what happens to the air from the time we breathe in up to the point at which we pronounce a sound. This is the branch of phonetics which is most relevant to anyone learning a foreign language, and draws heavily on aspects of human biology.

- **Acoustic phonetics** has a different focus, concentrating on the pitch, amplitude, and duration of sounds. This kind of phonetics would be important to anyone interested in the electronic production of music, for example, and is often studied as a branch of engineering.

- **Auditory phonetics** deals with the way in which sounds are registered by the ear. It is probably the least developed branch of phonetics, and would be essential for anyone wishing to work with people who have hearing or speech difficulties, e.g. for speech therapists.

Phonology, on the other hand, has a slightly different focus. It is less concerned with the processes of sound production than with the way in which those sounds join together to form a particular language. So when you learn German, you not only need to know how to pronounce the relevant sounds, but also how to *use* them in order to express meaning. One example would be knowing how to manipulate sounds in order to make plural forms from singular nouns – a process which is clearly very different in English and German.

Having said this, it is not always easy to separate the study of phonetics and phonology in this way. When learning a foreign language, the two disciplines are very closely related. The aim of this chapter is therefore to give you an overview of both the phonetics *and* phonology of German. We will begin by looking at the way in which sounds are produced in general, before turning to the pronunciation of German specifically. There we will be discussing some of the main difficulties with pronunciation which are experienced by learners of German as well as providing some practical tips on how to remedy them.

4.1   Analysing the sounds of language

4.1.1   *The International Phonetic Alphabet (IPA)*

In phonetics and phonology, it is important to distinguish between the way in which a sound is pronounced and the way it is normally written, in other words, between pronunciation and writing conventions. Take, for example, the following two words which are historically related. Think carefully about the way the *first* sound is pronounced in each case:

> German: *Vater*
> English: 'father'

It should be apparent that whereas the first sound of each word is spelled differently, their pronunciation is nonetheless the same. Now consider the following two words:

> German: *Sand*
> English: 'sand'

This time, the two initial sounds are spelled the same, but their pronunciation is different. Thus, the 's' in the German *Sand* is pronounced like the 'z' in the English word 'zoo'.

These kinds of differences mean that the alphabet we normally use when writing English and German is rather imprecise when it comes to describing the sounds of the two languages. If we want to compare the pronunciation of English and German, we therefore need a more accurate system of sound representation. It was with this kind of problem in mind that linguists developed the **International Phonetic Alphabet (IPA)** in the late nineteenth century. The IPA, however, goes beyond the description of English and German. This alphabet can be used to write down – or *transcribe* – the sounds of any of the world's languages. It is particularly useful for linguists who wish to transcribe the sounds of a language which has no written version at all. It is also invaluable when analysing accents and dialects, or different national varieties of the same language, e.g. the German spoken in Germany, Austria, and Switzerland.

In the IPA, the sound at the beginning of the words *Vater* and 'father' is represented by one **phonetic symbol** only: /f/. On the other hand, the initial sounds in *Sand* and 'sand' are represented by two different symbols: /z/ and /s/, respectively.

When describing individual sounds, phonetic symbols are usually written in slanted brackets, e.g. /f/, /z/ and /s/ or in square brackets, e.g. [f], [z] and [s]. (Square brackets are also used for transcribing whole words.) This compares to the letters of the conventional (Roman) alphabet, which are written in inverted commas, e.g. 'v', 'f' and 's'. The distinction between the two types of alphabet is very important when writing about sounds (i.e. in a book such as this) because we need to be able to differentiate clearly between pronunciation, on the one hand, and orthography, on the other.

Being able to read the International Phonetic Alphabet is enormously helpful to anyone learning a foreign language. This is because if you turn to any good German–English dictionary, and look up any word, not only a translation and grammatical information are given, but also the pronunciation of the word.

For example, take a bilingual dictionary and look up the German word *Ventilator*. Immediately after the entry itself, you will find the phonetic **transcription** of the word as follows: [vɛntilatɔʀ]. Not only will this tell you how to pronounce the sounds of that word, it will also show you where the stress falls. This is indicated by an apostrophe immediately before the syllable to be emphasised. Hence, the stress in the German *Ven-ti-'LA-tor* is quite different from the English *'VEN-ti-la-tor*.

Many people who use dictionaries cannot understand the IPA. This is a great pity because being able to read a phonetic transcription from the dictionary is the next best thing to asking a native speaker to pronounce a word out loud for you. Moreover, a knowledge of the phonetic alphabet can also be used to check the pronunciation of words in your mother tongue in a monolingual dictionary.

4.1.2   The organs of speech

The organs of speech are those parts of the body which are directly involved in the production or **articulation** of **speech sounds** (*see* Fig. 4.1).

The articulation of a speech sound begins from the moment we breathe in. The air enters our lungs, and is then expelled into the area known as the **vocal tract**. Languages which produce their sounds in this way are said to have a **pulmonic egressive airstream mechanism**. By contrast, many African, American Indian, and Indian languages also make sounds by *sucking in* the air as opposed to expelling it. This is known as an **ingressive airstream mechanism**, and results in sounds such as clicks.

Occasionally, English and German speakers also make use of the ingressive mechanism, for example, when trying to talk while out of breath, crying, or laughing. But the sounds of English and German are normally made egressively as air leaves the lungs and passes through the different parts of the vocal tract. The following sections will now give examples of what happens each step of the way.

THE WINDPIPE (TRACHEA)

Once the airstream leaves the lungs, it enters the **windpipe** or **trachea**. The lower part of the windpipe is roughly adjacent to the **oesophagus** or **food pipe** (*see* Fig. 4.1). When we swallow food, it is obviously intended to go down the food pipe and enter the stomach. But sometimes what we are eating 'goes down the wrong way', causing us to choke. What has actually occurred here is that the food has entered the *windpipe* as opposed to the *food pipe*. This does not normally happen because at the top end of the windpipe (above the voice box) is a 'lid' called the **epiglottis**. When we eat, this lid stays closed. When we speak, however, the epiglottis opens in order to let air through. This means that food is

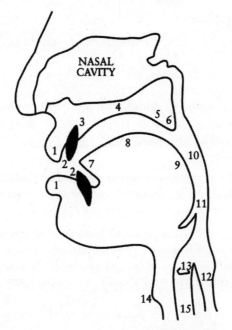

1. Lips
2. Teeth
3. Alveolar ridge
4. Hard palate
5. Soft palate or velum
6. Uvula
7. Tip of tongue
8. Blade of tongue

9. Back of tongue
10. Pharynx
11. Epiglottis
12. Food pipe or oesophagus
13. Vocal cords
14. Voice box or larynx
15. Windpipe or trachea

Fig. 4.1 The organs of speech in the vocal tract

more likely to go down the wrong way when we are eating and talking at the same time.

THE VOICE BOX (LARYNX)

The airstream now reaches the **voice box** or **larynx,** which is situated at the top of the trachea (but still inside it). This is one of the most important parts of the vocal tract.

As the air enters the voice box, it must pass through the **vocal cords** (or vocal folds), which consist of thin strips of tissue in the shape of two curtains. The space between the vocal cords is known as the **glottis.** The position of the glottis, in turn, affects what happens to the vocal cords.

There are three possibilities:

- If the glottis is *wide open*, then the air can pass through the vocal cords unobstructed.
- If the glottis is *slightly closed*, the air must force its way through, causing the vocal cords to vibrate.
- If the glottis is *completely closed*, then no sound can be made at all. This is usually caused by a temporary obstruction such as a particle of dust. When this happens, the blockage must be cleared (normally by coughing) before speech can resume.

The position of the glottis, and whether or not the vocal cords vibrate as the air passes through them, results in one of the most fundamental distinctions in the production of speech sounds. Try the following experiment:

- Place your fingers on your throat so as to cover the voice box.
- Pronounce the English sounds /p/ as in 'pat' and /b/ as in 'bat' (pronounce the initial sound only in each case as opposed to the whole word).
- With the first sound, /p/, you should not perceive any movement in the voice box.
- With the second sound, /b/, you should be able to feel the vocal cords vibrating inside the voice box.

Now try a similar experiment with the sounds: /f/ as in 'fine' and /v/ as in 'vine'. This time, cover your ears firmly with the palms of your hands, and pronounce each of the sounds in question, holding onto them for as long as possible. With /f/, you should not be able to hear anything other than the sound of the air passing through your lips. But with /v/, your whole head should be buzzing!

The principle which is at work here is known as the **voicing** of sounds. The first sound of each of the pairs we have discussed, that is, /p/ and /f/, does not involve the vocal cords vibrating since the glottis is wide open. These are therefore said to be **voiceless** sounds. By contrast, the second sound of the pairs, that is, /b/ and /v/, involves the air forcing its way through the slightly closed glottis, causing the vocal cords to vibrate. These sounds are therefore said to be **voiced**.

It might seem strange to think of some sounds as 'voiceless', i.e. 'having no voice', but this is quite logical. Think about what happens when you have laryngitis and 'lose your voice'. Are you genuinely unable to utter any sound at all? The answer is no. What you lose, in fact, is the capacity to produce *voiced* sounds. This is because the vocal cords are swollen and cannot vibrate. All you can do is *whisper*.

When we whisper, what we are doing is pronouncing all the sounds as though they were voiceless. In such cases, we lose the distinction between, say, 'pat' and 'bat'. (Try whispering these two words – can you hear a difference?) In practice, the only reason why we can still differentiate between such pairs of words is because they will usually make sense in the context of the sentence in which they occur. It is also helpful if we can *see* the person we are talking to in order to pick up visual clues. This is why whispering on the telephone does not normally guarantee very effective communication.

After the airstream has passed through the voice box and the epiglottis, it enters the **pharynx**. This area is a continuation of the food pipe, which connects the windpipe and voice box to the ears, nose, and throat. The upper part of the pharynx contains the tonsils, which are designed to intercept airborne particles which might cause infection.

THE UVULA

After the airstream has left the pharynx, it reaches a cone-shaped muscular structure in the back of the throat, known as the **uvula** (*see* Fig. 4.1). This is the part of the throat which hangs down, and which you can see if you open your mouth widely and look into a mirror.

When we speak English, the uvula does not normally move very much. In fact, it generally just hangs around doing nothing. However, in German the uvula is extremely important. This is the part of the throat which vibrates, for example, when the north German 'r' sound is produced as in the word *rot*. Some English speakers perceive this 'r' sound to be rather unpleasant because they associate it with coughing and spluttering. Some think it is an impolite sound to make, and try to avoid it. But inhibitions such as these must be overcome when speaking German, so it is a good idea to practise making the uvula vibrate. One way of doing this is by gargling – first with water and then without.

THE SOFT PALATE (VELUM)

The uvula is connected to a larger section of the mouth known as the **soft palate** or **velum** (*see* Fig. 4.1). This is the firm but fleshy area, which you can feel if you curl up your tongue, and run it along the roof of your mouth as far back as possible. The velum is important both in English and German, and is closely related to the production of sounds such as /k/ in 'cot' or *können* and /g/ in 'got' or *gönnen*.

In addition, however, German has a velar sound which does not generally occur in English. This is represented orthographically by 'ch' as in *Loch* or *Dach,* and by the phonetic symbol /x/. It is found in some varieties of English, notably Scottish English (as in 'Lo*ch* Ness'), but is unfamiliar to many other speakers of English.

We shall discuss the exact pronunciation of this velar sound later in this chapter. In the meantime, it is worth noting that it is the combination of the velar /x/ and the uvular 'r' sound, which results in the very 'throaty' or 'guttural' quality so often attributed to German.

THE ORAL TRACT AND NASAL CAVITY

The velum or soft palate is not simply a place where certain sounds are produced. It also has another important function. This is because it moves up and down, directing the airstream through the **oral tract** (≈ mouth) or **nasal cavity** (≈ nose). In total, there are four possible positions:

1. The velum is positioned in a way which allows air to escape from both the *oral tract and the nasal cavity* at the same time.
2. The velum is raised, the passage to the nasal cavity is blocked, and the air is expelled through the *oral tract*.
3. The velum is lowered, the oral tract is blocked, and the air must leave via the *nasal cavity*.
4. Both the oral tract and the nasal cavity are temporarily blocked, which means that air gathers behind the velum. Pressure then builds up until the air eventually escapes, causing a minor 'explosion'. The air is then expelled either through the *oral tract or the nasal cavity*.

Sounds which are produced by the first three positions are called **continuants** because the air *continues* to flow without being obstructed by the velum. By contrast, the fourth position produces sounds known as **stops** or **plosives** because the air is *stopped* by the velum, and then released, producing a small ex*plosion*.

Continuants include such sounds as /f/ or /v/ whereas stops/plosives would be /p/ or /b/. Try the following experiment in order to get a feel for the difference between these two types of sound:

- Hold a large sheet of paper in front of your mouth (hold it by the corner and not too firmly);
- Pronounce the continuant /f/ for as long as possible and observe how the paper moves;
- Now pronounce the plosive /p/ and see what happens to the piece of paper;
- What does the movement of the paper tell you about the difference in the airstream in each case?

Going back to the four positions of the velum, we can also say that most sounds of English and German are produced by the oral route, i.e. the air is expelled via the mouth (positions 1, 2 and 4). But both languages also have a small number of nasal sounds (positions 1, 3 and 4) such as /m/ as in *Mutter* or 'mother' and /n/ as in *nett* or 'nice'.

Sometimes, when we are ill, the velum swells up and is forced to remain in a *lowered* position. This means that much of the air which would normally leave via the oral tract must be expelled via the nasal cavity. It is this action which causes the temporary nasality in our speech typically associated with colds and flu.

English and German do not normally contain sounds which are articulated with the velum in the first position, i.e. where the air escapes through the oral tract and nasal cavity simultaneously. This is the way in which **nasal vowels** are produced, and is much more typical of French as in: _en France_. Sometimes, however, such nasal vowels also occur in German words of French origin, e.g. _Restaurant_ or _Balkon_.

THE HARD PALATE AND THE ALVEOLAR RIDGE

The soft palate is connected to the **hard palate**. This is the hard bony part at the front of the roof of the mouth (_see_ Fig. 4.1). It is when the middle of the tongue touches the hard palate, and air is expelled, that sounds such as the /j/ in _ja_ or 'yes' are produced.

The hard palate also connects with the **alveolar ridge**, though this time at the front of the roof of the mouth just above the teeth. If the tongue touches the alveolar ridge and air is expelled, sounds such as /t/ as in _Tag_, /d/ as in _dein_, /s/ as in _dass_, and /z/ as in _sein_ are produced.

THE TONGUE, LIPS AND TEETH

Finally, three parts of the mouth which need little explanation, although they are extremely important organs of speech, are the tongue, the lips and the teeth. The tongue, as we have already seen from previous examples, moves around and touches other areas of the mouth. But there are different parts of the tongue which help to produce sounds. For instance, with /t/, it is the part of the tongue just behind the tip which connects with the alveolar ridge. However, with /j/, it is the middle part of the tongue which touches the hard palate. We shall see later in this chapter how the movements of the tongue are also central to the articulation of vowels.

The lips are involved in sounds such as /p/, /b/ and /m/, as in _Pein, Bein_ and _mein_. By contrast, when air is expelled through the middle of the lips and teeth, sounds such as /f/ in _fein_ and /v/ in _Wein_ are produced.

The tongue, lips and teeth are used in the articulation of more or less the same sounds in English and German, and do not therefore present any great difficulty to the learner of German. Generally speaking, it is the sounds which are produced in conjunction with the alveolar ridge, the hard and soft palates, the uvula, and the glottis, which cause problems: in other words, sounds which are produced 'further back' in the vocal tract.

4.2   Describing German consonants

4.2.1   *The consonant chart*

Table 4.1 shows the consonants of German. When describing the consonants of any language, there are three pieces of information which can be given:

Table 4.1 The consonant chart with German sounds

PLACE→ MANNER↓	BILABIAL		LABIO-DENTAL		DENTAL		ALVEOLAR		PALATO-ALVEOLAR		PALATAL		VELAR		UVULAR		GLOTTAL	
VOICING→	−	+	−	+	−	+	−	+	−	+	−	+	−	+	−	+	−	+
PLOSIVE	p	b					t	d					k	g			ʔ	
FRICATIVE			f	v			s	z	ʃ	ʒ	ç	j	x				h	
AFFRICATE																		
NASAL		m						n						ŋ				
LATERAL								l										
ROLL								r								R		

(Adapted from MacCarthy, 1975: 62)

- **voicing**
  (whether the sound is voiced or voiceless as indicated by + or – on the chart);
- **place of articulation**
  (*where* in the vocal tract the sound is produced);
- **manner of articulation**
  (*how* the air passes through the vocal tract).

Using the information on the consonant chart, we can therefore say that:

/b/	= voiced bilabial plosive	/l/	= voiced alveolar lateral
/h/	= voiceless glottal fricative	/m/	= voiced bilabial nasal

It is important to realise that these labels are not assigned to the various sounds in an arbitrary fashion. Nor are they intended to confuse the student of German. They are in fact enormously helpful when trying to explain the many differences between the pronunciation of English and German.

4.2.2   Voicing of consonants

The first point when describing consonants is to differentiate between voiced and voiceless sounds. Table 4.1 contains many pairs of consonants, e.g. /p/ + /b/ or /s/ + /z/ etc. In such cases, the voiceless sounds are always on the left of the pair and the voiced sounds on the right. However, not all consonants belong to pairs in this way. Some voiced sounds such as /m/ and /n/, for example, have no voiceless partner, whereas some voiceless sounds such as /h/ have no voiced counterpart.

Practise saying the following pairs of consonants, focusing on the voiced and voiceless sound in each case. Note that in every other respect the pronunciation of the two sounds is identical.

voiceless		voiced	
/p/	*p*ink	/b/	*b*lau
/t/	*t*ot	/d/	*d*unkel
/k/	*k*urz	/g/	*g*elb
/f/	*f*risch	/v/	*w*ann
/s/	hei*ß*	/z/	*s*ingen

4.2.3   Place of articulation

The place of articulation refers to the precise area of the vocal tract in which a consonant sound is made. The production of sounds usually involves two organs of speech. In most cases, one of these organs moves and is referred to as the **active articulator**, whilst the other stays still and is known as the **passive articulator**.

The following sections describe the place of articulation from left to right on the consonant chart (*see* Table 4.1), that is:

bilabials → labio-dentals → dentals → alveolars → palato-alveolars → palatals → velars → uvulars → glottals

Note how the chart progresses from the *front* of the vocal tract (i.e. the lips) through to the *back* (i.e. the glottis). Thus, each of the set of sounds to be discussed is produced slightly further back in the vocal tract than the previous one.

BILABIALS

Bilabial sounds, as their name implies, involve both lips. In order to pronounce them, the upper and lower lips must be placed together. Examples of bilabials are:

voiceless bilabial	voiced bilabial
/p/ Pein	/b/ Bein
—	/m/ mein

Try pronouncing these three sounds, observing carefully the position of the lips. Note also that whereas /p/ and /b/ form a voiceless and voiced pair, /m/ is voiced and has no voiceless counterpart.

LABIO-DENTALS

Labio-dental sounds involve the lips and the teeth. For example:

voiceless labio-dental	voiced labio-dental
/f/ fein	/v/ Wein

Try pronouncing these two consonants, and observe how the air passes through the lips and the teeth, creating a slightly hissing sound.

DENTALS

Dental sounds involve the placing of the tongue between the teeth. This column of the consonant chart is empty because there are no sounds of German which are produced in this way. English, however, has two dentals:

voiceless dental	voiced dental
/θ/ *th*ing	/ð/ *th*is

These two sounds were originally found in Proto-Indo-European (see 2.1.1), although they were inherited by English but not German. For this reason, these sounds sometimes cause problems for native speakers of German (and many other languages) when they first begin to learn English – in the same way that those consonants of German which do not exist in English are often the most difficult for English-speaking learners of German.

In such cases, an interesting principle applies. When non-native speakers have difficulty pronouncing an unfamiliar sound of another language, they will usually opt for the next best thing, i.e. a sound which exists in their own language and is *closest* to the one they are attempting. Hence, a German native speaker in the early stages of learning English might pronounce 'thing' as 'sing', in other words, using the alveolar /s/ rather than the dental /θ/. In order to clarify this point for yourself, refer back to Table 4.1, enter the two English dentals in the correct boxes, and see where they stand in relation to /s/.

ALVEOLARS

Alveolar sounds are produced when the tongue makes contact with the alveolar ridge, i.e. the part of the roof of the mouth immediately above the teeth. This is the most common place of articulation for consonants of German (and English), hence there are many examples in Table 4.1.

Try pronouncing the following pairs of alveolar sounds, and observe closely which part of the tongue touches which part of the roof of the mouth:

voiceless alveolar	voiced alveolar
/t/ *T*isch	/d/ *d*ein
/s/ da*ss*	/z/ *s*ein
—	/n/ *n*ein
—	/l/ *L*inie
—	[r] *r*ot

The type of 'r' sound which is shown here is the one normally heard in southern Germany, Austria, and Switzerland. The precise difference between the various 'r' sounds will be discussed in the section on rolls on p. 95 and on allophones on p. 109 along with the reason why it is written in square as opposed to slanted brackets.

PALATO-ALVEOLARS

There are two **palato-alveolar** consonants in German:

voiceless palato-alveolar	voiced palato-alveolar
/ʃ/　Schuh	/ʒ/　Genie

For these sounds, the whole of the tongue is raised from the middle of the alveolar ridge to the front of the hard palate. If you are unfamiliar with /ʒ/, this is the sound which occurs in the French word *je*, or in English words such as 'leisure' and 'pleasure'.

PALATALS

Palatal consonants also involve the middle of the tongue making contact with the hard palate, but they are articulated further back in the mouth than the palato-alveolar sounds. Examples are:

voiceless palatal	voiced palatal
/ç/　ich	/j/　ja

The voiced consonant /j/ exists in both German and English, e.g. *ja* and 'yes'. On the other hand, its voiceless partner /ç/ only occurs in German, and may therefore be unfamiliar to native speakers of English. However, once you have grasped the basic distinction between voiced and voiceless sounds, this consonant is very easy to pronounce.

If you have problems with /ç/, try the following exercise:

- Place the palms of your hands firmly over your ears.
- Pronounce the voiced consonant /j/ (as in *ja*) and hold it for as long as possible.
- Check that you can hear the buzzing associated with voiced sounds.
- Now keep every other part of your mouth in the same position, but try to produce a voiceless sound instead of a voiced one (i.e. the vocal cords should no longer vibrate).
- You should be able to feel a hissing sound as the air glides over the roof of your mouth, but there should be no buzzing.
- This is the voiceless palatal consonant /ç/.
- Now try pronouncing /ç/ in the context of words such as *ich, mich, leicht* and *Früchte*.

VELARS

Velar consonants, as their name suggests, are articulated towards the back of the vocal tract in the velum or soft palate. The following sounds are velars:

voiceless velar	voiced velar
/k/　kaum	/g/　Gaumen
/x/　Loch	—
—	/ŋ/　sang

The velar consonants /k/ and /g/ occur in English words such as 'cot' and 'got', and do not therefore present the English-speaking learner of German with any particular difficulties. However, the other two velar consonants /x/ and /ŋ/ may be unfamiliar to the learner of German, though for different reasons.

/x/ does in fact occur in some varieties of English, especially Scottish English, but is generally unfamiliar to other speakers. Tips on how to pronounce this sound will be given in the section on fricatives on p. 91 since the relevant point here is not *where* the sound is pronounced (i.e. place of articulation) but *how* it is pronounced (i.e. manner of articulation).

By contrast, the voiced velar nasal /ŋ/ occurs in all forms of English, for example, in words such as 'ki*ng*' or 'sa*ng*'. The main reason why this consonant may be unfamiliar, however, is that it might not initially seem to constitute a sound in its own right. In terms of its pronunciation, it is half way between an alveolar /n/ and a velar /g/. Similarly, /ŋ/ is not represented orthographically by *one* letter of the alphabet, but by *two*: 'n' + 'g'.

Another reason why we may not immediately recognise /ŋ/ as a distinct consonant is that it does not occur at the beginning but only at the *end of words or syllables*, for example:

gi*ng*   gi*ng*+en
sa*ng*   sa*ng*+en

In spite of these apparent idiosyncrasies, the velar /ŋ/ is a very important sound in both English and German. There is, for example, a clear difference in meaning between pairs of words which contain /n/ and /ŋ/, respectively, for example, 'kin' and 'king' in English or *hin* and *hing* in German.

UVULARS

Uvular consonants involve movement of the uvula – the cone-shaped piece of muscle which hangs down in the back of the throat. The uvula *must* vibrate in order to produce the following sound, which occurs in most north German varieties:

voiceless uvular   voiced uvular

—   [R] *r*ot

English does not normally make use of the uvula, so this sound may seem unfamiliar to English-speaking learners of German.

GLOTTALS

Finally, having traced the articulation of the German consonants from the lips and teeth, through the alveolar ridge, to the hard and soft palates, and on to the uvula, we arrive at our last port of call: the glottis. This is the gap between the vocal cords, the position of which is so crucial to the voicing of sounds. In addition, however, this is also the place of articulation for two consonants:

voiceless glottal	voiced glottal
/h/ *Haus*	—
/ʔ/ ein Ei	—

There is no real difference between the way in which /h/ is pronounced in German and English, so this sound does not generally cause difficulty for English-speaking learners of German. Nevertheless, practise saying /h/ in order to get a feel for the *place* of articulation of this sound.

The second glottal consonant is known as the **glottal stop** or **glottal plosive,** and is represented by the phonetic symbol /ʔ/. This is the sound which sometimes replaces the /t/ in English words such as 'bu*tt*er' or even 'glo*tt*al'. It is very similar in terms of articulation to /h/, except /h/ is a continuant whereas /ʔ/ is a stop (see p. 82). In other words, it is possible to hold a /h/ sound for a long time, whereas /ʔ/ involves a blockage of the airstream as with sounds such as /p/ or /b/.

In British English, the glottal stop is often associated with *non-standard* accents or dialects. Sometimes, it is even dismissed as 'lazy' pronunciation, although this is quite inaccurate since the articulation of /ʔ/ requires no less effort than /t/. In German, however, the glottal stop is an extremely important part of *standard* pronunciation. In careful speech, this sound occurs before vowels at the beginning of words or syllables. So, for example, the phrase *ein Ei* contains two glottal stops: one before the *ein* and one before the *Ei*. Try pronouncing *ein Ei* both with and without the glottal stops. Without them, the phrase sounds like one word rather than two.

Now try the same exercise with the separable verbs *aufarbeiten* and *ausatmen*. Again, each word should contain two glottal stops, one before *auf* or *aus,* and one before *arbeiten* or *atmen*. It is very important to be aware of glottal stops in German since their omission is one of the features which gives the learner of German a 'foreign accent'.

4.2.4   *Manner of articulation*

Having looked at the place of articulation, i.e. *where* the sounds of German are produced, we will now look at the manner of articulation i.e. *how* the sounds are made. This means that we will be referring to the categories in the *vertical* column of Table 4.1, that is, the following types of sounds:

- plosives
- fricatives
- affricates
- nasals
- laterals
- rolls

PLOSIVES

On p. 82, we saw how the most important characteristic of **plosive** (or stop) consonants is the fact that the airstream is *stopped* as it passes through the vocal tract. This blockage is very brief, however, and after the pressure has built up, the air is soon released, causing a small *explosion*. Such sounds are to be distinguished from continuants where, as their name suggests, the airflow *continues* more or less uninterrupted on its passage through the vocal tract.

What makes the difference between the various kinds of plosive sounds is the *place* where they are articulated after the air has been released from behind the soft palate or velum. In this way, we can see how both the manner and the place of articulation coincide in order to produce different sounds.

Try saying the following sounds to yourself, and get a feel for the *manner* of articulation of plosive sounds:

voiceless plosives		voiced plosives	
/p/	Pein	/b/	Bein
/t/	Tag	/d/	Dach
/k/	*k*önnen	/g/	*g*önnen
/ʔ/	ein Ei	—	

FRICATIVES

As their name suggests, **fricatives** are those sounds where the airstream is manipulated in the vocal tract in such a way that *friction* is caused. There are four voiceless and voiced pairs of fricatives, and two voiceless fricatives with no voiced counterpart. Say the following sounds aloud:

voiceless fricatives		voiced fricatives	
/f/	*f*ein	/v/	Wein
/s/	hei*ß*	/z/	singen
/ʃ/	*Sch*nee	/ʒ/	Genie
/ç/	i*ch*	/j/	*j*a
/x/	Lo*ch*	—	
/h/	Haus	—	

Most of these sounds have already been discussed. However, one which has not yet been dealt with is the consonant represented by the phonetic symbol /x/ as in words such as *Loch* and *doch*.

This sound is unfamiliar to many English-speaking learners of German since it does not normally occur in English (although it can be heard in Scotland and in some regional English varieties, e.g. in Liverpool). As a result, many English speakers often replace it with the nearest English consonant: /k/. This leads to the mispronunciation of words such as *Loch* and *doch,* which then sound more like 'lock' or 'dock'. The key to getting this sound right rests on an understanding of its manner of articulation. Basically, if you are using the consonant /k/ where you should be saying /x/, you have the right *place* but the wrong *manner* of articulation. In other words, both /k/ and /x/ are velar sounds, but whereas the former is a plosive, the latter is a fricative. The way to remedy this problem is as follows:

- Practise pronouncing the velar plosive /k/ several times in quick succession.
- Get a feel for the mini-explosion which occurs as the air-stream is temporarily blocked.
- Now try to prevent that blockage from happening. Instead, the air must be allowed to flow freely, causing friction or a small vibration in the velum.
- The sound you should be producing is /x/, which may feel similar to the noise made when clearing your throat!
- Now say the words *Loch* and *doch* again. If they still sound like 'lock' and 'dock', then repeat the whole exercise.

AFFRICATES

Affricates are made up of two consonants: one fricative plus one plosive. There are two such sounds in German:

$$/p\underset{\smile}{f}/ \quad \text{as in } Apfel \text{ and } Pfanne$$

and

$$/t\underset{\smile}{s}/ \quad \text{as in } zu \text{ and } Zeit$$

Note how, when transcribed phonetically, affricates are written with a semi-circle underneath to show that they are pronounced as *one* sound. (It is precisely because they consist of *two* sounds, however, that they are not included in the consonant chart in Table 4.1.)

Both /p͡f/ and /t͡s/ tend to be unfamiliar to English-speaking learners of German. This is partly because they are the product of the second sound shift, which occurred in the predecessors of modern German but not English (see 2.1.3). It is for this reason that the English equivalents of the above words – 'apple', 'pan', 'to' and 'tide' – contain the plosives /p/ and /t/ as opposed to the affricates /p͡f/ and /t͡s/.

Of the two affricates /p͡f/ and /t͡s/, it is the latter which generally causes most difficulties. In fact, the inability to pronounce /t͡s/ accurately – and replacing it with /z/ or /s/ – is one of the main markers of an 'English accent'. Nevertheless, if you understand the relevant phonological principles, it is actually quite easy to get this sound right.

Just because the second sound shift did not introduce /t͡s/ into English words such as 'to' or 'time' does not mean that /t͡s/ never appears in English. In fact, this affricate can be found in many English words such as 'ca*ts*' or 'da*tes*'. What is different about the pronunciation of /ts̪/, however, is the *position* in which it may occur in the two languages. So, for example, in English, /ts̪/ only occurs *at the end* of words or syllables, e.g. 'ca*ts*', whereas in German, it is also found *at the beginning*, for example: *Zug* and *at the end*, for example: *Tanz*. Knowing how to produce this sound at the *beginning* of German words or syllables is, therefore, the key to pronouncing it correctly.

In order to learn the affricate /ts̪/, try the following short exercise:

- Say the English word 'cats'.
- Now say the imaginary word 'catsu'.
- Repeat 'catsu' many times, getting faster and faster.
- Now try dropping the initial 'ca'.
- What you are left with is the German sound /ts̪/ and the word *zu*.

It is not only English-speaking learners of German who may have problems with affricates. English also has two affricates which do not exist in the German sound system, and which are not always easy for German-speaking learners of English. These are /tʃ/ as in '*ch*ur*ch*' and /dʒ/ as in 'German*y*'. To familiarise yourself with these two affricates, try separating the plosive and the fricative in each case, e.g. /t/ + /ʃ/ and /d/ + /ʒ/, saying them slowly at first, and then more quickly, until they finally merge to form one sound.

Note also how the German pairs of affricates /p̪f/ and /ts̪/ consist exclusively of *voiceless* sounds. Now think about the English affricates: /tʃ/ is made up of two voiceless sounds, but /dʒ/ consists of two *voiced* sounds. In this sense, the affricates of German and English can be compared as shown in Table 4.2.

Table 4.2 German and English affricates

Affricate =	Plosive +	Fricative	Examples
German			
/p̪f/	/p/ (voiceless)	/f/ (voiceless)	*Pf*anne
/ts̪/	/t/ (voiceless)	/s/ (voiceless)	*Z*eit
English			
/tʃ/	/t/ (voiceless)	/ʃ/ (voiceless)	*ch*ur*ch*
/dʒ/	/d/ (voiced)	/ʒ/ (voiced)	*G*erman*y*

It is this difference between the voicing of affricates in English and German which often causes pronunciation problems for German-speaking learners of English. This is because native German speakers tend to be comfortable with *voiceless* affricates (which occur in German), but sometimes find the *voiced* affricate /dʒ/ problematical. What happens in such cases is the voiceless /tʃ/ is used where its voiced counterpart /dʒ/ is actually required. This results in words such as 'Germany' or 'German' being pronounced like '*Ch*ermany' or '*Ch*erman'.

NASALS

Nasal consonants are those sounds which are produced when the airstream is expelled via the nasal cavity rather than the oral tract. There are three nasal sounds in German:

voiceless nasal	voiced nasal
—	/m/ *m*ein
—	/n/ *n*ein
—	/ŋ/ Di*ng*

Generally speaking, /m/ and /n/ do not cause difficulties for English-speaking learners of German since they also occur in English. However, the velar nasal /ŋ/ may lead to some minor pronunciation problems. This is because, in English, the sounds represented orthographically by the letters 'ng' are not always pronounced in the same way. Take the following words:

English word	spelling	pronunciation
finger hunger	'ng'	/ŋ/+/g/
singer ringer	'ng'	/ŋ/

Can you distinguish between the pronunciation of the nasal sounds here? Normally there is a noticeable difference between 'finger' and 'hunger', on the one hand, and 'singer' and 'ringer', on the other. (Note, however, that some regional varieties of English have /ŋ/+/g/ in all four cases, whereas others have only /ŋ/.)

German, by contrast, does not have this distinction. This means that 'ng' is pronounced differently in the following pairs of English and German words:

				spelling	pronunciation
English	finger	hunger	younger	'ng'	/ŋ/+/g/
German	*Finger*	*Hunger*	*jünger*	'ng'	/ŋ/

Say these three pairs of English and German words aloud to yourself, and make sure you are absolutely certain of the difference in their pronunciation. If they still sound the same in the two languages, then try again.

LATERALS

The only **lateral** sound in German is /l/ as in:

voiceless lateral	voiced lateral
—	/l/ *laut*

Laterals are so called because of the position of the tongue, which is curled up to touch the alveolar ridge with the sides remaining down, allowing the air to escape *laterally* (i.e. on either side). One way to test this is by putting the tongue in the right position for pronouncing /l/, then sucking the air in sharply instead of expelling it. The stream of cold air which you can feel travels either side of the tongue.

Producing the consonant /l/ in German does not normally present any great difficulty to the English-speaking learner of the language. This is because the required sound is virtually identical with the /l/ in English words such as 'loud'. There is, however, a slightly different problem where this sound is concerned.

Unbeknown to many of its speakers, the English sound system contains two different types of /l/. For example, take the word 'little'. In this word, there are two 'l' sounds: one at the beginning and one at the end. But their pronunciation is quite distinct. The first 'l' is pronounced with the front of the tongue on the alveolar ridge, whereas the second is pronounced further back with the middle part of the tongue. In phonetic terms, these are known as a 'clear l' and 'dark l' (or 'front l' and 'back l'), and are represented by the phonetic symbols [l] and [ɫ], respectively:

clear/front	dark/back
[l]	[ɫ]
*li*t	*t*le

Practise saying these two types of /l/, and make sure you can distinguish clearly between them. Note also that, in English, the latter 'dark l' only occurs *at the end* of words or syllables.

The main problem for English-speaking learners of German is to avoid reproducing the 'dark l' in those positions where it would normally occur in English. This is because standard German requires a clear, 'front l' in *all* positions (though some dialects contain the 'dark l').

Now practise saying the following words, concentrating specifically on the pronunciation of /l/:

faul	*fallen*	*viel*	*Halle*	*Held*

Make absolutely certain that you are not using the second type of /l/ sound in 'little', but the first.

ROLLS

Rolls (sometimes known as *trills*) are sounds which involve one of the organs of speech hitting another several times in quick succession. In music the term 'trill' is used to describe the playing of two successive notes in rapid alternation. Other useful comparisons are drum rolls or the warbling sound made by some birds. In German – but not English – this principle of rolling or trilling is central to the articulation of the 'r' sounds, whereby there are two possibilities:

voiceless roll	voiced roll	place of articulation
—	[r]	alveolar
—	[R]	uvular

The first type of 'r' is produced when the tongue touches the alveolar ridge. If this occurs several times and very quickly, then the resulting sound is an **alveolar roll**. This is represented by the phonetic symbol [r]. This kind of 'r' sound is very similar to the one which occurs in Spanish or Italian.

The second possibility is that the 'r' is produced much further back in the vocal tract. The back of the tongue is raised towards the uvula. The friction, which occurs as the air passes through, causes the tongue to touch the uvula. If contact is made several times, then the resulting sound is known as an **uvular roll**, represented by the phonetic symbol [R]. This 'r' has a very 'throaty' quality, and is also close, in phonetic terms, to the velar fricative /x/ in *Loch* or *doch* (*see* Table 4.1).

These two types of 'r' represent regional **variants** of the same sound. Basically, the uvular [R] occurs in northern varieties of German, whereas the alveolar [r] is typically heard in southern Germany, Austria, and Switzerland. Native speakers of German are generally consistent in terms of which variant they use. For this reason, non-native speakers are not encouraged to mix the two, but to opt for one or the other.

Learning to pronounce the 'r' sounds correctly in German is not always easy for native speakers of English, and it frequently takes a lot of practice to get them right. It is important, however, to listen carefully to the way in which native speakers of German pronounce their 'r' sounds, and to try to imitate them.

4.2.5   Summary of consonant descriptions

Now that all aspects of the German consonants have been described, Table 4.3 summarises the details of each sound. Remember that three pieces of information are relevant to consonants: voicing, place of articulation, and manner of articulation.

Table 4.3 Description of the German consonants

Phonetic symbol	Voicing	Place of articulation	Manner of articulation	Example
/p/	voiceless	bilabial	plosive	*Pap*ier, hal*b*
/b/	voiced	bilabial	plosive	*b*raun, ha*b*en
/t/	voiceless	alveolar	plosive	*T*ag, Han*d*
/d/	voiced	alveolar	plosive	*d*och, Län*d*er
/k/	voiceless	velar	plosive	*k*ommen, Zu*ck*er
/g/	voiced	velar	plosive	*g*elb, Fra*g*e
/ʔ/	voiceless	glottal	plosive	ein Ei, ab*a*rbeiten
/f/	voiceless	labio-dental	fricative	*v*ier, A*ff*e
/v/	voiced	labio-dental	fricative	*W*agen, Kla*v*ier
/s/	voiceless	alveolar	fricative	*Sz*ene, hei*ß*
/z/	voiced	alveolar	fricative	*s*o, le*s*en
/ʃ/	voiceless	palato-alveolar	fricative	*Sch*nee, A*sch*e
/ʒ/	voiced	palato-alveolar	fricative	*G*enie, Eta*g*e
/ç/	voiceless	palatal	fricative	*Ch*emie, mi*ch*
/j/	voiced	palatal	fricative	*J*anuar, bri*ll*ant
/x/	voiceless	velar	fricative	Bu*ch*, la*ch*en
/h/	voiceless	glottal	fricative	*H*aus, Ge*h*alt
/m/	voiced	bilabial	nasal	*m*ein, i*mm*er
/n/	voiced	alveolar	nasal	*n*ein, a*n*ders
/ŋ/	voiced	velar	nasal	Di*ng*, hä*ng*en
/l/	voiced	alveolar	lateral	*l*ang, fa*ll*en
[r]	voiced	alveolar	roll	*r*ot, Stra*ß*e
[R]	voiced	uvular	roll	*r*ot, Stra*ß*e

4.3   Describing German vowels

When asked to name the vowels of English, most native speakers would probably reply 'a', 'e', 'i', 'o', 'u'. There might also be some debate as to whether 'y' is a vowel or a consonant. In reality, however, there are many more vowel sounds, both in English and in German.

In the previous section, we saw how the conventional Roman alphabet is much too vague to describe German consonants. It will therefore come as no surprise to discover that the same problem applies to vowels. So, for example, the letter of the English alphabet 'e' is pronounced quite differently in the following two words: 'bed' and 'below'.

Similarly, the sounds represented by the letter 'o' are not the same in these two German words: *Ofen* and *offen*. Once again, we see that the conventional alphabet often uses the *same letter* in order to represent what are, in fact, *different sounds* (and vice versa). Thus, when trying to discuss vowels – and help learners of German with their pronunciation – a much more systematic approach is needed.

4.3.1   *The difference between consonants and vowels*

In order to understand the way in which the vowels of a language are articulated, it is useful to begin by comparing them with consonants. Try the following experiment:

- Pronounce the consonant sounds /l/ and /f/ out loud, as in the English word 'leaf' [lif].
- Now say the vowel in the middle of this word, /i/, holding on to it for as long as possible.
- Pronounce the sounds again in quick succession: /l/, /f/, /i/, /l/, /f/, /i/, etc.
- Can you observe a physical difference in the way the two consonants are produced when compared to the vowel? If not, repeat the exercise several times.

The crucial distinction between consonants and vowels lies in what happens to the airstream as it passes through the vocal tract. With consonants, a clear obstruction is caused by one or more of the organs of speech, e.g. the tongue, lips, teeth, alveolar ridge, etc. With vowels, however, the air flows much more freely. It is this *lack of significant obstruction* to the airstream which is characteristic of vowels.

But if there is no real obstruction where vowels are concerned, how is it possible to produce vowel sounds which differ *from one another*? Try pronouncing the vowels in the following English words, and then alternating quickly between the two:

$$/i/ \quad \text{'leaf'}$$
$$/ɪ/ \quad \text{'lift'}$$

What happens when vowels such as /i/ and /ɪ/ are articulated is the following. A *chamber* is created within the oral tract through which the airstream must pass. It is when slight changes are made to the *shape* of this chamber that different vowel sounds are then produced. The three main organs of speech responsible for modifying the shape of the oral tract in this way are the soft palate (velum), the lips, and the tongue.

Another important aspect of consonants is the issue of voicing – in other words, whether or not the vocal cords are vibrating. This action produces the distinction between voiced and voiceless consonants, resulting in pairs such as /p/ and /b/. We have already seen how, even though /p/ is voiceless, it is still audible because of the way in which the lips block the passage of air. By contrast, because there is no genuine obstruction to the airflow where vowels are concerned, vowel sounds must normally be voiced – otherwise they cannot be heard.

To test this hypothesis, try the experiment which was used to identify the voicing of consonants in section 4.2.2. Put your hands over your ears, and pronounce the vowel sounds /i/ and /ɪ/ in 'leaf' and 'lift', respectively, holding on to them for as long as possible. You should be able to feel the same buzzing sensation which is associated with voiced consonants. Now try *devoicing* these vowels, i.e. articulating them without any vibration of the vocal cords. You should find that it is still possible to produce them, but that they are barely audible. Once again, what you are doing is whispering. Whenever we whisper, what we are in fact doing is converting all (voiced) vowels and all voiced consonants into voiceless sounds.

Because the differences between vowel sounds are quite subtle, their description is undoubtedly more complex than that of consonants. For example, explaining the difference in phonetic terms between /i/ and /ɪ/ is rather more difficult than describing the distinction between /p/ and /v/, where various organs of speech are clearly involved. Nonetheless, it is still helpful to outline some of the main ways in which vowel sounds are made, so that we can explore some of the typical pronunciation problems experienced by foreign learners of German.

4.3.2 Vowel articulation

When describing the articulation of vowels, the three most significant features are the position of:

- the soft palate or velum
- the lips
- the tongue.

THE SOFT PALATE (VELUM)

The soft palate or velum has two main functions in the production of consonants. It is the place of articulation for velar sounds, and its movements also direct the airstream through the vocal tract. If the soft palate is raised, the air escapes through the oral tract. If it is lowered, the air is released via the nasal cavity.

Where vowels are concerned, the position of the soft palate is also very important. In the case of both German and English vowels, it is almost always raised, and the airstream expelled via the oral tract. Consequently, most vowel sounds in the two languages are produced *orally* as opposed to *nasally*.

However, it is also possible for the soft palate to be positioned in such a way that the air escapes via the nasal cavity and the oral tract *simultaneously*. This is the main characteristic of so-called nasal vowels which frequently occur in French, for example, in *en France*.

THE LIPS

The position of the lips is crucial to the articulation of vowels. Generally speaking, the lips are either **spread** or **rounded**, although there is some scope for variation between these two positions.

The vowel systems of both English and German use spread and rounded lips. For the following sounds, the lips are spread: /i/ 'feel' or *Spiel* whereas, here, the vowels are pronounced with rounded lips: /u/ 'you' or *gut*.

THE TONGUE

The tongue is a very flexible speech organ and, where consonants are concerned, it moves around the mouth to touch other parts of the oral tract, e.g. the teeth, alveolar ridge, hard palate, etc.

For the articulation of vowels, however, the space within which the tongue can move around is much more restricted. This almond-shaped space is called the **vowel area** (*see* Fig. 4.2(i)). The outer edges of the vowel area are then known as the **vowel limit**.

The tongue movements which are permissible within the vowel area are very clearly defined. This is because, if the tongue crosses the vowel limit and touches another organ of speech, then a *consonant* is produced. Consequently, in order to articulate vowels and not consonants, the tongue must remain *inside* the vowel limit.

In Fig. 4.2(ii) it is possible to indicate the various types of **tongue movements** which may occur. These are measured in terms of the highest point of the tongue along two planes. First, the tongue can move from front to back, i.e. along the *horizontal* axis. Second, it can move up and down, i.e. on a *vertical* axis.

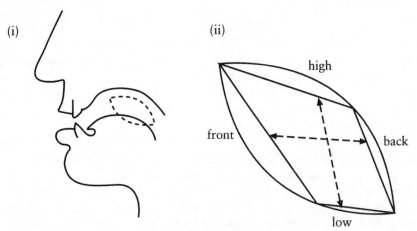

Fig. 4.2 The vowel area

Fig. 4.3 shows the stylised version of the vowel area which is normally used to describe vowels. The position of the tongue along the two planes is indicated by the terms: **front, central and back** (horizontal axis) and **high, mid-high, mid-low and low** (vertical axis).

If you go to the doctor's with a sore throat, you will normally be asked to open your mouth and produce the sound /ɑ/. This can be described as a *low vowel*. With this sound, the tongue will be in the lowest possible position, thus allowing the doctor to take a look at the back of the throat. Were you to say /u/, on the other hand, you would be producing a *high vowel*. In other words, the tongue would be in the highest possible position, therefore, blocking the doctor's view completely.

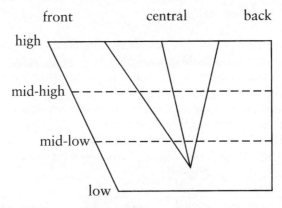

Fig. 4.3 The vowel figure

4.3.3 The German vowel figure

Now that the basic principles behind the articulation of vowel sounds have been described, we can take a look at the different vowels of German. Fig. 4.4 shows the vowel figure, but this time with the German sounds indicated and numbered. There are three main features of these sounds which are relevant to the learner of German. These are:

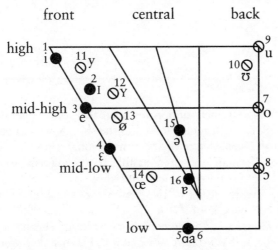

Fig. 4.4 The German vowel figure

- length of vowels, i.e. whether they are long or short;
- lip-rounding, i.e. whether the lips are spread or rounded;
- whether the vowel is made up of one sound (monophthong) or two sounds (diphthong).

LENGTH OF VOWELS

An important feature of German vowels is that most can be paired with another on account of length. In other words, each of the sounds from 1 to 14 on Fig. 4.4 has a partner – the first is **long** whereas the second is **short** (*see* Table 4.4). These long and short vowels are represented in the vowel figure by odd and even numbers, respectively. Some linguists use the terms 'lax' and 'tense' to describe short and long vowels, respectively. In addition, some follow the convention of indicating the long vowels by use of a colon, e.g. /a:/, /e:/, /i:/ etc., though this will not be adopted here.

Table 4.4 German vowels according to length

German word	Phonetic symbol	Vowel number	Vowel length
v*ie*l	/i/	1	long
T*i*sch	/ɪ/	2	short
T*ee*	/e/	3	long
B*e*tt	/ɛ/	4	short
k*a*m	/ɑ/	5	long
M*a*nn	/a/	6	short
S*o*hn	/o/	7	long
St*o*ck	/ɔ/	8	short
g*u*t	/u/	9	long
m*u*ss	/ʊ/	10	short
k*ü*hl	/y/	11	long
h*ü*bsch	/ʏ/	12	short
sch*ö*n	/ø/	13	long
zw*ö*lf	/œ/	14	short

(Examples from MacCarthy, 1975: 20)

Vowel length is extremely important from the point of view of correct pronunciation. But note how the long and the short vowel in each pair are represented by the same letter of the conventional alphabet. This means that learners of German are often unable to distinguish between those words which contain a long vowel and those where a short vowel is required. This, in turn, leads to two typical pronunciation errors where English-speaking learners of German are concerned: *short vowels are sometimes lengthened* and *long vowels are sometimes shortened*.

In order to check that you are not making this mistake, practise saying the pairs of vowel sounds in Table 4.4, making sure that there is a clear distinction between the length in each pair. If you cannot hear a difference, then you are doing something wrong.

The only exception to this principle of pairing are the two short vowels, 15 /ə/ and 16 /ɐ/, which are also known as **schwa** and **dark schwa**, respectively. Although both are short, central vowels, the dark schwa /ɐ/ is articulated with the tongue slightly lower and further back in the vowel area than schwa /ə/. The difference between these two sounds may be fairly subtle from the point of view of the English-speaking learner of German, but it is significant enough to change the meaning of some pairs of words. Practise saying the following out loud, focusing on the final vowel sound in each case:

schwa /ə/	dark schwa /ɐ/
Wette	Wetter
Liebe	lieber
Besuche	Besucher

Can you hear a difference between the vowels in question? If not, try again.

LIP-ROUNDING

The correct positioning of the lips is crucial if the German vowel sounds are to be articulated correctly. There are two positions for the lips: spread or rounded, although there is a certain amount of variation between the two.

On Fig. 4.4, each vowel is accompanied by a circle, which provides a key to lip-rounding. Those sounds requiring rounded lips are indicated by a circle with a line through it; those requiring spread lips or neutral lip-positioning are indicated by a black dot. The vowels of German can therefore be divided into three main groups as summarised in Tables 4.5, 4.6 and 4.7. Practise pronouncing each of these groups of vowels, paying specific attention to the position of the lips.

Table 4.5 Vowels requiring lip-rounding

German word	Phonetic symbol	Vowel number
Sohn	/o/	7
Stock	/ɔ/	8
g*u*t	/u/	9
m*u*ss	/ʊ/	10
k*ü*hl	/y/	11
h*ü*bsch	/Y/	12
schön	/ø/	13
zwölf	/œ/	14

Table 4.6 Vowels requiring spread lips

German word	Phonetic symbol	Vowel number
*vi*el	/i/	1
T*i*sch	/ɪ/	2
T*ee*	/e/	3
B*e*tt	/ɛ/	4

Table 4.7 Vowels requiring neutral lip-positioning

German word	Phonetic symbol	Vowel number
k*a*m	/ɑ/	5
M*a*nn	/a/	6
Gebäude	/ə/	15
Wass*er*	/ɐ/	16

For the native speaker of English, the idea of lip-rounding is not wholly unfamiliar. This is because there are a number of English vowels which also require rounded lips, for example, in words such as 'box' or 'food'. These are similar (though not identical) to the German vowels 8 and 9 in *Stock* and *gut*, respectively. However, these vowel sounds (along with 7 and 10) have something else in common. Not only do they require lip-rounding, they are also *back* vowels, that is to say, they are articulated with the highest point of the tongue at the back of the vowel area.

By contrast, German also has a set of vowels requiring lip-rounding, and which are produced with the highest point of the tongue at the *front* of the vowel area. These are the so-called front, rounded vowels, and are numbered 11, 12, 13 and 14. They occur in words such as: *kühl, hübsch, schön, zwölf*.

Because there are no front, rounded vowels in English, these are sounds which sometimes cause problems. Having said this, it is perfectly possible for English speakers to pronounce them – it is simply that they require *very protruded lips*. Say the four words above out loud, and make sure that your lips are sticking out as far forward as possible. If you try to keep your lips flat and still, it is unlikely that you will be able to articulate these vowels properly.

MONOPHTHONGS AND DIPHTHONGS

All of the vowels discussed so far have consisted of just one sound. These are called **monophthongs**. However, there is an additional type of vowel, which is made up of *two* sounds. These are referred to as **diphthongs**.

We saw earlier how some consonants, such as /t͡s/ and /p͡f/, are also made up of two sounds. These were known as affricates. Diphthongs can therefore be thought of as the vocalic equivalent of affricates. As can be seen from Table 4.8, there are three diphthongs in German.

Table 4.8 The German diphthongs

German word	Phonetic symbol	Vowel number
*ei*n	/aɪ/	17
*au*f	/aʊ/	18
n*eu*	/ɔɪ/	19

Diphthongs occur when two vowels merge in order to form one. In other words, the diphthong /aɪ/ in the word *ein* is made up of the two sounds: /a/ plus /ɪ/. If you pronounce these two vowels separately – but in very quick succession – you find yourself *moving* from the first vowel, /a/, to the second, /ɪ/, until they join, producing /aɪ/. For this reason, diphthongs are also referred to as **moving vowels**. Similarly, the two diphthongs 18 and 19 involve a transition from /a/ to /ʊ/ and /a/ to /ɪ/, respectively. This movement from one vowel to another is illustrated in Fig. 4.5.

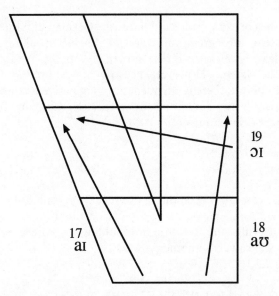

Fig. 4.5 The vowel figure with German diphthongs

The articulation of *monophthongs*, by contrast, does not involve any movement. For this reason, single vowel sounds such as /a/, /ɛ/, /ɪ/, etc. are also known as **steady vowels**.

English has many more diphthongs than German. In addition to the three German examples described above, there are another five, as illustrated in Tables 4.9 and 4.10. Pronounce these English words and, once again, try to get a feel for the way in which the vowels are *moving* in each case.

Table 4.9 The diphthongs of English also occurring in German

English word	German word	Phonetic symbol
light	*ein*	/aɪ/
out	*auf*	/aʊ/
toy	*neu*	/ɔɪ/

Table 4.10 The diphthongs of English not occurring in German

English word	Phonetic symbol
late	/eɪ/
chair	/ɛə/
home	/əʊ/
tour	/ʊə/
here	/ɪə/

Achieving the correct pronunciation for the German diphthongs does not normally present any great difficulty to English-speaking learners of German, not least because the three German diphthongs are also part of the English sound system. However, because there are so many more diphthongs in English, there is a tendency among native English speakers to convert long vowels into diphthongs when speaking German. Typical words where this might occur are:

Tee	[te]	*viel*	[fil]
Sohn	[zon]	*gut*	[gut]

In each of these cases, it is essential to produce a monophthong, i.e. a steady vowel which does not move, as opposed to a diphthong. Practise saying these words, making sure that you are 'holding on' to the vowel, i.e. not allowing it to slip towards another vowel.

4.3.4 Summary of vowel descriptions

Table 4.11 summarises the German vowel sounds and their descriptions.

4.4 Analysing units of sound

At the beginning of this chapter, a distinction was made between phonetics and phonology. Phonetics is the study of the physical production of speech sounds. Phonology, on the other hand, is more concerned with the function

Table 4.11 Description of the German vowels

Number	Phonetic symbol	Monophthong/ diphthong	Length	Description	Position of lips	Example
1	/i/	M	Long	High front	Spread	viel, ihnen
2	/ɪ/	M	Short	High front	Spread	ich, Mitte
3	/e/	M	Long	Mid-high front	Loosely spread	Regel, Schnee
4	/ɛ/	M	Short	Mid-low front	Slightly spread	Ende, Gäste
5	/a/	M	Long	Low, central	Neutral	Abend, Name
6	/a/	M	Short	Low, central	Neutral	Apfel, Hand
7	/o/	M	Long	Mid-high, back	Rounded	ohne, groß
8	/ɔ/	M	Short	Mid-low, back	Loosely rounded	offen, Sonne
9	/u/	M	Long	High, back	Strongly rounded	Urlaub, du
10	/ʊ/	M	Short	High, back	Rounded	unser, Mutter
11	/y/	M	Long	High, front	Strongly rounded	über, Bücher
12	/ʏ/	M	Short	High, front	Strongly rounded	füllen, hübsch
13	/ø/	M	Long	Mid-high, front	Strongly rounded	Öl, schön
14	/œ/	M	Short	Mid-low, front	Strongly rounded	öfters, können
15	/ə/	M	Short	Mid*, central	Neutral	eine, Gebäude
16	/ɐ/	M	Short	Mid-low, central	Neutral	der, Wasser
17	/ai/	D	—	6 to 2	Loosely rounded	ein, klein
18	/au/	D	—	6 to 10	Loosely rounded	auf, blau
19	/ɔi/	D	—	8 to 2	Loosely rounded	neu, deutsch

Note: *'Mid' refers to a position between mid-low and mid-high.

of those sounds in the context of a particular language. Technically, what we have dealt with so far are the articulatory principles behind the production of German sounds – in other words, German phonetics. What we have not yet considered is the way in which those sounds work together to form a system of meaning which is specific to German – i.e. German phonology.

4.4.1   Minimal units of sound: phonemes

Consider the English words 'pat' and 'bat'. These two words are almost identical. Indeed, their only distinguishing feature is the fact that /p/ is a voiceless consonant, whereas /b/ is voiced. Phonetically speaking, the difference between these two sounds is fairly minimal. But phonologically speaking, it is enormous.

However small the distinction between /p/ and /b/, every native speaker of English understands its significance. This is because the difference between these two sounds is important enough to change the *meaning* of pairs of words such as the following:

> 'pat'   'bat'
> 'pet'   'bet'
> 'pit'   'bit'

In German, the difference between /p/ and /b/ is equally important. Thus, by voicing or not voicing the initial consonant, we can change the meaning of word pairs such as *Pein* and *Bein*.

When sounds are significant enough to affect the meaning of words in this way, they are known as **phonemes**. Phonemes, then, are the basic units of sound – or building blocks – of a language. One of the main characteristics which differentiates German from, say, English or Greek, is the fact that each language is made up of its own unique set of phonemes.

Recognising the phonemes of a given language is easy. If you take any two sounds, and can find pairs of words which have different meanings because of those sounds, then you have identified phonemes. For example, the consonants /f/ and /k/ are clearly phonemes of English because they distinguish words such as:

> 'fat'   'cat'
> 'fit'   'kit'

The same goes for the vowels /ɪ/ and /a/ as in:

> 'big'   'bag'
> 'lid'   'lad'

Pairs of words such as these are known as **minimal pairs**, and the principle which is at work is one of **contrast**. In other words, in order to identify phonemes of a language, you need to find pairs of sounds which *contrast* sufficiently in order to change the meaning of two words.

When different languages share a common history, it is to be expected that their phonemes are fairly similar. Since German and English are both Germanic languages, it is unsurprising to find that the same types of sounds often have the same effect on meaning. Hence, /f/ and /k/ produce minimal pairs in both languages, e.g. 'fat' and 'cat' or *fein* and *kein*. The same applies to /ɪ/ and /a/ as in the English words 'big' and 'bag' and the German words *Mist* and *Mast*.

Nevertheless, it is crucial to be aware of the fact that, even though many of the phonemes of German and English are the same, there are still a number of important differences. Take, for example, the voiceless palatal fricative /ç/, which occurs in the German word *ich*. This consonant does not exist in the English sound system. In other words, it is *not* a phoneme of English, and carries no meaning as a result. A typical pronunciation error, therefore, is to replace this German sound with one which does exist in English, for example, /ʃ/ as in 'sugar' (which is sometimes perceived to be the 'nearest' sound to /ç/).

However, both /ç/ *and* /ʃ/ are phonemes of German. This means that they contrast in a way which leads to minimal pairs such as: *mich* (me) and *misch!* (mix!). To a non-native learner of German, the difference between these two sounds may seem irrelevant. But it is important to realise that, by not pronouncing them correctly, you may actually change the meaning of the words in question. So, for example, you could end up saying: 'She likes *mix*' when what you really mean is: 'She likes *me*'.

Two further sounds which do not constitute phonemes of English are the vowels /y/ as in *fühlen* (to feel) and /Y/ as in *füllen* (to fill). Because *neither* of these sounds exists in English, it is very easy for the English speaker to underestimate the importance of distinguishing between them. But, once again, it must be remembered that the difference between /y/ and /Y/ is as important in German as the difference between /ɪ/ and /a/ in English. If you therefore confuse these two German phonemes, you could end up saying something like 'I *fill* good today' or 'Please *feel* my cup with coffee'!

Not every pronunciation error will result in nonsensical sentences. Moreover, German speakers will often still understand you because of the overall context in which the sentence is uttered. But by thinking about potential errors such as these, it is possible to appreciate how the basic units of sound sometimes work differently in German and English. Learning a foreign language requires that you be sensitive to the way in which the sound system of the other language may differ from that of your mother tongue.

4.4.2   *Variation in sounds: allophones*

Phonemes are those sounds which are important enough to affect the meaning of words. However, sometimes the pronunciation of a sound can vary *without* changing meaning. Take the example of the consonant /l/. In section 4.2.4, we saw how there are two possible variants of this sound in English. In the word 'little', each of these variants occurs once. Thus, the first consonant is a clear or front [l] (pronounced with the front of the tongue), whereas the final consonant is a dark or back [ɫ] (pronounced with the back of the tongue). If you were to mix up these two types of /l/ sound, you would not change the meaning of the word 'little'. However, you would sound very odd.

What is happening here is that the choice between the two /l/ sounds depends on their position within the word 'little'. Thus, the clear, front [l] occurs *at the beginning* of the word, whereas the dark, back [l] occurs *at the end*. The two sounds are, in fact, quite distinct – but not in a way which affects meaning. They are not therefore phonemes of English, they are **allophones**.

Allophones, then, are different ways of pronouncing the same phoneme. The principle which is used to identify them is known as **complementary distribution**. In other words, allophones *complement* one another because they are *distributed* in different parts of words and syllables. Each allophone is also said to be contextually determined, i.e. the *context* in which it occurs *determines* which variant is appropriate. However, unlike phonemes, allophones *never* contrast. This is why they cannot change the meaning of words.

In linguistics, it is customary to distinguish between phonemes and allophones through differing transcription conventions. Thus:

- slanted brackets are used at the phonemic level, e.g. /.../, producing a **broad transcription**;
- square brackets are used at the allophonic level, e.g. [...], producing a **narrow transcription**.

To go back to the example of /l/, we can say that this English phoneme has two allophones: the front, clear [l] and the back, dark [ɫ]. The additional signs which are sometimes used to modify the original phonetic symbol – such as the horizontal dash in [ɫ] – are called **diacritics**. Another example of a diacritic is the **tilde** which indicates nasalisation in vowels of French origin, e.g. [ã] in *Restaurant* [RɛstoRã] or [õ] in *Balkon* [balkõ].

Let us now turn to a more specific example of the way in which the study of allophones relates to the pronunciation of German. So far in this chapter, we have talked about /r/ sounds in fairly general terms. But now try saying the following three words. Is the pronunciation of /r/ the same in each case?

- *rot*
- *hart*
- *Wasser*

Clearly, the pronunciation of the basic phoneme /r/ varies quite radically in each of these three contexts. But in order to understand what is happening here, we need to think in terms of allophones rather than phonemes. The various types of /r/ sound can therefore be described as follows:

rot → [ʀot] or [rot]

Here we have an 'r' sound occurring at the beginning of a word, and there are two main ways in which it can be pronounced. In the first case, we have the uvular roll indicated by the symbol [ʀ]. In the second case, there is the alveolar roll indicated by the symbol [r].

In section 4.2.4, we saw how the occurrence of these two sounds varies geographically. Thus, [r] tends to be heard in southern Germany, Austria and Switzerland, whereas [ʀ] is more typical in northern Germany. (It is also worth noting that, while [ʀ] is often taught to non-native speakers as the 'correct pronunciation', Switzerland and Austria have their own standard varieties of German where [r] is considered the standard variant.)

Now take:

hart → [haʁt] or [hɑt]

This time, 'r' is occurring between a vowel and a consonant. Again, there are two possibilities for its pronunciation. In careful German speech, this sound would be pronounced as an uvular fricative, represented by the symbol [ʁ]. (This is not unlike the velar fricative /x/ as in *Loch*.) Alternatively, in fairly rapid speech, this 'r' sound may disappear completely. However, if this happens then the preceding short vowel /a/ would be lengthened to [ɑ].

Finally, take:

Wasser → [vasɛʀ] or [vasɐ]

Here we have an 'r' sound at the end of a word. Although it is technically possible to pronounce the /ɛ/ and the /ʀ/ separately in very careful speech, this would be quite unusual. It would be much more common for these two sounds to be replaced by the single vowel known as 'dark schwa'. As we saw in 4.3.3, this sound is represented by the symbol [ɐ].

In conclusion, we have seen how this basic unit of sound – the phoneme /r/ – has several allophones which occur in different parts of words without changing the meaning of those words:

PHONEME	ALLOPHONES
/r/	[r] [ʀ] [ʁ] [ɐ]

It has also become clear that the occurrence of allophones may be affected by other factors, for example, the speaker's region or country of origin, as well as the speed at which he or she is talking.

Sources and recommended reading

- The most comprehensive accounts of German pronunciation written for foreign learners of the language are Hall (1992) and MacCarthy (1975), both of which also have accompanying tapes for pronunciation practice.

- Other useful summaries can be found in Chapter 2 of Fox (1990), Chapter 6 of Russ (1994) and Chapter 4 of Kürschner (1989).
- Good general introductions to phonetics and phonology are Chapters 5 and 6 of Fromkin and Rodman (1993) and Chapters 22 and 27 of Crystal (1997).
- A useful dictionary of phonetics and phonology is Trask (1996).

Exercises

1. Write the phonetic symbol for the consonants represented by italicised letters in the following words. State whether the sound is voiced or voiceless, and give its place and manner of articulation.

   Example: *b*raun /b/ Voiced bilabial plosive

   1. *sch*ön
   2. *M*aus
   3. *V*ater
   4. Han*d*
   5. Lo*ch*

   6. *w*o
   7. *Ch*emie
   8. la*ng*
   9. *s*ehen
   10. *J*ournalist

2. Consider the italicised vowel sounds in the following words, and fill in the table accordingly. The first one has been done for you (note that all are monophthongs).

WORD	PHONETIC SYMBOL	VOWEL NUMBER	VOWEL LENGTH	DESCRIPTION	POSITION OF LIPS
1. L*ie*be	/i/	1	Long	High front	Spread
2. R*e*cht					
3. M*a*ß					
4. gr*ü*n					
5. bess*e*r					
6. B*oo*t					
7. g*u*t					
8. m*ü*ssen					
9. K*ö*nig					
10. müd*e*					

3. Identify the phonemes which differentiate the following minimal pairs. Say the words out loud and make sure that you are distinguishing clearly between the pronunciation of each pair.

Examples:	Nuss/Bus	/n/ and /b/
	füllen/fallen	/Y/ and /a/

1. mein/nein
2. schön/schon
3. Kiste/Küste
4. lieber/Liebe
5. über/aber

6. wusste/wüsste
7. mich/misch
8. Stahl/Stall
9. hing/hin
10. Blüten/bluten

4. Read the following passage aloud. Then write it out using the conventional alphabet.

[maɪn nɑmə ɪst maʀia ʃmɪt/ɪç bɪn fynfʊntt͜svant͜sɪç jɑʀə alt ʊnt vonə ɪn manhaɪm/ɪç hɑbə aɪnə t͜svaɪt͜sɪmɐvonʊŋ ɪn deɐ ʃtatmɪtə/ɪç hɑbə dʀaɪ kat͜sən di mɪtsi ʃnʊki ʊnt pɪŋko haɪsən/ɪm juli fɑʀə ɪç ɪn ʊʀlaʊp/ɪç veɐdə t͜svaɪ vɔxən aʊf kʀeta feɐbʀɪŋən/ɪç fʀɔɪə mɪç ʃon zeɐ dɑʀaʊf]

5. Transcribe the following words using the International Phonetic Alphabet (use phonemes not allophones):

1. muss
2. dabei
3. deutsch
4. gebraucht
5. Österreich

6. Schule
7. schließlich
8. Gründe
9. handfest
10. Themen

6. In phonetic terms, what do the following groups of sounds have in common? If in doubt, refer back to Tables 4.3 (p. 97) and 4.11 (p. 107).

Example: /l/, /b/, /a/, /r/   They are all *voiced* sounds.

1. /f/, /x/ and /z/
2. /a/, /ɪ/ and /ɛ/
3. /t/, /d/ and /ʔ/
4. /y/, /i/ and /ɛ/
5. /x/, /g/ and /ŋ/

6. /p/, /f/ and /t͜s/
7. /h/ and /ʔ/
8. /aɪ/, /aʊ/ and /ɔɪ/
9. /l/, /t/ and /n/
10. /y/, /u/ and /o/

7. Now that you understand the way in which sounds are articulated, it is possible to reconsider certain historical developments in the German language which were discussed in Chapter 2.

Re-read section 2.1.2 and study Table 2.1 on the Germanic sound shift (p. 13–15). Then identify the phonetic symbols involved in each sound shift, and describe the *exact* phonetic changes which occurred in the following cases. What do the changes within each group have in common?

Group A	*Group B*
1. 'p' → 'f'	1. 'b' → 'p'
2. 't' → 'th'	2. 'd' → 't'
3. 'k' → 'h'	3. 'g' → 'k'

8. Now re-read section 2.1.3 and study Table 2.2 on the High German
   sound shift (p. 16–18). Then identify the phonetic symbols and the *exact*
   phonetic changes which occurred in Groups A and B. What do the
   changes within each group have in common?

Group A	Group B
1. 'p' → 'pf'	1. 'p' → 'f' or 'ff'
2. 't' → 'z'	2. 't' → 'ss' or 'ß'
3. 'k' → 'ch'	3. 'k' → 'ch'

9. Describe the two *consonant* sounds which differentiate the following
   pairs of English and German words. (Note that the vowels also differ in
   some cases.)

   Example: bed/*Bett*
   English: /d/   voiced alveolar plosive
   German: /t/   voiceless alveolar plosive

1. thick/*dick*	6. apple/*Apfel*
2. book/*Buch*	7. out/*aus*
3. hand/*Hand*	8. ten/*zehn*
4. father/*Vater*	9. love/*Liebe*
5. milk/*Milch*	10. open/*offen*

|5|

Putting the sounds together

In Chapter 4, the sounds of German were analysed on an individual basis. We looked at the vowels and consonants, and described the way in which each separate sound is articulated. These separate sounds are also known in linguistics as **segments**.

But now consider this English word: 'medicine' [mɛdɪsɪn]. When we utter a word such as this, we do not pronounce each segment in complete isolation, i.e. finishing one sound before we begin the next. If we did, we would have to say: [m] + [ɛ] + [d] + [ɪ] + [s] + [ɪ] + [n]. In order to articulate the individual sounds as carefully as this, we would have to speak extremely slowly. In fact, we would probably not make very good communicators at all since most people would find such a way of talking rather irritating and would soon stop listening. In practice, what happens when we speak is that we *merge* small groups of consonants and vowels in order to form **syllables**. Sometimes, a word may consist of one syllable only. In other cases, two or more are joined together. The word 'medicine', for example, is made up of three syllables: [mɛ] + [dɪ] + [sɪn].

We can see therefore how, in the same way that we merge certain letters of the alphabet in order to produce 'joined-up writing', we also link the individual sounds of language when speaking in order to form syllables, words, and eventually whole sentences. This results in what is known in linguistics as **connected speech**.

However, as soon as we begin to connect the individual segments in this way, a number of important processes start to take place. Because we have not quite finished pronouncing one sound before we begin the next, the articulation of a sound may be *influenced* by the other sounds which surround it. In some cases, a sound may even be dropped altogether. In faster speech, for example, many English speakers would be much more likely to pronounce 'medicine' as follows: [mɛd] + [sɪn].

Two main changes have occurred here. First of all, the /ɪ/ in the second syllable has disappeared. Second – and as a direct result of losing /ɪ/ – the segments have re-formed in order to make two syllables instead of three. These kinds of processes are the product of so-called **co-articulatory effects.** In other words, the fact that sounds are articulated together with other sounds – i.e. *co-articulated* – means that their pronunciation will sometimes change as a result. Co-articulatory effects are a permanent feature of natural, everyday speech in all languages. If we wish to achieve authentic-sounding pronunciation in any foreign language, it is therefore extremely important to have an understanding of the main changes which are likely to occur.

However, this process of connecting the individual segments of a language can be taken a step further. Once we start to put syllables and words together in order to form whole sentences, two additional factors come into play. First of all, there is **stress,** i.e. which part of a word or sentence is given extra emphasis. Second, there is **intonation,** i.e. how the **pitch** of our voice rises or falls in the course of articulating a phrase or sentence.

Stress and intonation are often considered to be a more or less separate branch of phonology, which is then referred to as **supra-segmental phonology** (i.e. *over and above* the segments). But this does not mean that stress and intonation have no influence on the pronunciation of individual sounds. For example, with 'medicine', we find that it was only possible to lose the vowel, /ɪ/, because the syllable in which it occurred was not being stressed:

[mɛ + dɪ + sɪn]   (first syllable stressed, second and third syllables unstressed)
[mɛd + sɪn]   (second, *unstressed* syllable lost)

In practice, therefore, stress and intonation are very closely related to the various co-articulatory effects which typify connected speech.

5.1   The structure of syllables

Syllables are a familiar concept, and most people have little difficulty counting the number of syllables in a given word. For example:

- 'word'   has one syllable;
- 'language'   has two syllables;
- 'alphabet'   has three syllables.

In linguistics, however, it is customary to use more technical terminology in order to describe the syllabic structure of words. For example, we can say that:

- 'word'   is **monosyllabic;**
- 'language'   is **bi-** or **disyllabic;**
- 'alphabet'   is **trisyllabic.**

Alternatively, 'language' and 'alphabet' can simply be referred to as **polysyllabic.**

But even though most people find it relatively easy to identify the *number* of syllables in a word, this does not necessarily mean that they are entirely sure what a syllable really is. So what exactly is a syllable? Syllables are basically small clusters of vowels and consonants which are articulated together, i.e. without a pause in between. Hence the word 'alphabet' consists of three syllables. This can be indicated with the use of full stops as follows: al.pha.bet.

In turn, these three syllables consist of the following clusters of vowels and consonants:

VC	CV	CVC
al	fa	bɛt

The key to understanding the structure of German syllables lies in discovering which consonants and vowels may or may not occur together. This is because one of the main differences between languages is the fact that their rules of **syllabification** vary. Thus, German and English differ in the types of syllabic structure which they allow.

In order to find out more about the structure of syllables in any language, it is useful to begin by thinking about words which *do not exist* in that language. Take, for example, **Meu* [mɔɪ]. This word would be perfectly possible in German. However, it does not exist – as indicated by the asterisk. We can therefore say that **Meu* constitutes what is known in linguistics as an **accidental gap** – although there is no such word at the moment, this is purely accidental. **Meu* might be invented at some time in the future, perhaps as a new brand-name for ice-cream or soap.

Now consider the word **Tschmlunki* [tʃmlʊŋki]. Again, this is not a German word. However, the reason why it does not exist is different than in the case of **Meu*. This is because **Tschmlunki* is made up of a combination of sounds that is not permitted in German, i.e. it contains four consonants before the first vowel. We can therefore say that this kind of word constitutes a **systemic gap** – the *system* of German syllabification does not allow it.

When trying to understand which sets of vowels and consonants may or may not occur together in a particular language, systemic gaps are extremely important. Accidental gaps, on the other hand, are of little more than passing interest since it is possible that new words will be formed from such gaps in the future. The branch of phonology which is specifically concerned with describing the vowel/consonant sequences permissible within different languages is known as **phonotactics**.

5.1.1   German syllabification

Generally speaking, the following combinations of vowels and consonants are possible in German:

(C) (C) (C) V (C) (C) (C) (C)

In other words: a syllable *must* contain at least one vowel. This vowel may then be preceded by up to three consonants and/or followed by up to four consonants.

Monosyllabic words which illustrate these combinations are as follows, although not all the possibilities are included here since there are some accidental gaps:

V	*Ei*	VC	*Uhr*	VCC	*Art*
CV	*Kuh*	CVC	*Buch*	CVCC	*Wolf*
CCV	*Schnee*	CCVC	*Stein*	CCVCC	*Stern*
CCCV	*Stroh*	CCCVC	*Strick*	CCCVCC	*Strumpf*
VCCC	*Angst*	VCCCC	*Ernst*		
CVCCC	*Dunst*	CVCCCC	*Herbst*		
CCVCCC	*Brunst*				

(Source: Fox, 1990: 47)

However, knowing that German organises its syllables in this way is not, in itself, particularly helpful to the foreign learner of the language. These rules do not, for example, explain why words such as *Fpmustf* or *Snudt* are not permissible, even though the consonants and vowels are technically in the right order. Furthermore, when pronounced in a different sequence, the very same sounds form the words *Strumpf* and *Dunst*, respectively. What we really need to know therefore are the *positions within syllables* in which certain kinds of consonants and vowels may or may not occur in German.

In the next two sections, we will look more closely at some of the rules which limit the occurrence of consonants and vowels within German syllables. But first it is important to introduce one terminological distinction: syllables which end in one or more consonants are known as **closed**, whereas syllables which end in a vowel are referred to as **open**.

Examples of words with *closed* syllables are:

Hand	[hant]
Platz	[plats]
Schrank	[ʃʀaŋk]

Examples of words with *open* syllables are:

du	[du]
sie	[zi]
wo	[vo]

5.1.2 Consonants

There are a number of different rules relating to the positions within syllables in which consonants may or may not occur, but in this section we shall be looking at two examples only. Most German consonants can occur at the *beginning of syllables and words*. There are, however, two important exceptions: /ŋ/ and /s/. Here we encounter both a similarity and a difference with English. For example, /ŋ/ cannot occur at the beginning of syllables and words in either German or English.

The voiceless alveolar fricative, /s/, on the other hand, is different. In English, this consonant is frequently found at the beginning of syllables and words, for example, in 'ab.sence' or 'say'. But this is not permitted in standard German, where the voiced /z/ is required. This, in turn, leads to a common error among English-speaking learners of German who sometimes pronounce words such as *Ab.we.sen.heit* or *sa.gen* with the voiceless /s/, when they should be using the voiced /z/. Practise saying these two German words, making sure that you are using the voiced and not the voiceless consonant.

Another extremely important rule of syllabification similarly relates to the distinction between voiced and voiceless consonants. In German, the voiced plosives and fricatives /b/, /d/, /g/, /v/, /z/, and /ʒ/ (collectively known as **obstruents**) are not permitted *at the end of syllables or words*. This is a rule of German phonotactics known as ***Auslautverhärtung***, and can be best summed up with reference to the examples contained in Table 5.1.

Table 5.1 Examples of *Auslautverhärtung*

Non-final →voiced	Word-final →voiceless	Syllable-final →voiceless
[b] (*Liebe*)	[p] (*lieb*)	[p] (*lieblich*)
[d] (*Hände*)	[t] (*Hand*)	[t] (*handlich*)
[g] (*Wege*)	[k] (*Weg*)	[k] (*Wegrand*)
[v] (*brave*)	[f] (*brav*)	[f] (*Bravheit*)
[z] (*Felsen*)	[s] (*Fels*)	[s] (*Felsblock*)
[ʒ] (*beiges*)	[ʃ] (*beige*)	[ʃ] (*beigefarben*)

Source: Hall, 1992: 28

Most students of German acquire the correct pronunciation of words such as these without ever realising that there are strict rules governing which types of sound may occur in which position. However, in order to be certain that you are familiar with the principle which is at work here, practise saying these words out loud several times, focusing on the consonants in question. Make absolutely sure that you are using the voiced and voiceless consonants in the right places.

Finally, because it is very long-winded to say 'at the end of words or syllables' every time we want to describe phonotactic rules, linguistics uses a more precise concept, namely, **salient**. The term **salient-initial** then refers to a sound which occurs at the beginning of a syllable or word. This compares to **salient-final**, which describes a sound occurring at the end of a syllable or word.

In conclusion, the two rules outlined in this section are:

- /ŋ/ and /s/ are not permitted in salient-initial position in German;
- the voiced obstruents, /b/, /d/, /g/, /v/, /z/, and /ʒ/, are not permitted in salient-final position in German.

5.1.3 Vowels

There are two important considerations when describing the position of vowels in German syllables:

- whether the syllable is stressed or unstressed;
- whether the syllable is open or closed.

Generally speaking, *all* the vowels of German may occur in *unstressed* syllables. However, there are some limits regarding which vowels may occur in *stressed* syllables. For example, schwa /ə/ and dark schwa /ɐ/ cannot occur in stressed positions, only *unstressed* positions:

Wette	[vɛtə]
Wetter	[vɛtɐ]

In these examples, the stress is falling on the *first* syllable in each case, i.e. [vɛt] and *not* on the schwa or dark schwa contained in the final syllable.

The distinction between closed and open syllables is also significant where vowels are concerned. Generally speaking, if a syllable is closed (i.e. ends in one or more consonants), then *any* of the German vowels may occur. If, however, a syllable is open (i.e. ends in a vowel), then only *long* vowels may normally occur:

du	[du]
sie	[zi]
wo	[vo]

Practise saying these words out loud, making sure that you are using long and not short vowels.

5.2 Co-articulatory effects

We saw how the pronunciation of individual sounds may vary according to their position within a given syllable or word. These changes are the result of so-called co-articulatory effects, which typify all natural, connected speech. The three most important types of co-articulatory effect which are found in German are:

- assimilation;
- elision;
- vowel reduction.

5.2.1   Assimilation

Assimilation is the process whereby one sound takes on the qualities of a neighbouring sound. This process may take place in two different directions. If a sound influences one which follows it, then this is known as **progressive assimilation**. On the other hand, if a sound influences one which precedes it, this is referred to as **regressive assimilation**. Assimilation can also be *partial* or *total*.

Where consonants are concerned, there are three aspects of pronunciation which may be affected by assimilation:

- place of articulation;
- manner of articulation;
- voicing.

ASSIMILATION OF PLACE

Say the following words and phrases out loud. Begin by pronouncing them very slowly, concentrating specifically on the alveolar nasal, /n/, which is in bold type:

anpassen	[anpasən]
in Position	[ɪn pɔzɪtsjon]
Einbahnstraße	[aɪnbanʃtRasə]
diesen Ball	[dizən bal]
einmal	[aɪnmal]
kann man	[kan man]

Now try speeding up your pronunciation. Do you notice any change to the way in which you are articulating the /n/ sound?

What tends to happen in faster speech is that before you have quite finished pronouncing the /n/ in question, you have already started to prepare for the next consonant. This, in turn, leads to a slight change or *modification* in the way in which /n/ is articulated. Thus, the alveolar nasal /n/ begins to sound more like the bilabial nasal [m]:

anpassen	[ampasən]	(before /p/)
in Position	[ɪm pɔzɪtsjon]	
Einbahnstraße	[aɪmbɑnʃtʀɑsə]	(before /b/)
diesen Ball	[dizəm bal]	
einmal	[aɪmmɑl]	(before /m/)
kann man	[kam man]	

The explanation for this change may not, at first, be obvious. This is because, in each of the three pairs of words and phrases above, /n/ is followed by a different consonant, that is, /p/, /b/ or /m/, respectively.

However, these three consonants have something in common: they are all *bilabial* sounds. In other words, their *place of articulation* is the same. What is happening, therefore, is that before the articulation of the alveolar /n/ is complete, the pronunciation of a bilabial consonant has already begun. This then leads to a partial modification of the *alveolar* /n/ sound to a *bilabial* [m]. This is an example of assimilation of place of articulation. Note also that such assimilation can occur both between two syllables or between two words. To sum up this rule, we can say: /n/ may be assimilated to [m] before the bilabial consonants /p/, /b/, and /m/.

Note how we also need to differentiate here between phonemes and allophones. The *phoneme* in question is /n/. This is the sound which carries meaning. But recall the discussion in section 4.4 where we saw how phonemes may sometimes be pronounced in slightly different ways without changing the meaning of the word in which they occur. These different variants of phonemes are called *allophones* and are written in square brackets. What we have seen here is that one possible variant of the phoneme /n/ is the allophone [m]. This change will not occur every time – only when the conditions are right, for example, when /n/ is followed by a bilabial consonant such as /p/, /b/ or /m/.

A similar process occurs in the following pairs of words and phrases:

/n/ → [ŋ]	*Einkauf*	[aɪŋkaʊf]	(before /k/)
	mein Kaffee	[maɪŋ kafe]	
	Unglück	[ʊŋglʏk]	(before /g/)
	in Gefahr	[ɪŋ gəfaʀ]	

This time, however, the alveolar nasal /n/ has been assimilated to the velar nasal [ŋ]. This is because the consonants which follow are the velar plosives, /k/ or /g/. The result is that the place of articulation has changed from an *alveolar* nasal /n/ to a *velar* nasal [ŋ].

It is worth noting that if you speak very slowly and carefully, there will probably be no real change to the consonants we have looked at here. However, as soon as you begin to speed up your pronunciation, then assimilation almost always occurs – even if it is sometimes only partial as opposed to total. Assimilation is therefore a very important aspect of authentic-sounding German speech. Indeed, in many cases, it would be a failure to assimilate which would sound rather odd.

Practise pronouncing all of the above examples out loud. Try each example once without and once with assimilation. Can you hear the difference?

ASSIMILATION OF MANNER

Now consider the following words and phrases:

/b/ → [m]	*zum Beispiel*	[tsʊm maɪʃpil]	(after /m/)
/d/ → [n]	*Bundesrepublik*	[bʊnnəsʀepublik]	(after /n/)
/g/ → [ŋ]	*ungefähr*	[ʊŋŋfɛɐ]	(after /ŋ)

In these examples, a slightly different type of assimilation is occurring. Here the *plosive* consonants /b/, /d/, and /g/ are changing to become *nasal* sounds like the [m], [n], and [ŋ] sounds which precede them, respectively.

This time, it is not the place of articulation which is being assimilated but the *manner*. Moreover, the change is taking place in a different direction: the nasal sounds /m/, /n/, and /ŋ/ are influencing the plosive sounds which follow them. This is, therefore, an example of progressive assimilation. This process is not typical of careful pronunciation, and need not necessarily be imitated by the non-native speaker. But it is certainly found in rapid, colloquial German speech.

ASSIMILATION OF VOICING

There are two ways in which the voicing of consonants can be assimilated. First, a voiced consonant can become voiceless – a process known as *devoicing*. Second, a voiceless consonant can become voiced – a process referred to as *voicing* (see section 3.2.2).

In the following examples, the voiced plosives, /b/, /d/, and /g/, and the voiced fricative, /z/, are being devoiced because of the voiceless consonants which precede them – again, a form of progressive assimilation:

/z/ → [z̥]	*Fischsuppe*	[fɪʃz̥ʊpə]	(after /ʃ/)
/b/ → [b̥]	*Regensburg*	[ʀeɡənsb̥ʊɐk]	(after /s/)
/d/ → [d̥]	*aufdrücken*	[aʊfd̥ʀʏkən]	(after /f/)
/g/ → [g̊]	*maßgeblich*	[mɑsg̊epliç]	(after /s/)

Pronounce each of these words, concentrating specifically on the consonant which is being devoiced in each case.

Note how a special diacritic is being used here to indicate devoicing, namely, a small circle written directly under or over the sound in question. It would, of course, be possible to simply use the phonetic symbol for the equivalent voiceless consonant, but this is not the convention. This is because a distinction is being made between a *voiceless* consonant, on the one hand, and a *devoiced* consonant, on the other. Voiceless consonants such as /s/, /p/, /t/ and /k/ are *phonemes* of German. This means that they can change the meaning of the words in which they occur. But the devoiced consonants [z̥], [b̥], [d̥], and [g̊] are merely *allophones* of /z/, /b/, /d/, and /g/. As a result, they do not lead to changes in meaning.

One reason why it is important to distinguish between a voiceless and a devoiced consonant is that the process of devoicing is sometimes only *partial*, as in the following examples:

/j/ → [j̊]	*Hans-Jakob*	[hansj̊akɔp]	(after /s/)
/v/ → [v̥]	*das Wetter*	[das v̥ɛtɐ]	(after /s/)
/ʀ/ → [ʀ̥]	*mit Recht*	[mɪt ʀ̥ɛçt]	(after /t/)
/l/ → [l̥]	*auflegen*	[aʊf l̥eɡən]	(after /f/)

Practise pronouncing these examples, concentrating on the partial devoicing which is occurring.

Finally, the opposite process to devoicing is *voicing*. This refers to those cases where voiceless consonants become voiced. It should be stressed, however, that this is typical only of *very informal* speech and some regional dialects of German. It should not generally be adopted by non-native speakers, at least not in the early stages of learning the language. Examples are:

/s/ → [z]	*weiß er*	[vaɪzɐ]
/t/ → [d]	*hat er*	[hadɐ]
/f/ → [v]	*hoff' ich*	[hɔvɪç]

Note also how this process of voicing is occurring **intervocalically**, i.e. between two vowels. This is because, as you may recall, all vowels are normally voiced (see 3.3.1). In other words, the voiceless consonant is being voiced because it is occurring between two *voiced* vowels.

5.2.2 Elision

Elision is the process whereby sounds are lost completely or *elided*. There are three main types of elision which are relevant to learners of German:

- elision of schwa;
- reduction of double consonants;
- elision of /t/.

ELISION OF SCHWA

One of the most important processes in German connected speech is the loss of schwa, i.e. /ə/ before nasal consonants. This occurs most frequently in the context of verbs, adjectives, and some plural nouns, which end in the suffix *-en*. For example:

verb:	*treten*	[tRetn̩]
adjective:	*guten*	[gutn̩]
noun:	*Ratten*	[Ratn̩]

In such cases, a new diacritic – a line beneath the /n/ – is being used to indicate the loss of schwa. The resulting form constitutes what is known as a **syllabic**. This is because, although schwa has been lost, /n̩/ still constitutes a syllable in its own right.

Not all examples of elision of schwa are quite as straightforward as the three we have just looked at. This is because in some cases, the loss of schwa also leads to assimilation:

/ən/ → [m̩]	*Lippen*	[lɪpm̩]	(after /p/)
	gaben	[gabm̩]	(after /b/)
/ən/ → [ŋ̍]	*locken*	[lɔkŋ̍]	(after /k/)
	wegen	[vegŋ̍]	(after /g/)

In other words, the same types of progressive assimilation begin to occur which were described in section 5.2.1, i.e. the place of articulation of the alveolar nasal /n/ is changed to produce either the bilabial [m] or the velar [ŋ].

Note also that schwa can be elided in the middle of words in a way which leads to syllabics:

/ən/ → [n̩]	*Reisende*	[Raɪzn̩də]	(after /z/)
/ən/ → [m̩]	*Lippenstift*	[lɪpm̩ʃtɪft]	(after /p/)
/ən/ → [ŋ̍]	*fliegende*	[fligŋ̍də]	(after /g/)

Furthermore, schwa is sometimes lost before /l/, resulting in a different type of syllabic:

Handel	→ [handl̩]
handeln	→ [handl̩n]

All of the above forms are very typical of relaxed, informal speech and, in some cases, rapid, formal speech. They should therefore be practised and imitated by the non-native learner of German.

Finally, another example of the loss of schwa affects first person verb endings. This occurs in both present and past tense forms, and is a typical feature of very relaxed conversational style. For example:

ich mache	→ *ich mach'*	[ɪç max]
konnte ich	→ *konnt' ich*	[kɔnt ɪç]

REDUCTION OF DOUBLE CONSONANTS

This is a fairly straightforward process whereby two identical consonants are reduced to one. For example:

/tt/ → [t]   *mitteilen*   [mɪtaɪln̩]
/nn/ → [n]   *annehmen*   [anemm̩]

Note also that two consonants may sometimes be the same due to assimilation which has already taken place:

/sʃ/   *Eisschrank*   [aɪsʃʀaŋk]
[ʃʃ]   *Eisschrank*   [aɪʃʃʀaŋk]
[ʃ]   *Eisschrank*   [aɪʃʀaŋk]

Finally, there are sometimes cases where syllabics which have already been assimilated are then elided. For example:

/mən/   *kommen*   [kɔmən]
[mm]   *kommen*   [kɔmm̩]
[m]   *kommen*   [kɔm(m̩)]

The convention here is to place parentheses (brackets) around the elided syllabic. However, since it is also possible that this reduced form might be ambiguous – it could mean *komm!* or *kommen* – this type of elision can only occur in situations where there will be no confusion regarding meaning.

ELISION OF /t/

There are two main contexts in which /t/ is likely to be elided, as illustrated in the following examples.

- the /t/ element in the affricate /t͜s/ is lost:

/nt͜s/ → [ns]   *ganz*   [gans]   (after /n/)
/lt͜s/ → [ls]   *hältst*   [hɛlst]   (after /l/)
/st͜s/ → [ss]   *auszugehen*   [aʊssugen]   (after /s/)

- /t/ is elided following a fricative:

/stl/ → [sl]   *festlich*   [fɛslɪç]   (after /s/)
/ftl/ → [fl]   *Häftling*   [hɛflɪŋ]   (after /f/)
/çtl/ → [çl]   *Frauenrechtlerin*   [fʀaʊənʀeçlərɪn]   (after /ç/)

This type of elision is fairly typical of relaxed conversation, and can therefore be imitated by non-native speakers.

5.2.3   *Vowel reductions*

Most of the co-articulatory effects which have been discussed so far relate to consonants. However, vowels are also subject to a number of changes, collectively known as **vowel reductions**.

Consider the following question: *Hast du ihn gesehen?* In careful speech, this would probably be pronounced as follows:

[hast du in gəzeən]

In more relaxed speech, however, the pronunciation might be more like:

[has dʊ ɪn gəzeṇ]

In this version, the long vowels contained in both *du* and *ihn* have been shortened: /u/ to /ʊ/ and /i/ to /ɪ/, respectively. (The final /t/ in *hast* has also been assimilated to the /d/ of *du*, and *-en* in *gesehen* has been reduced to a syllabic.)

But in very fast speech, the short /ʊ/ in *du* might be reduced even further to schwa. For example:

[has də ɪn gəzeṇ]

Finally, in extremely casual, colloquial speech, the question might even be pronounced as follows:

[has ṇ gəzeṇ]

Here the pronunciation has changed quite radically: the word *du* has been elided completely and *ihn* has been reduced to a syllabic following the loss of schwa. Practise saying all four variants of the above question, getting a feel for the changes to the vowels which occur as the style becomes increasingly relaxed.

Clearly, there are many different changes which may affect vowels in German. Vowels may be:

- shortened (i.e. a long vowel becomes short);
- reduced to schwa;
- elided completely.

But there is an additional factor behind such changes which must be highlighted. This is because, unlike the co-articulatory effects which relate to consonants, it is not simply the neighbouring sounds which are causing these reductions. In fact, it is only possible to reduce the vowels in *du* and *ihn* in this way because they are occurring in *unstressed* positions. Note, for example, that if you wanted to ask the question slightly differently, stressing the *du* or *ihn*, such vowel reductions could not possibly occur:

Hast DU ihn gesehen?	[du]	(long vowel)
Hast du IHN gesehen?	[in]	(long vowel)

What we are beginning to see, therefore, is how the pronunciation of individual sounds may also be affected by patterns of *stress*.

5.3   Stress

Connected speech is primarily concerned with the way in which the pronunciation of individual sounds is affected by neighbouring sounds. But in the previous section, we began to see how an additional factor may also come into play, namely, *stress*. Stress is the first of two *supra-segmental* features to be discussed in the remainder of this chapter, the second being intonation.

When learning a foreign language, it is extremely important to know which part of words and sentences are going to be emphasised. This is because if we pronounce all the sounds of a language correctly but get the stress patterns wrong, we would still have a strong foreign accent.

Sometimes, however, stress patterns have implications which go beyond the question of 'accent'. Consider, for example, the following word: [kafe]. Knowing where the stress falls in a word such as this is crucial not only in terms of pronunciation. In this case, there are two possibilities, and which of these you choose actually changes the *meaning* of the word. Hence:

[ka'fe]	*(das) Café*	(café, coffee house)
['kafe]	*(der) Kaffee*	(coffee)

From this example, we can see how a familiarity with the basic patterns of stress in a foreign language is important from the point of view of both pronunciation *and* meaning. (Note also how stress is indicated by an apostrophe which is placed immediately before the syllable to be emphasised.)

Finally, stress does not only affect individual words as in the above examples, it also affects the pronunciation and meaning of whole sentences. In this section, we shall therefore be looking at two different kinds of stress:

- word stress
- sentence stress.

5.3.1   Word stress

When describing the stress patterns of German words, there are two factors which need to be taken into account: the *structure* and the *origin* of the word in question. The structure of a word can be broken down into two main elements: **roots** and **affixes**. The roots of a word carry the basic semantic meaning, e.g. *geh-, sing-,* or *lieb-*. Affixes, on the other hand, convey grammatical information. Affixes can also be divided into **prefixes** (which occur before the root), e.g. *ge-, ver-, ent-,* and **suffixes** (which occur after the root), e.g. *-ung, -lich, -keit.*

The second important factor is the origin of the word. Here it is useful to recall our discussion of the historical development of German in Chapter 2.

There we saw how Germanic languages underwent an important change in their stress patterns known as *der germanische Akzentwandel* (see 2.1.2). This meant that there was a general shift in emphasis to the *first* syllable of Germanic words. Romance languages such as French, on the other hand, have retained the more variable patterns of stress which typified Proto-Indo-European.

Broadly speaking, this distinction still applies to Germanic and Romance languages today. But German, of course, also contains a number of foreign (or non-Germanic) words which do not follow Germanic stress rules. Instead, such words adhere to the patterns more typical of the other Indo-European languages from which they are derived. This means that modern German has a mixture of stress patterns.

STRESS IN GERMAN WORDS

The rule for words of Germanic origin is fairly simple: the stress normally falls on the root and not the affix. Pronounce the following words, concentrating specifically on where the emphasis occurs in each case:

> '*machen*
> *ge'macht*
> *ver'reisen*

If the word has more than one syllable but no clearly identifiable affix, then the stress still falls on the first syllable:

> '*Tafel*
> '*Boden*
> '*Schwester*

There is, however, one context where an affix may be stressed: in separable verbs. This is because, in such cases, the prefixes are actually meaningful in the semantic sense, as opposed to simply carriers of grammatical information:

> '*aufstehen*
> '*hinfahren*
> '*zumachen*

This also means that there are markedly different stress patterns for pairs of identical verbs, where one is separable and the other inseparable:

separable verb (prefix stressed)		inseparable verb (root stressed)	
'*umgehen*	(to circulate)	*um'gehen*	(to avoid)
'*durchsetzen*	(to carry through)	*durch'setzen*	(to intersperse with)
'*übertreten*	(to step over)	*über'treten*	(to overstep)

Practise saying these pairs of verbs, focusing on the different stress patterns in each.

STRESS IN FOREIGN WORDS

The rule for foreign words – i.e. words which are not of Germanic origin – is also fairly straightforward. Normally the main stress falls on the final syllable:

> *Demon'strant*
> *Ingen'ieur*
> *Universi'tät*

One exception to this rule is a small group of foreign suffixes, which are not generally stressed. These include *-us, -o, -a* and *-ik*:

> *'Zirkus*   *'Drama*
> *'Konto*   *Ling'uistik*   (BUT *Mus'ik, Phys'ik*)

COMBINATION OF GERMAN AND FOREIGN WORDS

Not all stress patterns are quite as clear-cut as the examples we have looked at so far. What happens, for example, when a word is partly Germanic and partly foreign in origin? The answer is twofold. If there is a foreign root and a German suffix, then there is no conflict of interest – both the rules for German and foreign words can be satisfied simultaneously. Hence: *na'türlich*. Here, the final syllable of the foreign root is stressed, e.g. *na'tür*, and the German suffix, *-lich*, remains unstressed.

If, however, a word contains a German root and a foreign suffix, then there is a conflict. In such cases, it is the foreign suffix which is normally stressed. Hence:

> *Liefe'rant*
> *Wäsche'rei*

COMPOUNDS

Many German words, for example, *Bahnhof* or *Bundeskanzler*, are composed of more than one word. These are known as **compounds**. The individual words which make up compounds are, of course, normally subject to their own particular stress patterns. But what happens when they occur together? Which word takes precedence? In such cases, there are a number of different possibilities.

Generally speaking, if two monosyllabic words are joined together to form a compound, then it is the first element which is stressed. Hence:

> 'Bahnhof
> 'Hochhaus
> 'Frühstück

If, however, one element of the compound is a polysyllabic word, then something different occurs. Both elements of the compound can be stressed, but with more emphasis placed on the first than on the second. This is known as **primary** and **secondary stress**. Hence:

> 'Bundes ,kanzler
> 'Auto ,bahn
> Fa 'milien ,name

Practise saying these words aloud, getting a feel for the different degrees of stress. Note also how secondary stress is indicated by a comma before the second element to be emphasised.

Sometimes there are cases where primary stress may in fact occur on the second word in the compound. This is in those compounds where it is the second part which carries the more important meaning:

> Oster 'montag
> Zwei 'zimmerwohnung
> Jahr 'zehnt

This pattern is also found in a number of place-names:

> Trave 'münde
> Saar 'brücken
> Bremer 'haven

Finally, it is occasionally even possible to place primary stress on *all* the individual words in a compound. This occurs in hyphenated words where the meaning of each part is considered to be of equal importance:

> 'Baden- 'Württemberg
> 'Klaus- 'Dieter
> 'schwarz- 'rot- 'gold

5.3.2   Sentence stress

It is not only individual words, but also whole phrases and sentences which are subject to different levels of emphasis. This is known as **sentence stress** or **rhythm**. Three things can be said about this particular type of stress.

Read the following three sentences aloud, articulating each slightly faster than the previous one. Concentrate on the stress patterns which are indicated in each case:

1. *'Mein 'Vater 'fährt 'morgen 'früh zum 'Frankfurter 'Flughafen* (slow)
2. *Mein 'Vater fährt 'morgen 'früh zum 'Frankfurter 'Flughafen* (medium)
3. *Mein 'Vater fährt morgen 'früh zum Frankfurter 'Flughafen* (fast)

The first point to be made here is that sentence stress normally falls on the most meaningful units of the sentence. In sentence 1, all elements are being considered equally meaningful (with the exception of *zum*). This would be an example of someone speaking in a very deliberate fashion. Of course, we do not speak like this most of the time for fear of irritating the people we are talking to (although it might be necessary if we were dictating a letter or were on the telephone with a poor connection). In normal conversation, we therefore tend to speed things up a little, as in sentence 2 or 3.

Once we speak more quickly, however, the patterns of stress begin to change. If you look again at the above examples, you will see that there are fewer stressed elements in sentence 3 than in 2 and 1, respectively. The elements which are now most likely to be stressed are the so-called **content words**, e.g. nouns, verbs, and adjectives. Those parts which remain unstressed will be the **function words**, e.g. articles, pronouns, and prepositions, etc.

The second point relates to the very regular or rhythmical way in which the stress falls in *all three* sentences. Irrespective of how many words or syllables are stressed, note how the space between the stressed elements is always fairly even. Languages which are characterised by this kind of stress pattern, such as German and English, are known as **stress-timed**. Romance languages, on the other hand, have a different rhythm. French and Spanish, for example, tend to give more equal weighting to the various syllables throughout a sentence, and are therefore referred to as **syllable-timed**.

This distinction between stress- and syllable-timing explains what is perhaps one of the most fundamental phonological differences between the Germanic and Romance languages. It is also why, to the ears of a native German or English speaker, French or Spanish may sound as though they are being spoken very quickly. In reality, however, this impression is not being created by the speed at which such languages are articulated – it is simply the very regular, rhythmical way in which the emphasis falls on the individual syllables.

Because German and English have rather similar patterns of sentence stress, achieving the correct patterns should not present any great difficulties for learners of German, but this does bring us to the third and final point. Once we begin to speak more quickly and prioritise some syllables and words over others, then the kinds of elision and reduction processes described in sections 5.2.2 and 5.2.3 will also start to take effect.

In sentence 3, for example, only the three most important elements of meaning are being emphasised: *Vater, früh,* and *Flughafen*. This means that certain processes of reduction are likely to occur in the remaining unstressed syllables and words. For example, the reduction of the suffix /ən/ to the syllabic is much more likely to occur in the unstressed word *morgen* [mɔɐgn̩] than in the stressed word *Flughafen* [flughɑfən]. In sentence 1, on the other hand, this kind of reduction would not be possible in either of these two words because both are being stressed equally.

5.4   Intonation

The second supra-segmental feature which is important for learners of German is *intonation*. Whereas stress can be described as the prominence given to certain syllables and words over others, intonation is concerned with changes in *pitch*. Pitch, in turn, is determined by the speed at which our vocal cords vibrate – the faster they vibrate, the higher the pitch. When we speak, our voice pitch is constantly changing due to the differing speeds at which the vocal cords vibrate. This then results in the rising and falling patterns of intonation which make our speech characteristically human. If you think of the way robots speak, it is precisely their lack of intonation which makes them sound so mechanical and monotone.

Through intonation we convey a range of emotions and intentions such as politeness, enthusiasm, anger, caution, gratitude, disbelief, etc. By changing our intonation, we can also communicate to the people with whom we are talking whether or not we expect a reply or further comment on what we have said. To some extent, of course, the way we use intonation relates to our own personalities and the types of situations in which we find ourselves, i.e. whether or not we are in the habit of expressing enthusiasm, or when and where we are likely to be polite or impolite. But even allowing for individual differences in the way we make use of intonation, the patterns available to us are still fairly fixed.

The problem when learning foreign languages is that intonational patterns are likely to be different to those of our own language. Yet getting those patterns right is crucial if we want our feelings to be interpreted correctly by our interlocutors. We need to be aware that using inappropriate patterns of intonation may mean that, whereas we think we are saying one thing, others perceive us to be saying something quite different. Sometimes this can have tremendous consequences for the social relationships in which we engage. German and English, for example, have rather different ways of conveying politeness and sympathy through intonation.

5.4.1   The nucleus

It is easy to claim that changes in intonation occur when the pitch of our voices rises and falls, but what does this sound like in practice? Consider the following sentence: *Ich komme heute nachmittag.* Instead of pronouncing this sentence in the usual manner, try humming it, i.e. saying it as a series of 'mms'. Can you identify a point in the sentence at which the pitch changes? If you are applying the correct intonation, you should find that there is a noticeable downward shift in pitch just before the *nach* in *nachmittag*:

↓

Ich komme heute nachmittag

The point at which there is a significant change in pitch within an utterance – whether upwards or downwards – is known as the **nucleus**. Note that the nucleus is always a *stressed* syllable. Identifying the nucleus in any phrase or sentence is the key to describing intonational patterns.

5.4.2   *Typical patterns of German intonation*

There are five main patterns of intonation which are relevant to anyone learning German. Understanding these patterns depends first on finding the nucleus, and second, on a familiarity with the kinds of meanings they convey.

THE FALL

↘
Gut!

↘
Schade!

↘
Ich komme sofort!

In these utterances, there is a sharp fall in pitch at the nucleus (indicated by an arrow in each case). This falling intonation signals that the utterance is complete, and that the speaker does not expect any further response. A similar pattern occurs in English, but the German fall is slightly sharper and more pronounced. Practise saying the above phrases, focusing on the steep fall in pitch.

THE RISE

↗
Hier?

↗
Wo?

↗
Siehst du ihn?

The rise is the opposite of the fall, and its meaning is also the reverse. All three of the above utterances are questions. Through rising intonation, the speaker is therefore signalling that he or she expects a response from the interlocutor – in other words, an answer to the question. Again, this pattern also exists in English, but the rise is steeper in German. Practise this rise with the three examples above.

LEVEL PITCH

⟵ ──────────────────────⟶   ↘

Wenn du heute nachmittag kommst, (wirst du ihn treffen)

This pattern of intonation is used when the speaker intends to add more information to what has already been said. The pitch remains fairly even across the whole of the utterance. The main difference between German and English is that, in English, there would be an upward shift in pitch here. Practise saying this sentence, focusing specifically on the level pitch which typifies the first half of the sentence – in the second half the pitch will fall. Do not allow the pitch to rise when saying *kommst*.

THE RISE–FALL

↗ ↘
Wunderbar!
↗ ↘
Danke!
↗ ↘
Es hat geklappt!

This quite radical change in pitch is used to express enthusiasm in statements, commands, and questions. It is similar to the English pattern, except that both the rise and the fall are steeper. Practise this rise–fall pattern in the three examples above.

THE FALL–RISE

↘ ↗
Kommt er <u>wirklich</u>?
↘ ↗
Ist das <u>unser</u> Wagen?
↘ ↗
Hast <u>du</u> das gemacht?

This fall–rise pattern is used to accompany the emphasis which is already being placed on *wirklich, unser,* and *du*. A similar change in pitch occurs in English, except that it tends to be followed by another fall, producing a fall–rise–fall pattern. This, however, must be avoided. Say the above sentences out loud, concentrating specifically on *not* allowing the pitch to drop a second time after the rise.

5.4.3   Avoiding patterns of English intonation

Although the intonational patterns of German and English are in many respects quite similar, there are two specific patterns in English which do *not* occur in German. Avoiding these types of intonation is therefore essential for anyone who wishes to achieve authentic-sounding pronunciation in German.

THE LOW RISE

What's the matter?   (reassuring)

Come along!   (gentle command)

Don't worry!   (encouraging)

The low rise in English is used in situations where falling intonation might sound aggressive or unsympathetic. Try saying each phrase twice – once with a low rise in pitch, and once with falling intonation. Can you discern the different kinds of meaning conveyed by these two types of intonation?

There are two problems where the low rise is concerned: one for native German speakers and one for native English speakers. First, since there is no low rise in German, native German speakers often replace it with falling intonation when speaking English. This, however, may unintentionally convey impoliteness or a generally unsympathetic attitude – something which occasionally leads to intercultural misunderstandings between German and English speakers when speaking English.

Second, when the low rise is used by English speakers of German, it sounds quite foreign. Since German has no strict equivalent to the low rise, however, it tends to convey the same sorts of meanings in different ways. For example, German often uses additional words combined with falling intonation. In the following sentences, the particles *mal*, *schon* and *wohl* are used to soften what is being said:

Warten Sie mal einen Augenblick!   (gentle, pleading command)

Es wird schon klappen.   (encouraging)

Sie werden wohl kommen.   (reassuring)

Practise saying each of these sentences, focusing on the particle and the falling intonation which replaces the English low rise.

THE RISE–FALL–RISE

The second intonational pattern of English which does not occur in German is the rise–fall–rise. This is used in English to convey hesitation, concession, warmth, or general encouragement. For example:

⬈ ⬊⬈
Peter   (hesitant, appealing)

⬈ ⬊⬈
I hope not   (sympathetic)

⬈ ⬊⬈
She sings well
(but her acting's terrible)   (concession)

Again, given that German does not share this intonational pattern, it uses different means in order to convey the same kinds of sentiments. Possible equivalents of the above examples might therefore be:

Du, Peter!   (addition of personal pronoun *du*)
Ich hoffe nicht
Singen kann sie gut,   (falling intonation)
(aber nicht schauspielen)   (word order change)

Sources and recommended reading

- See Hall (1992), Chapters 5 and 6, for a good introduction to German stress/intonation and connected speech as well as many useful exercises.
- See MacCarthy (1975), Chapters 2, 3, and 4, for a summary of German stress and intonation.
- Fox (1990), Chapter 2, contains a more advanced discussion of connected speech and supra-segmental phonology.
- Good general introductions to English phonetics and phonology are Chapter 6 of Fromkin and Rodman (1993) and Chapters 27 and 29 of Crystal (1997).
- A useful dictionary of phonetics and phonology is Trask (1996).

Exercises

1. Using your knowledge of German syllabification, divide the following words into syllables.

> *Example:*   mögen   mö.gen

1. nämlich	6. Schmetterlinge
2. halbtags	7. aufregend
3. einige	8. Marianne
4. gemacht	9. gerade
5. hatte	10. ausatmen

2. The following words do not exist in German. Are they accidental or systemic gaps? If they are systemic gaps, say which rule of syllabification is being broken.

> *Examples:*   *dauf* [dauf]   accidental gap
>   *sun*   [sun]   systemic gap (/s/ cannot occur in initial position)

1. la	[la]	6. len	[lən]
2. gnuk	[ŋuk]	7. bing	[bɪŋ]
3. Schmenk	[ʃmɛŋk]	8. Gromp	[gRɔmp]
4. bag	[bag]	9. Tmrpfan	[tmʀpfan]
5. Zunk	[ts̪ʊŋk]	10. Gacht	[gaxt]

3. The German rule of *Auslautverhärtung* states that voiced obstruents (plosives and fricatives) cannot occur in salient-final position. Tick the appropriate column in the following tables to indicate whether the voiced or voiceless consonant will occur in each individual word.

[t] or [d]?

	[t]	[d]
1. Länder		
2. Land		
3. Landkarte		
4. Rind		
5. Rinder		
6. Rindlein		

[p] or [b]?

	[p]	[b]
1. halb		
2. halbtags		
3. halbieren		
4. Dieb		
5. Diebstahl		
6. Diebe		

[k] or [g]?

	[k]	[g]
1. Tag		
2. Tage		
3. täglich		
4. fliegen		
5. flog		
6. Flüge		

4. Name the processes of assimilation that have occurred in the words listed below, e.g.:

   - voicing
   - devoicing
   - change in place of articulation
   - change in manner of articulation

   Example: Schrank   [ʃʀaŋk]   /n/ → [ŋ]

   Assimilation of place of articulation.
   The *alveolar* nasal /n/ has changed to the *velar* nasal [ŋ] before the *velar* plosive /k/.

1. Auflage	[aʊfl̩agə]	6. hoff' ich	[hɔvɪç]
2. Einkauf	[aɪŋkaʊf]	7. Kravatte	[kʀavatə]
3. weit besser	[vaɪp bɛsɐ]	8. Magnet	[maŋnet]
4. maßgeblich	[masĝeplɪç]	9. schönes Stück	[ʃønəʃʃtʏk]
5. hat sein	[hat z̥aɪn]	10. Bundesrepublik	[bʊnnəsʀepublik]

5. When schwa is lost in German *-en* endings, one of three syllabics occurs: [n̩], [m̩] or [ŋ̍]. Transcribe the following words phonetically, and then say which syllabic would occur in each case, and why.

   Example: Lippen   [lɪpm̩]   [m̩] occurs after bilabial plosive /p/

1. haben	6. fallen
2. müssen	7. Bomben
3. Schinken	8. lesen
4. gaben	9. Sachen
5. sagen	10. Sitten

6. Mark the syllable which contains the primary stress in the following words. If in doubt refer to a good dictionary.

> *Example*:   Paket → Pa'ket

1. Erzbischof	8. Grammatik
2. Eisenbahn	9. Maschine
3. Offizier	10. Fahrkarte
4. zwischendurch	11. Literatur
5. musikalisch	12. Politik
6. barfuß	13. Protest
7. gewährleisten	14. Demokratie

7. Imagine the following sentences are being spoken moderately quickly. Where would the stress be likely to fall in each case?

1. Das kannst du nicht machen.
2. Wir fahren übermorgen nach London.
3. Wie weit von Ihrem Haus ist die neue Schule?
4. Das kann ich mir überhaupt nicht vorstellen.
5. Heidelberg ist eine wunderschöne Stadt aber Wien gefällt mir besser.
6. Mein Bruder studiert Germanistik und Anglistik an der Universität Hamburg.
7. Ich reite und schwimme sehr gern.
8. Was halten Sie davon, wenn wir das erst morgen besprechen?
9. Ich habe schon gar keine Lust mehr, in Urlaub zu fahren.
10. Die deutsche Satzbetonung zu beschreiben ist nicht einfach.

6

The structure of German words

In Chapters 4 and 5, we saw why it is useful to study the sounds of German if we want to pronounce words clearly and be sure that we are actually saying what we mean. This, however, is only one of the things we need to learn when acquiring a new language. All students of foreign languages are aware that, even with the best pronunciation in the world, they will not get very far if they do not know a fairly large number of *words*.

But what exactly is a word? This may seem like a rather strange question, since most people would probably claim to know the answer. Consider the following four definitions:

1. Words are pronounced separately.
2. Words are written with a space either side.
3. Words are units of meaning.
4. Words are units of grammar.

These are all perfectly acceptable suggestions. Yet, from a linguistic point of view, each is problematical.

The first answer suggests that words are somehow related to sounds, since their pronunciation occurs separately. But think of what it is like listening to a language you do not understand. Can you really tell where one word ends and another begins? Moreover, in Chapter 5 on connected speech, we saw how the pronunciation of the same word may actually change due to the sounds of the words which precede or follow it. In conclusion, pronunciation would not appear to be a very reliable guide to the concept of word.

The second definition proposes that words are written separately, hence there is a link with orthography. In German and English, of course, it is generally true that words are written with a space either side, although there are languages where this is not the case, e.g. Sanskrit. But even in English there are examples which are not so clear-cut. Why, for example, is 'tea bag' written as two words, whereas 'teacup' is only one? And what about the use of hyphens? Which of the following is correct: 'washing machine' or 'washing-machine'? Moreover, why does German have only *one* word for the same object, e.g. *Waschmaschine*? We are beginning to see that writing conventions are not particularly helpful when trying to define the concept of word.

A similar problem occurs with the idea that words have a particular meaning of their own. By comparing German and English, for example, we can see that these two languages have very different ideas about the *amount* of meaning which can be contained in a single word. Hence, in German, the following is possible:

Donaudampfschifffahrtsgesellschaftskapitänskajütenschlüssel

whereas the English equivalent would be something like:

The key to the cabin of the captain of the Danube steam navigation company

On the other hand, this could be seen as just another difference in orthographic conventions, whereby German allows a single written word to contain 'more' meaning than English.

Finally, there are difficulties with the suggestion that there is a relationship between individual words and grammar. Take, for example, the verb forms *hat* and *ist*. While it is true that the suffix *-t* conveys the sense of *er* or *sie*, to what extent does it do this alone? Is it not true to say that the grammatical meaning of these verbs only really becomes clear when they occur *together* with the necessary personal pronouns, e.g. *sie hat* or *er ist*?

All in all, we can see how there are serious problems trying to find suitable criteria with which to define the concept of 'word'. It is with these difficulties in mind that linguists have found it better to put aside some of the more traditional explanations, and adopt a rather different approach. In order to do this, they have divided the study of words into two main areas. Thus, **semantics**, which we shall explore in Chapter 8, is specifically concerned with word meaning, whereas **morphology** deals with the form of words, that is to say, their structure and grammar.

6.1   Describing and analysing words

Grammar is a familiar term to most students of foreign languages. Grammar books describe the structure and the rules of the language we are trying to learn. In linguistics, however, it is customary to differentiate between two particular types of grammar:

the grammar of words   = morphology
the grammar of sentences = syntax

In reality, of course, it is not always possible to divide the study of word and sentence grammar as neatly as these labels imply. But for the purposes of this book, it will be nonetheless useful to adhere to such a distinction. Thus, in Chapter 7, we shall look at syntax, whereas in this chapter we shall be concentrating on morphology, that is, the description and analysis of individual words.

6.1.1   Minimal units of meaning: morphemes

We can see why, from a linguistic point of view, the concept of 'word' is rather vague. This is why, in morphology, it is customary to break words down into smaller, more manageable units. Hence, *Möglichkeiten* can be divided up as follows: *Mög+lich+keit+en*. From this example, we can see that there are different components within the word which can then be analysed:

Mög-	carries meaning in the sense of 'possible'
-lich	turns the word into the adjective *möglich*
-keit	converts the adjective into the noun *Möglichkeit*
-en	changes the noun from the singular to the plural *Möglichkeiten*

These individual components are known in linguistics as **morphemes**. Morphemes can be thought of as the 'building blocks' from which words are made. In addition, morphemes constitute minimal units of meaning in the same way that *phonemes* are the smallest meaningful units of sound (see 4.4).

Morphemes should not, however, be confused with syllables, even if the two concepts do sometimes coincide (see 5.1). For example, the word *Mög+lich+keit+en* contains four syllables as well as four morphemes, whereas *mach+t* is made up of one syllable but two morphemes. By contrast, *aber* has two syllables but only one morpheme.

Now that we have found a different way of looking at the structure of words, let us take another example. Here are five words divided into their respective morphemes:

> *Spiel*
> *ge+spiel+t*
> *Spiel+er*
> *spiel+t*
> *spiel+en*

There are four things which can be said about the way in which words such as these have been constructed. (Some of this will already be familiar from the discussion of stress patterns in 5.3.1, where we also saw how it was necessary to break words down into smaller units.)

LEXICAL MORPHEMES

First, all five of the above words contain the **root** morpheme *Spiel*. This is the part of the word which carries meaning in the lexical sense, e.g. 'play'. For this reason, roots are also sometimes known as **lexical morphemes**.

GRAMMATICAL MORPHEMES

The last four words in the above list each contain an affix, for example, *ge-*, *-t*, *-er*, or *-en*. Affixes are those parts of words which carry meaning in the grammatical sense, e.g. past tense, infinitive etc. For this reason, they are also known as **grammatical morphemes**.

Affixes can be further divided into prefixes (which occur before the root) such as *ge-*, and suffixes (which occur after the root) such as *-t*, *-er*, and *-en*.

Sometimes, a single word may contain two affixes, for example, *ge-* and *-t* as in *gespielt*. This kind of affix is known as a **circumfix** because it goes 'around the root'. However, strictly speaking, a circumfix is only *one* morpheme. This is because the grammatical meaning which is being indicated – in this case, past tense – is simply the same information divided into two parts. In morphology, a circumfix may also be referred to as a **discontinuous morpheme** or **discontinuous affix**.

It is also important to note that just because the first of the five words, *Spiel*, contains no affix does not mean that it has 'no grammar'. Sometimes, grammatical meaning – in this case, 'noun, singular' – is conveyed through the *absence* of an affix. This is what is known as a **zero affix**.

FREE AND BOUND MORPHEMES

The morphemes contained in the five words in the above list not only look different, they also behave differently. Some, such as *Spiel*, can stand alone. These are therefore referred to as **free morphemes**. Others, such as *ge-*, *-t*, *-er*, and *-en* cannot stand alone. These are known as **bound morphemes**.

Affixes are always bound, since they must occur together with a root. However, it is not possible to say that all roots are free. *Spiel* is a free morpheme, but the root *mög-* (in *Möglichkeiten*) is bound.

LEXEMES AND WORD FORMS

Finally, having broken down *Spiel, gespielt, Spieler, spielt,* and *spielen* into separate morphemes, let us now consider them again as whole words. What would happen if you were to look up each of these words in a dictionary? Which ones would you find?

The answer is that the dictionary would list those items which contain lexical meaning and can therefore stand on their own, e.g. *Spiel, Spieler,* and *spielen*. These types of words are known as **lexemes**. By contrast, you would not normally find those items which cannot meaningfully stand alone, e.g. *gespielt* and *spielt*. This is because these are simply grammatical variants of the original lexemes. Such grammatical variants are known as **word forms**.

In conclusion, it is worth remembering for the future that, if you cannot find a particular item in a dictionary, it is possible that you are looking for a word form rather than a lexeme.

6.1.2   Word classes

So far, it has been suggested that linguists prefer to think in terms of morphemes rather than words. However, in the discussion of word forms and lexemes above, we began to see how it is still sometimes necessary to talk about 'words'. One reason for this is that you cannot look up morphemes in a dictionary!

Another reason why it is important not to forget about words entirely is because most grammar books still use this concept in order to describe the rules and regulations of languages. They tend to divide words into different **word classes**, e.g. nouns, verbs, adjectives, etc. Word classes are groups of words which behave in the same way grammatically.

In order to be certain that you understand the terminology which is generally used in discussions of grammar and morphology, here is a brief outline of the main types of word class.

NOUNS

Nouns are words which are used to name people (*Mann, Frau, Kind*), objects (*Tisch, Schule, Haus*) or concepts (*Hass, Idee, Wetter*). In grammatical descriptions, it is customary to distinguish between **animate** (living) and **inanimate** (non-living) nouns.

All German nouns – whether animate or inanimate – are classified in terms of **gender**. There are three categories of gender, masculine, feminine, or neuter, hence: *der Mann, der Tisch, der Hass, die Frau, die Schule, die Idee, das Kind, das Haus, das Wetter*. English, by comparison, has a system of **biological**, but not **grammatical gender**. In other words, it tends to think of only animate nouns as male or female (he/she), while describing most inanimate nouns such as 'table' and 'weather' as neuter (it).

Nouns can be further classified in terms of **countability**. For example, **countable nouns** include *Mann* (*zwei Männer*) and *Idee* (*viele Ideen*). **Non-countable nouns** are *Hass* and *Wetter*. Note that, in some cases, countability varies between languages. Thus, 'information' is non-countable in English (*informations → pieces of information), but countable in German (*Informationen*). Conversely, 'sport' is countable in English (sports), but non-countable in German (*Sporte → Sportarten).

DETERMINERS

Determiners are those words which precede the noun in order to give more precise information about number or status. In other words, they describe or *determine* the noun.

The most common type of determiners are **articles**, e.g. *der, die, das, ein, eine*. These can be sub-divided into the **definite article** (*der, die, das*) and the **indefinite article** (*ein, eine*). Articles are referred to in this way because they tell us how specific or definite the status of a noun is. For example, if I say: 'I have <u>a</u> book' or *ich habe <u>ein</u> Buch*, then I am referring to an *indefinite* object – the book could be one of several. If, however, I say: 'I have <u>the</u> book' or *ich habe <u>das</u> Buch*, then this is very *definite*. Indeed, I can only be talking about one particular book – perhaps, for example, the one you lent me yesterday.

Other types of determiner include:

- **demonstratives**, e.g *dieser* and *jener*, which are used to distinguish one noun from another, i.e. 'this one' as opposed to 'that one'.
- **possessives**, e.g. *mein, dein, sein, ihr, unser, euer, ihr, Ihr*, which describe *possession*, i.e. 'my book', 'your book', etc.
- **interrogatives**, e.g. *welcher...?, was für...?,* which are used in questions, i.e. 'which book?' or 'what sort of book?'
- **quantifiers**, e.g. *alle, einige, manche, viele,* which say something about the *quantity* of nouns being referred to, i.e. 'all books', 'a few books', 'some books', 'many books'.

PRONOUNS

Pronouns are words which can stand *in place of* nouns. The most common type are **personal pronouns**, e.g. *ich, du, er, sie, es, wir, ihr, sie, Sie*. Thus, in the following sentences, *der Mann* and *er* are grammatical equivalents:

der Mann schläft   (determiner + noun)
        er schläft   (pronoun)

Relative pronouns such as *der, die, das* are used to introduce relative clauses, for example:

der Mann,   *der* schläft
die Frau,   *die* schläft
das Kind,   *das* schläft

From this example, we can also see that it is possible for the same word to belong to more than one word class. Thus, in the above sentences, *der, die* and *das* are functioning as relative pronouns, whereas earlier we saw how they may also act as definite articles.

ADJECTIVES

Adjectives attribute certain qualities to nouns, such as size, age, colour, *das große Buch, das neue Buch,* or *das rote Buch.*

Comparative adjectives are used to *compare* the quality of one noun with another, e.g. *mein Buch ist größer (als dein Buch)* or *dein Buch ist älter (als mein Buch).* Note how English and German usually form comparative adjectives by adding the same suffix (*-er*), e.g. 'big/bigger' and *groß/größer.* This is because the two languages are historically so closely related.

Superlatives are those adjectives which describe the highest degree of quality, for example, *dieses Buch ist am ältesten* or 'this book is the oldest'. Note, once again, how both English and German use the same suffix, *-est,* in order to express the superlative.

VERBS

Verbs are those words which are used to express actions, events, or states of mind, e.g. *laufen, geschehen, denken* ('run', 'happen', 'think').

In English and German, most verbs require a **subject**. This is normally the person who is performing the action in question, e.g. *ich schlafe* or 'I sleep'. Many verbs also require a **direct object**, e.g. *ich kaufe ein Buch* or 'I buy a book'.

In grammar books and dictionaries, it is customary to distinguish between those verbs which occur *with* a direct object and those which occur *without.* Thus, *kaufen* or 'buy' are said to be **transitive verbs** because they must normally be accompanied by a direct object, e.g. *ich kaufe ein Buch* or 'I buy a book' (in other words, you must buy *something*). But *schlafen* and 'sleep' are said to be **intransitive verbs,** since they stand alone with their subject e.g. *ich schlafe* or 'I sleep'. When you look up a verb in the dictionary, check whether it is transitive or intransitive, so that you know how to use it correctly. This is indicated by the abbreviations *vt* and *vi,* respectively.

Sometimes, transitive verbs such as *kaufen* (buy) can be also be used in an intransitive way. Hence, it is possible to say *ich kaufe ein Buch* (I am buying a book) or *ich kaufe* (I am buying). However, such verbs are still really transitive, since even if you say 'I am buying' (i.e. on the stock market), the implication is that you are buying *something* (e.g. shares).

Verbs can also be divided into two other categories. **Finite verb** forms are those which tell us something about the subject, e.g. *(ich) schlafe* or *(er) liest.* These compare to **infinitive** (or non-finite) forms such as *schlafen* or *lesen,* which do not tell us who is doing the sleeping or reading. Infinitive verbs are very general in terms of their reference; the number of possible subjects is said to be *infinite.*

ADVERBS

Adverbs are those words which accompany and describe *verbs*, e.g., *er kam schnell* or 'he came quickly'. Adverbs therefore have the same function with respect to verbs that adjectives have *vis-à-vis* nouns.

Another function of adverbs is to qualify adjectives, for example, *sie ist sehr reich* or 'she is very rich'.

Finally, adverbs do not only refer to individual verbs and nouns. In some cases, they apply to whole sentences. For example:

Heute fahre ich nach Hause.	Today I'm going home.
Sie hat nie Zeit.	She never has time.

These kinds of adverbs are known as **sentence adverbs**.

PREPOSITIONS

Prepositions are words which accompany nouns, pronouns, and other word classes in order to express a relationship of *position*. When learning prepositions in German, it is extremely important to know which cases they are used with. The following take the accusative case:

bis, durch, für, gegen, ohne, um

whereas these occur with the dative:

aus, außer, bei, gegenüber, mit, nach, seit, von, zu

The following take either the accusative or the dative:

an, auf, entlang, hinter, in, neben, über, unter, vor, zwischen

And finally, these four prepositions take the genitive case, although it is not uncommon to hear them used with the dative in informal, spoken German:

(an)statt, trotz, während, wegen

CONJUNCTIONS

Conjunctions are words such as *und* (and), *aber* (but), *oder* (or), *weil* (because), *wenn* (if/when) and *dass* (that). Sometimes, conjunctions are used to connect or join two words:

du und ich	you and I	(i.e. two pronouns)
klein aber teuer	small but expensive	(i.e. two adjectives)
fahren oder laufen	drive or walk	(i.e. two verbs).

Alternatively, they may be used to connect different parts of a sentence:

> *Susanne fuhr am Montag <u>und</u> Peter fuhr am Dienstag.*
> Susanne left on Monday *and* Peter left on Tuesday.
>
> *Susanne fuhr am Montag, <u>weil</u> sie am Dienstag arbeiten musste.*
> Susanne left on Monday *because* she had to work on Tuesday.

MODAL PARTICLES

Modal particles are a group of words such as *doch, aber, ja, nur, mal, eigentlich, wohl, schon*, etc. They are particularly common in spoken German, and are often used to add extra emphasis or convey the speaker's attitude to what is being said. For example, the tone of the statement *Er ist gestern gekommen* can be modified subtly with the help of modal particles, as follows:

Statement	Implication
Er ist <u>wohl</u> gestern gekommen.	I assume he came yesterday, but you might tell me otherwise.
Er ist <u>ja</u> gestern gekommen.	I know for sure that he came yesterday (for example, because something then happened).
Er ist <u>doch</u> gestern gekommen.	I am contradicting you. You claimed that he didn't come yesterday, but I know that he did.

INTERJECTIONS

Finally, **interjections** are words or exclamations which convey emotional meaning such as 'Gosh!', 'Yuk!' or 'Agh!' in English, and *Pfui!* or *Ach!* in German. These types of words are interesting since they do not form grammatical relationships with other words, that is to say, they do not have to fit in grammatically with the rest of a sentence.

6.2   Words and grammar

Earlier in this chapter, a distinction was made between lexemes and word forms. Lexemes are those items which contain lexical meaning and are therefore listed in dictionaries, e.g. *Spiel, Spieler*, and *spielen*. These compare to word forms, which express grammatical rather than lexical meaning, and do not normally have their own dictionary entry, e.g. *spielt* and *gespielt*. In this section, we shall be concentrating on the structure of word forms.

To return to the example of the root morpheme *spiel-*. As we have already seen, this root might change to become the word forms *spielt* or *gespielt*. Another way of saying this is that the root has been inflected – it has been moulded into a new shape with the help of affixes. The branch of morphology concerned with the way in which the same roots are inflected to produce new word forms is known as **inflectional morphology**.

In this section, we shall look at two types of inflectional morphology central to the study of German. In 6.2.1, we analyse the ways in which verbs are inflected to mark grammatical information. This process is known as **conjugation**. Then, in 6.2.2, we shall look at the ways in which nouns, pronouns, determiners, and adjectives are similarly inflected. This is known as **declension**.

6.2.1   Verb conjugation

One of the first things we have to learn when acquiring a foreign language is how to conjugate verbs in the correct manner. So, for example, we must know how to inflect an infinitive such as *lieben* in order to produce the following finite forms:

ich liebe	*wir lieben*
du liebst	*ihr liebt*
er/sie/es liebt	*sie/Sie lieben*

Every time we conjugate a verb in this way, German requires that five different grammatical categories be expressed. These are: person, number, tense, mood, and voice.

PERSON

Persson tells us *who* is the subject of the verb, whereby there are three possibilities. The 1st person can be *ich* or *wir*, the 2nd person is *du, ihr* or *Sie*, and the 3rd person is *er/sie/es* or *sie*.

NUMBER

Number tells us *how many* subjects are being referred to. There are only two possibilities in German and English: **singular** or **plural**.

Together, person and number produce the following classifications, which are often used in grammar books:

	singular	plural
1st PERSON	*ich liebe*	*wir lieben*
2nd PERSON	*du liebst*	*ihr liebt*
3rd PERSON	*er/sie/es liebt*	*sie lieben*

German differs from English in that it distinguishes between singular and plural forms of the 2nd person, e.g. *du* and *ihr*. In addition, German marks formality and informality through the use of *Sie* and *du/ihr*, respectively. However, the polite form *Sie* does not mark number, i.e. the singular and plural forms are the same. In terms of its endings, it then follows the 3rd person plural.

TENSE

Tense is a familiar term to most language learners, and is used to express categories of time such as past (*ich liebte*), present (*ich liebe*), and future (*ich werde lieben*).

MOOD

Mood is used to describe attitudes of fact, desire, possibility, etc. and can be divided into two categories. The **indicative** conveys certainty or objectivity (e.g. *er liebt, er hat geliebt*) whereas the **subjunctive** expresses doubt or tentativeness (e.g. *er liebe, er hätte geliebt*).

VOICE

Voice describes the relationship between the verb and its subject, which can be either **active** or **passive**. For example, in the active form *ich liebe*, it is *I* who is doing the loving. In the passive form, *ich werde geliebt*, someone else is doing the loving, and it is *I* who is being loved.

Tables 6.1 and 6.2 summarise the various forms of German verbs with respect to tense, mood, and voice.

Table 6.1 Active verb forms

Tense	Indicative mood	Subjunctive mood
Present	*er liebt*	*er liebe*
Imperfect	*er liebte*	*er liebte*
Perfect	*er hat geliebt*	*er habe geliebt*
Pluperfect	*er hatte geliebt*	*er hätte geliebt*
Future	*er wird lieben*	*er werde lieben*
Future perfect	*er wird geliebt haben*	*er werde geliebt haben*
Present conditional	—	*er würde lieben*
Past conditional	—	*er würde geliebt haben*

Table 6.2 Passive verb forms

Tense	Indicative mood	Subjunctive mood
Present	*er wird geliebt*	*er werde geliebt*
Imperfect	*er wurde geliebt*	*er würde geliebt*
Perfect	*er ist geliebt worden*	*er sei geliebt worden*
Pluperfect	*er war geliebt worden*	*er wäre geliebt worden*
Future	*er wird geliebt werden*	*er werde geliebt werden*
Future perfect	*er wird geliebt worden sein*	*er werde geliebt worden sein*
Present conditional	—	*er würde geliebt werden*
Past conditional	—	*er würde geliebt worden sein*

SAME AFFIXES, DIFFERENT INFORMATION

The five grammatical categories which must be reflected by verbs are not contained in just any part of the verb. It is the root or verb stem *lieb-* which conveys the *lexical* information (i.e. 'love'). On the other hand, it is the affix which normally contains the *grammatical* information relating to person, number, tense, mood, and voice. For example:

lieb+E	*lieb+EN*	(root + suffix)
lieb+ST	*lieb+T*	
lieb+T	*lieb+EN*	

An important exception to this rule are those verbs where tenses are formed by ablaut (see 2.1.2). In these forms, tense is marked *within* the stem, e.g. *ich sang, ich blieb, ich ging*, etc.

But having looked at these examples, a problem arises: how can the same affixes mark different grammatical categories? For example, *-e* can mark both the 1st person form of the present indicative, *ich liebe,* and the 3rd person form of the present subjunctive, *er liebe.* Similarly, *-en* might indicate the infinitive form, *lieben,* the 1st person plural, *wir lieben,* or the 3rd person plural, *sie lieben.* To put the question another way: if the same affix is carrying different grammatical information, how is it possible for German verbs to function without causing confusion?

The answer to this problem lies partly in the fact that grammatical meaning is not expressed by verbal affixes alone. For example, person and number in German verbs only really make sense in conjunction with the personal pronouns, *ich, du, er/sie/es,* etc. Similarly, tense, mood, and voice often rely on additional words within a sentence in order to gain their overall meaning. In this respect, we can see how conjugation is not simply a question of morphology – it also involves sentence structure or syntax.

A further way in which morphology and syntax are closely linked is where the marking of tense, mood, and voice is concerned. This is because these categories sometimes involve the use of more than one verb. Consider the following forms:

Imperfect	Perfect
ich liebte	*ich habe geliebt*
du liebtest	*du hast geliebt*
er/sie liebte	*er/sie hat geliebt*
wir liebten	*wir haben geliebt*
ihr liebtet	*ihr habt geliebt*
sie/Sie liebten	*sie/Sie haben geliebt*

From this example, we can see that while the imperfect form consists of one verb only, the perfect requires two verbs. Another way of saying this is that the imperfect contains a **main verb** (*lieben*) whereas the perfect has an **auxiliary verb** (*haben*) plus a main verb (*lieben*). Any tense which is formed with one verb only is referred to as **simple tense**. This is why the imperfect tense is sometimes referred to as the 'past simple'. This compares to a tense formed with the help of one or more auxiliary verbs which is known as a **compound tense**.

But if more than one verb is being used in a sentence, how do you know where to mark such categories as person and number? Here, there are two points worth noting. First of all, a German clause may contain no more than three auxiliary verbs. For example:

structure	German	English
1. main verb	*er liebt*	he loves
2. one auxiliary + main verb	*er wird geliebt*	he is loved
3. two auxiliaries + main verb	*er ist geliebt worden*	he has been loved
4. three auxiliaries + main verb	*er wird geliebt worden sein*	he will have been loved

Second, the endings for person and number are always marked *at the first possible opportunity* and *once only*. Thus, in example 1, the 3rd person singular ending is contained in the only verb which occurs: *lieben*. However, in sentences 2, 3, and 4, these endings are marked by the *first* auxiliary verb which occurs. In 2 and 4, this verb is *werden* (→ *wird*), whereas in sentence 3, it is *sein* (→ *ist*).

In section 6.2.2, we shall see how this principle of marking grammatical information at the first possible opportunity and once only also applies to declension.

SAME INFORMATION, DIFFERENT AFFIXES

In the previous section, we looked at the way in which the same affixes are sometimes used to express different grammatical information. Here we will see how the reverse is also true, i.e. the same grammatical information is sometimes conveyed by different affixes.

When asked which affix marks the 2nd person singular verb form, *du*, most learners of German would probably reply *-st* (e.g. *du machst, du gehst*, etc.). But now think about the *du*-forms of the following verbs. Are they really all the same?

reiten	(to ride)	*reizen*	(to irritate)
sagen	(to say)	*bleiben*	(to stay)
atmen	(to breathe)	*segnen*	(to bless)
baden	(to bathe)	*widmen*	(to dedicate)
wissen	(to know)	*(sich) wappnen*	(to prepare oneself)

The answer to this question is clearly no. In fact, the 2nd person singular forms vary as follows:

du reit+est	*du reiz+t*
du sag+st	*du bleib+st*
du atm+est	*du segn+est*
du bad+est	*du widm+est*
du weiß+t	*du wappn+est (dich)*

What we can see therefore is that the same grammatical information – 2nd person singular – is being expressed by three different suffixes: *-est, -t,* and *-st*. Can you now identify a rule which tells you which affix is used in which situation? (Tip: you may need to refer back to Chapter 4 on phonology.)

The answer is to be found in the type of sound which precedes the suffix /st/ in each case. The rule can be summarised as follows:

1. /ɛ/ must be added to /st/ when the verb stem ends in an alveolar plosive such as /d/ or /t/, e.g. *du bad+est* and *du reit+est.*
   The same rule applies after the double plosive consonants /tm/, /dm/, /gn/ and /pn/, e.g. *du atm+est, du wid+mest, du segn+est* and *du wappn+est.* In such cases, an additional /ɛ/ is required because it phonetically difficult to pronounce three plosives in succession, e.g. /dst/ or /tst/, and impossible to pronounce four, e.g. /tmst/, /dmst/, /gnst/ or /pnst/.
2. /s/ must be dropped from /st/ if the verb stem already ends in the alveolar plosive /s/, e.g. *du weiß+t* and *du reiz+t.*
   It is important not to be misled by spelling here – remember that 'ß' and 'z' represent the sounds /s/ and /ts/, respectively, both of which end in /s/.
3. Finally, in all other cases, the affix /st/ can be used, e.g. *du bleib+st* and *du sag+st.*

In Chapter 4, we saw how the pronunciation of a phoneme such as /r/ can sometimes vary *without* actually changing its meaning. These different forms of /r/ were then referred to as allophones. Allophones are written in square brackets, as opposed to phonemes, which are written between slanted brackets (*see* 4.4.2 and Table 6.3).

Table 6.3 Allophones of the phoneme /r/

Allophone	Lexeme	Phonetic transcription
[R] or [r]	rot	[ʀot] or [rot]
[ʁ]	hart	[haʁt]
[ɐ]	Wasser	[vasɐ]

In morphology, a similar principle applies. Thus, it is possible for the pronunciation of a morpheme – in this case /st/ – to vary *without* changing its meaning. The three endings [ɛst], [t], and [st] are therefore examples of what are known in linguistics as **allomorphs** (*see* Table 6.4).

Table 6.4 Allomorphs of the morpheme /st/

Allomorph	Word form	Phonetic transcription
[ɛst]	badest, atmest,	[bɑdɛst],[ɑtmɛst]
	reitest, segnest	[ʀaɪtɛst],[zegnɛst]
	widmest, wappnest	[vɪdmɛst], [vapnɛst]
[t]	weißt, reizt	[vaɪst], [ʀaɪt̯st]
[st]	bleibst, sagst	[blaɪpst], [zɑkst]

A more technical way of saying this is that the affixes [ɛst], [t], and [st] are *phonologically determined allomorphs of the morpheme* /st/. In other words, the pronunciation of /st/ is determined – or influenced – by the sound which precedes it in each case. But despite their differing pronunciation, the three allomorphs are still carrying the same grammatical meaning – they are all used to mark the 2nd person singular form of finite verbs.

6.2.2   Declension

We have already seen how verbs are inflected in order to express five different grammatical categories: person, number, tense, mood, and voice. This is known as conjugation. A similar process also applies to nouns, pronouns, determiners, and adjectives. The way in which these types of words are inflected is referred to as *declension*.

Every time a noun occurs in German *three* grammatical categories must be indicated:

1. **Number** tells us how many nouns there are, whereby there are only two possibilities: singular (*das Kind*) and plural (*die Kinder*).
2. **Gender** indicates whether the noun is masculine (*der Mann*), feminine (*die Frau*), or neuter (*das Kind*). In other words, there are three possibilities.
3. **Case** tells us about the relationship between the noun and any other nouns or verbs which occur in the same sentence. Here there are four possibilities:
   (a) If the noun is performing the action associated with the verb, then it occurs in the **nominative case**, e.g. *der Mann* *schreibt*. Another way of saying this is that the noun *der Mann* is the subject of the verb *schreibt*. Hence, the nominative case is sometimes referred to as the **subject case**.
   (b) If the noun is having the action performed upon it, then it occurs in the **accusative case**, e.g. *der Mann schreibt einen Brief*. In this sentence, *der Mann* is the subject of the verb *schreibt*, whereas *einen Brief* is the object which is being written. For this reason, the accusative case is sometimes known as the (**direct**) **object case**.

(c) If the noun is only indirectly related to the verb, then it occurs in the **dative case**, e.g. *der Mann schreibt der Frau einen Brief*. In this sentence, *der Frau* is also the object of the verb *schreibt*, but she is a different kind of object to *einen Brief*. Unlike the letter she is not 'being written'. Instead, she is 'being written *to*'. Another way of saying this is that *der Frau* is the indirect object of the verb. Hence, the dative case is also sometimes referred to as the **indirect object case**.

(d) Finally, the **genitive case** describes a relationship between two nouns, e.g. *der Brief des Mannes*. In this sentence, the first noun *der Brief* belongs to the second noun *des Mannes*. Because a relationship of ownership is being expressed, the genitive case is sometimes known as the **possessive case**.

For the English-speaking learner of German, having to memorise the correct forms for gender and case can seem very perplexing. One of the reasons for this is that English does not appear to mark these categories. Some people therefore think that German has 'more grammar' than English. But while English nouns are not differentiated according to grammatical gender, it is not true to say that English does not mark case – it just does so less often and in a different way to German. So, for example, the dative case in English can be indicated by the preposition 'to':

the man writes a letter to the woman

English has marked the dative case by adding another word ('to') to the determiner ('the') and noun ('woman'). German does not need to add a new word – it simply inflects one which already exists. Hence, the determiner, *die*, in *die Frau* is inflected to *der* in order to create the dative form:

der Mann schreibt der Frau einen Brief

However, even English has some forms which are inflected to mark grammatical information, e.g. the genitive case as in: *the man's letter*. Note how the possessive is also indicated by the use of /s/ in German, e.g. *der Brief des Mannes*. Again, this is because the two languages are so closely related in historical terms.

AGREEMENT

It is not only nouns and pronouns which must convey the appropriate grammatical categories every time they are used. Any determiner or adjective accompanying the noun must also indicate its relationship to that noun, e.g. *der gute Mann* or *ein guter Mann*. Another way of saying this is that the determiner and adjective must 'agree with' the noun. This is what is known in linguistics as **agreement** or **concord**.

In German, there are two groups of adjectival suffixes, which are classified as *strong* and *weak endings*. But before we turn to adjectives, let us look at the different forms of one kind of determiner, the definite article. Study the forms contained in Table 6.5.

Table 6.5 Declension of definite articles in German

	Masculine	Feminine	Neuter	Plural
nominative	der	die	das	die
accusative	den	die	das	die
dative	dem	der	dem	den
genitive	des	der	des	der

Now look at the group of adjectival endings in Table 6.6, known as strong endings.

Table 6.6 Strong adjectival endings

	Masculine	Feminine	Neuter	Plural
nominative	gut-er	gut-e	gut-es	gut-e
accusative	gut-en	gut-e	gut-es	gut-e
dative	gut-em	gut-er	gut-em	gut-en
genitive	gut-en	gut-er	gut-en	gut-er

Can you see any similarity between these strong adjectival endings and the forms of the definite article? If you look closely, it should become clear that many of the affixes which follow /d/ in the definite article are virtually identical to the strong adjectival endings, for example:

$$d\text{-}er \rightarrow gut\text{-}er \qquad d\text{-}em \rightarrow gut\text{-}em$$
$$d\text{-}en \rightarrow gut\text{-}en \qquad d\text{-}as \rightarrow gut\text{-}es$$

To put this in morphological terms: the endings on the definite article and the strong endings on adjectives are, in fact, the *same morpheme*. In other words, they are carrying the same grammatical information. Now look at the so-called weak adjectival endings in Table 6.7. These are much less differentiated.

Table 6.7 Weak adjectival endings

	Masculine	Feminine	Neuter	Plural
nominative	gut-e	gut-e	gut-e	gut-en
accusative	gut-en	gut-e	gut-e	gut-en
dative	gut-en	gut-en	gut-en	gut-en
genitive	gut-en	gut-en	gut-en	gut-en

It is at this point that we can make an interesting comparison between the declension of determiners and adjectives, on the one hand, and verb conjugation, on the other. In the previous section, we saw how the verb endings for person and number must always be placed *once only* and *at the first possible opportunity*. For example:

er <u>liebt</u>   er <u>ist</u> geliebt worden

er <u>wird</u> geliebt   er <u>wird</u> geliebt worden sein

A similar principle also applies to determiners and adjectives. Thus, the grammatical information conveying number, gender, and case may be carried by *either* the determiner *or* the strong endings on adjectives. But the golden rule is that this information cannot be carried by both. In other words, it must occur *once only* and *at the first possible opportunity*.

Consider the following:

gut-er Mann   gut-e Frau   gut-es Kind   gut-e Leute

These examples contain no determiner. The adjective is therefore the only place where the necessary grammatical information can occur. In other words, number, gender, and case must be conveyed through strong endings placed on the adjective itself, e.g. *gut-<u>er</u>, gut-<u>e</u>, gut-<u>es</u>*, and *gut-<u>e</u>*. The same applies to the following examples where a determiner occurs in the form of the indefinite article *ein*:

ein gut-er Mann   eine gut-e Frau   ein gut-es Kind   gut-e Leute

Here, the indefinite article *ein/e* is not providing the necessary grammatical information (even though it could technically). Thus, number, gender, and case must be indicated at the *next* possible opportunity, i.e. through strong endings placed on the adjective. (Where the plural is concerned, there is no article, so the same principle applies as in the previous examples.)

However, the following examples are completely different:

der gut-e Mann   die gut-e Frau   das gut-e Kind   die gut-en Leute

This time, the determiner – the definite article – already contains the strong endings needed to mark number, gender, and case. But recall how this information may occur once only. As a result, the adjective which follows the article is *not* allowed to contain a strong ending – it must have a weak ending: *-e* or *-en*.

There are, of course, one or two problems with this analysis. It would be perfectly reasonable to ask why the strong and weak forms of the masculine adjectival endings are the same for the nominative and accusative cases, e.g. *-en*. The answer lies, in fact, in the complex history of the language, although we need not go into this in more detail here. Similarly, the masculine and neuter strong adjectival endings in the genitive case, e.g. *-en*, are unlike their respective determiner, *des*. Again, the reason for this is historical – the determiner *des* is, in fact, derived from the genitive marker /s/ rather than from the suffix *-en*.

Another apparent exception to the rule of marking grammatical information once only is where adjectives occur in so-called **apposition**, i.e. side-by-side. So, more than one strong ending *is* permitted in a phrase such as *ein guter, billiger Wein*. This is because the two adjectives belong to the same word class. As we saw in section 6.1.2, words which belong to the same class behave in the same way grammatically.

LEARNING PATTERNS OF DECLENSION

Can the English-speaking learner of German ever learn all the different patterns of declension? Is it ever possible to get all the endings right? The answer is yes, but the method is perhaps unattractive: at first, there is probably no alternative to patiently memorising the various forms by heart. However, by studying declension from the perspective of morphology, it should be clear that learning the correct endings is an important and worthwhile task. This is because declension is extremely meaningful in German.

But there is another point where some extra knowledge about language can be helpful: what is the best source of information when trying to learn patterns of declension? Memorising declension tables is a start, but it will not generally work in isolation. This is because you also have to know how to apply declension when actually speaking and writing German. To learn how to do this, you need as much exposure to 'real' language as possible.

Many students have their most intensive period of contact with 'real' German on a so-called 'year abroad' or a six-month period of their degree where they study or work in a German-speaking country. This is an excellent opportunity to improve one's command of the language in a way which cannot normally be achieved in the home country. Nevertheless, Chapter 10 shows how there are many kinds of variation in the German language. Not only do written and spoken styles differ, but spoken German has a number of regional and national dialects. This has important consequences for foreign students.

In Chapter 5 on connected speech, we saw how, in colloquial German, speakers often assimilate sounds. This may mean that it is no longer possible to differentiate clearly between, say, an accusative and a dative ending. Thus, *den großen Ball* might be pronounced: [den gʀosm̩ bal]. Similarly, in some regional dialects, the suffix /n/ is frequently dropped altogether. Hence, *die großen Banken* might be pronounced: [di gʀosə baŋkə].

The fact that precise patterns of declension are lost in many spoken varieties of German has both advantages and disadvantages for the foreign learner. The main advantage is that it is often possible to achieve quite authentic-sounding German, while at the same time eliding endings or pronouncing them in a rather muffled way! The disadvantage is that this 'mumbling' has its limits even when speaking – in formal situations you will always be expected to articulate the correct endings clearly. Moreover, the 'mumbling' approach can never be extended to written German. Indeed, written language still has very strict norms for declension, which must be adhered to. Therefore, it is important to realise that the only way to learn patterns of declension properly is through *reading* and not simply *speaking* German.

6.3   Creating new vocabulary

In section 6.2, we explored some of the ways in which affixes may be used to inflect roots, thereby creating new word forms. We now turn to the way in which new *lexemes* are produced in German, i.e. words which have their own lexical meaning, and are therefore listed in dictionaries. There are two main ways in which lexemes can be created. Let us return to the example of *Spiel*.

First of all, the affix *-er* might be added to the root lexeme *Spiel* in order to form the new lexeme *Spieler*. Another way of saying this is that *Spieler* has been *derived* from *Spiel*. The branch of morphology which deals with this kind of word formation is known as **derivational morphology**. This will be dealt with in section 6.3.1.

The second way in which new lexemes may be formed is when two roots are joined together. So, for example, the noun *Spiel* might be added to a second noun *Platz* in order to produce the new lexeme *Spielplatz*. This process is known as **compounding**.

6.3.1   Derivation

Before we consider some examples of derivational morphology, let us take another quick look at inflection. The following new word forms have been created from the root *spiel-*. What do they have in common?

spiel- → *gespielt, spielt, spielte*

You may have noticed that all of these *inflected forms* belong to the same word class. In other words, they are all different types of verb.

Now look at the following lexemes which have been derived from the root lexeme *Spiel*:

Spiel → *Spieler, spielerisch, verspielen*

Three new lexemes have been created here from the original noun *Spiel*: the first is also a noun (*Spieler*), whereas the second is an adjective (*spielerisch*), and the third is a verb (*verspielen*). We can therefore see how *derived forms* can belong either to the same or to a different word class as the original lexeme. This is typical of derivational morphology. Indeed, the fact that all different classes of lexemes can be created means that derivation is a much more inventive way of producing new words than inflection.

New lexemes are normally formed with the help of affixes. These affixes can be divided into three groups: those which change the word class, those which maintain it, and those which can do both; *see* Table 6.8, Table 6.9 and Table 6.10.

Table 6.8 Class-changing affixes

Affix	Example	Change	
-er	*fahren → Fahr+er*	verb	→ noun
-heit	*schön → Schön+heit*	adjective	→ noun

Table 6.9 Class-maintaining affixes

Affix	Example	Change	
-chen	*Tisch →Tischchen*	noun	→ noun
ver-	*lieben → verlieben*	verb	→ verb

Table 6.10 Class-maintaining or class-changing affixes

Affix	Example	Change	
-lich	*Sprache → sprachlich*	noun	→ adjective
-lich	*bewegen → beweglich*	verb	→ adjective
-lich	*reich → reichlich*	adjective	→ adjective

Once we look at lexemes in this way, we can see that the changes can be considered from two different points of view. On the one hand, we can say that *fahren, schön, Tisch, lieben, Sprache, bewegen* and *reich* are the **source lexemes**: they are the original forms from which the new lexemes are derived. On the other hand, *Fahrer, Schönheit, Tischchen, verlieben, sprachlich, beweglich* and *reichlich* are the **target lexemes**: they are the newly derived forms or the end products. (It is not always easy to identify the precise source lexeme, but the general principle is to take the shortest, most commonly used word.)

With this distinction in mind, we can now find new ways of describing patterns of word formation. Depending on whether the source lexeme was a noun, a verb, or an adjective, we can say that the target lexeme is **denominal, deverbal,** or **deadjectival,** respectively; *see* Table 6.11.

Table 6.11 Source lexemes

Source lexeme	Target lexeme	Process
Weib	→ *weiblich*	denominal
bewegen	→ *beweglich*	deverbal
neu	→ *neulich*	deadjectival

Looking at things from the opposite point of view, we can say that if the target lexeme is a noun, verb, or adjective, then the processes which have occurred are **nominalisation, verbalisation,** or **adjectivalisation,** respectively; *see* Table 6.12.

Table 6.12 Target lexemes

Source lexeme	Target lexeme	Process
drohen	→ *Drohung*	nominalisation
rein	→ *reinigen*	verbalisation
Frucht	→ *fruchtbar*	adjectivalisation

Furthermore, if there is a change of word class, we can combine the two processes as shown in Table 6.13.

Table 6.13 Word class changes

Source lexeme	Target lexeme	Process
Weib	→ *weiblich*	denominal adjectivalisation
bewegen	→ *beweglich*	deverbal adjectivalisation
drohen	→ *Drohung*	deverbal nominalisation
rein	→ *reinigen*	deadjectival verbalisation

Now that we have considered the types of changes which occur as a result of derivation, we can look more closely at some of the technical aspects of word formation. As we shall see, adding a new affix to an old root is only one way of creating a new lexeme. Altogether there are three main types of derivation:

EXPLICIT DERIVATION

This type of derivation occurs where new lexemes are formed with the *explicit* help of affixes:

root + suffix:	*fahr-* → *Fahr+t*
prefix + root:	*fahr-* → *Ge+fahr*
root + circumfix:	*fahr-* → *ge+fahr+en*

IMPLICIT DERIVATION

Implicit derivation does not involve the use of affixes, but concerns only the root lexeme. There are two ways in which this occurs. The first possibility is that a morpheme within the root is replaced by another. This is what is known as a **replacive process**. There are three types of replacive process: *ablaut*, *umlaut*, and *ablaut + umlaut*:

replacive processes	
ablaut:	*fahr-* → *fuhr*
umlaut:	*fahr-* → *fähr-* (e.g. *Fähre*)
ablaut+umlaut:	*fahr-* → *führ-* (e.g. *führen*)

The second type of implicit derivation is where no change is made to the root at all, or where the root lexeme is an infinitive verb which is turned into a noun. This is known as **zero derivation** or **conversion**. For example:

zero derivation/	*lauf-* → *der Lauf*
conversion:	*laufen* → *das Laufen*

EXPLICIT + IMPLICIT DERIVATION

Finally, this type of derivation involves both the addition of affixes *and* a replacive process:

prefix + ablaut:	*steh-* → *Verstand*
umlaut + suffix:	*Stadt* → *Städtchen*
circumfix + ablaut:	*Berg* → *Gebirge*

Now look at the following three groups of words. All are nouns which have been derived from other lexemes, i.e. they are the product of nominalisation. Can you see anything which they might have in common?

Group A	Group B	Group C
Lehr+er	*Lehrer+in*	*Mäd+chen*
Red+ner	*Bedeut+ung*	*Büch+lein*
Tisch+ler	*Fahr+t*	*Rät+sel*
Tepp+ich	*Sauber+keit*	*Mäd+erl*
Kön+ig	*Mann+schaft*	*Mües+li*
Früh+ling	*Explo+sion*	*Vier+tel*
Pal+ast	*Revolu+tion*	*Niv+eau*
Profess+or	*Gesund+heit*	*Dick+icht*
Sena+tor	*Biolog+ie*	*Etik+ett*
Tour+ismus	*Bäcker+ei*	*Dog+ma*
Zykl+us	*Vill+a*	*Vent+il*
Doktor+and	*Promen+ade*	*Nikot+in*
Komödi+ant	*Demont+age*	*Hear+ing*

Group A	Group B	Group C
Kapit+än	*Eleg+anz*	*Dat+um*
Funktion+är	*Resid+enz*	*Stud+ium*
Demokr+at	*Mus+ik*	*Dynam+it*
Athl+et	*Viol+ine*	*Essen*
Fris+eur	*Hepat+itis*	*Ge+red+e*
Phys+iker	*Neur+ose*	
Kompon+ist	*Skep+sis*	
Bio+loge	*Universi+tät*	
Astro+nom	*Manik+üre*	
Gang	*Nat+ur*	
Lauf		

What distinguishes these three groups of nouns is their gender: Group A are masculine, Group B are feminine, are Group C are neuter. We can see therefore that there is a clear link between different types of derivation and the gender of any noun which is produced. Here are some of the basic rules which might help you to predict the gender of nouns in future.

Nouns formed with the following suffixes are normally MASCULINE:

-er, -ner, -ler, -ich, -ig, -ling, -ast, -or, -tor, -ismus, -us, -and, -ant, -än, är, -at, -et, -eur, -iker, -ist, -oge, -nom.
Exceptions: *die Butter, das Fieber, das Labor.*

Nouns formed with these suffixes are usually FEMININE:

-in, -ung, -t, -keit, -schaft, -sion, -tion, -heit, -ie, -ei, -a , -ade, -age, -anz, -enz, -ik, -ine, -itis, -ose, -sis, -tät, -üre, -ur.
Exceptions: *das Sofa, der Papagei, das Genie, der Atlantik, das Abitur.*

Nouns formed with these suffixes are generally NEUTER:

-chen, -lein, -sel, -erl, -li, -tel, -eau, -icht, -ett, -ma, -il, -in, -ing, -um, ium, -it.
Exceptions: *der Profit, die Firma.*

But what about those nouns formed without the help of affixes? Here, some other rules apply:

- Lexemes formed by ablaut alone are normally MASCULINE, e.g. *der Gang (gehen), der Biss (beißen), der Stand (stehen), der Verstand (verstehen).*
  Exceptions: *das Maß (messen), das Schloss (schließen), das Verbot (verbieten).*
- Those lexemes formed by zero derivation or conversion are a little more complex:
  if they are derived solely from the root of the verb, then they too are usually MASCULINE, e.g. *der Lauf (laufen), der Sitz (sitzen), der Rauch (rauchen).*Exceptions: *das Leid (leiden), das Soll (sollen).*

if, however, they are infinitive verb forms converted into **verbal nouns**, then they are always NEUTER, e.g. *das Gehen, das Stehen, das Laufen, das Sitzen, das Rauchen*. These are equivalent to the English **gerund**, *-ing*, e.g. *going, standing, running, sitting, smoking*, etc.

- Finally, those nouns which contain the circumfix *Ge-/-e* are almost always NEUTER, e.g. *das Gerede, das Getue, das Gebirge*.
  Exception: *der Gedanke*.

Of course, very few linguistic rules are completely watertight and, as we have seen, there are some exceptions to these categories. Nonetheless, it should be clear how a basic understanding of derivation can help the learner of German to remember a considerable number of noun genders more easily.

6.3.2   Compounding

We have already seen how new lexemes can be derived by combining old roots with new affixes (or by changing the root itself). Compounding, by comparison, is different. This time, new lexemes are formed by joining two roots together. For example:

Spiel+karte	playing card
Spiel+automat	amusement machine
Spiel+film	feature film

Sometimes, more than two roots are added together, forming so-called **complex compounds** such as:

Glatt+eis+warn+dienst	black ice warning service
Lampen+schirm+fabrik	lampshade factory
Schorn+stein+feger+meister	master chimney sweep

Having said this, it is important to note that it is not necessary for a compound to be *written* as one word in order to be a compound. All the German and English words listed above are compound forms. Where the two languages differ is in terms of writing conventions. Thus, while English sometimes joins its compounds together, e.g. 'lampshade', it often prefers to keep them separate, e.g. 'playing card' or even use hyphens, e.g. 'playing-card'. German, on the other hand, is much more consistent, tending to write its compounds as one word. This is what sometimes makes German words seem so much longer than their English equivalents. But it does not, of course, imply that German is a language with 'more meaning' than English.

In German, there are three main types of compounds:

1. Compound adjectives such as *dunkelblau, dauerarbeitslos*.
2. Compound verbs such as *kaltpressen, Staub saugen*.
3. Compound nouns such as *Haustür, Schlüsselloch*.

Nouns are by far the most common type of compound. It is therefore worth remembering one of the basic rules of word formation in German: the gender of compound nouns is always taken from the *final* noun. For example:

die Tür	→ *die Haustür*	(but *das Haus*)
das Loch	→ *das Schlüsselloch*	(but *der Schlüssel*)

or to return to an earlier example:

der Donaudampfschifffahrtsgesellschaftskapitänskajütenschlüssel

(BUT *die Donau, der Dampf, das Schiff, die Fahrt, die Gesellschaft, der Kapitän, die Kajüte!*)

Another way of looking at compounds is in terms of the relationships of meaning which obtain between the different roots. All compounds, whether adjectives, verbs, or nouns, can be placed in one of two groups:

Subordinating compounds are those where the second element of the compound is being *described* by the first:

hellgrau	a grey which is light	= light grey
die Milchkanne	a jug for milk	= milk jug
die Drehtür	a door which turns	= revolving door

Coordinating compounds, on the other hand, display *equal* meaning between the two elements. Nevertheless, the meaning of the new compound form is still more than the sum of the original parts:

die Strumpfhose	socks which are also trousers	= tights
der Stadtstaat	a state which is also a city	= city–state
der Mähdrescher	a mower and a thresher	= combine harvester

These kinds of compounds often occur with place-names consisting of two areas which have been united for political or administrative reasons:

Schleswig-Holstein
Elsass-Lothringen
Baden-Württemberg

In Chapter 5, we also saw how such lexemes have a special pattern of stress. Thus, primary stress is placed on *both* components: e.g. *'Schleswig-'Holstein, 'Elsass-'Lothringen, 'Baden-'Württemberg* (see 5.3.1). This is in order to reflect the fact that each of the two regions is equal in terms of political status.

Finally, not all compounds simply consist of two or more roots which have been added together. Consider the following words:

der Landsmann	*Land+s+mann*	fellow country-man	= compatriot
der Meeresgrund	*Meer+es+grund*	bottom of the sea	= sea-bed

Why do such words contain an extra affix in-between the two root lexemes? The answer is that the /s/ and /əs/ are historical forms of the genitive case derived from *des Lands Mann* or *des Meeres Grund*. These inflected forms, which have then been retained in the new compound noun, are known as **linking morphemes**.

But what about the following compounds?

die Einbildungskraft	*Ein+bild+ung+s+kraft*	power of imagination
der Arbeitsplatz	*Arbeit+s+platz*	work-place

In these examples, it is not possible to explain the occurrence of /s/ in grammatical terms. This is because both *Einbildung* and *Arbeit* are feminine nouns which would not normally be inflected with the genitive /s/. Another possibility, therefore, is that /s/ is a kind of linking morpheme which facilitates pronunciation. In other words, the fricative /s/ is 'interrupting' the /ŋ/ and /k/ in *Einbildungskraft* or the /t/ and /p/ in *Arbeitsplatz,* making them easier to pronounce. Whatever the explanation may be, however, these types of morpheme cannot be considered meaningful in the lexical or grammatical sense. For this reason, they are often referred to as **empty morphemes**.

Sources and recommended reading

- A thorough account of German morphology and word classes can be found in Chapters 3 and 4 of Fox (1990).
- For more information on morphology and especially word formation, see Russ (1994).
- See Durrell (1992), Chapters 2–5, for an accessible summary of German grammar.
- Durrell (1991) contains detailed explanations of the different word classes in German, and Durrell, Kohl and Loftus (1993) has many relevant exercises for self-study.
- See Schmidt-Veitner and Wieland (1995) for exercises on noun gender.
- Kürschner (1989), Chapters 5 and 6, provides a good summary of morphology and word classes (in German).
- For general introductions to morphology, see Chapter 16 of Crystal (1997) and Chapter 2 of Fromkin and Rodman (1993).

- Both Hurford (1994) and Wright and Hope (1996) contain detailed descriptions of English word classes and grammatical terminology.

Exercises

1. Divide each of the following words into their respective morphemes.

    Example: unbedingt → un+be+ding+t

    1. Bahnhof
    2. vergessen
    3. Spionage
    4. gelb
    5. Demokratisierung
    6. grausam
    7. unbeeindruckt
    8. gestern
    9. Bedeutung
    10. bleiben

2. Divide the words in the following sentence into their respective morphemes. Then state whether each of the morphemes is lexical or grammatical and free or bound. The first one has been done for you.

    Auf dem Schreibtisch liegt ein grünliches Büchlein
     ↓
     lexical
     free

    Auf   _____

    dem   _____

    Schreibtisch _____

    liegt   _____

    ein   _____

    grünliches   _____

    Büchlein   _____

3. State whether the following 20 words are word forms or lexemes by ticking the appropriate column. If you cannot decide, refer to a dictionary.

WORD	WORD FORM	LEXEME
1. Bücher		
2. lachen		
3. gebacken		
4. saß		
5. Bleistift		
6. Grammatik		
7. Tisch		
8. schlief		
9. Deutschland		

WORD	WORD FORM	LEXEME
10. gesprochen		
11. Wörter		
12. laufen		
13. Geschäfte		
14. Feuer		
15. springen		
16. Mütter		
17. Risiken		
18. hätte		
19. Funde		
20. offen		

4. Read, and make sure you understand, the following text:

Marion Gräfin Dönhoff – Dame am Puls der 'Zeit'

Liberaler Journalismus und preußische Prägung, Fortschritt und die notwendige Selbstbeschränkung in der Freiheit: Themen, die Marion Gräfin Dönhoff (86), die große alte Dame des politischen Journalismus, bewegen. Sie war im Widerstand gegen Hitler; 1946 ging sie in die neugegründete Redaktion der Hamburger Wochenzeitung 'DIE ZEIT'. 22 Jahre später wurde sie Chefredakteurin – 1973 wechselte sie in die Position der Herausgeberin. Kürzlich feierte ihre 'ZEIT' (Auflage 484 000) 50. Geburtstag. Das Motto der Gräfin: 'Ohne Schreiben könnte ich nicht leben.'

(Source: Deutschland. *Zeitschrift für Politik, Kultur und Wissenschaft*, 2, 1996)

Now state the class to which each individual word belongs, using the following abbreviations:

N	– Noun	Adj	– Adjective
V	– Verb	Adv	– Adverb
Det	– Determiner	Prep	– Preposition
Pro	– Pronoun	Conj	– Conjunction

5. Fill in the correct endings for the following words. Then state whether the endings are weak or strong, and say why.

> *Example:* Er ist ein schön___ Film. → Er ist ein schönER Film.
> (no strong ending on ein, hence strong ending on *schön*)

1. Wir gehen in ein neu___ Theaterstück.
2. Es stand in der heutig___ Zeitung.
3. Es ist ein lustig___ Buch.
4. Wir lesen gern die klassisch___ Dichter.

5. Ich sah es in ein___ Zeitschrift.
6. Ich lese gerade einen neu___ Roman.
7. Es ist das best___ aber auch das teuerst___ Wörterbuch.
8. Es war eine sehr romantisch___ Geschichte.
9. Steht es vor deinem groß___ Bücherregal?
10. Hast du das klein___ schwarz___ Heft?

6. Consider the following pairs of lexemes where the second has been derived from the first. Then state the following information:

- type of change
  (e.g. verb to noun/deverbal nominalisation)
- the linguistic process(es)
  (e.g. affix, umlaut, ablaut, zero derivation/conversion)
- type of derivation
  (e.g. explicit, implicit, explicit + implicit)

> *Example:* nass → Nässe
>   Type: adjective → noun (deadjectival nominalisation)
>   Process: umlaut + suffix -*e*
>   Derivation: explicit + implicit

1. Sport → Sportler
2. leiden → Leidenschaft
3. essen → Essen
4. brauchen → brauchbar
5. krank → kränklich
6. Haus → hausieren
7. treiben → Getriebe
8. Mode → modisch
9. beißen → bissig
10. lang → langsam

7. Provide the correct form of the definite article for the following nouns. Which rule of derivation allows you to predict the gender in each case?

> *Example:* Leistung → *die* Leistung (affix -*ung*)

1. Schema
2. Dynamit
3. Panik
4. Natur
5. Wurf
6. Basis
7. Teppich
8. Betrieb
9. Flucht
10. Machen

7

The structure of German sentences

In Chapter 6 we saw how linguists divide the study of grammar into two main areas: *morphology* deals with the grammar of words, while **syntax** focuses on the grammar of sentences. Now look at the following sentences:

> I drink several cups of tea a day.
> We could go shopping tomorrow.

It is part of your knowledge about English which tells you that these sentences are grammatical or well-formed. In this respect, they differ from the following:

> *Drink tea several a cups day I of.
> *Shopping could tomorrow we go.

These sentences are clearly ungrammatical or ill-formed (hence the asterisk). They break all the rules of syntax which a speaker of English must know in order to use the language correctly.

As children, we learn the syntactic rules of our mother tongue without any conscious effort. Even though these rules are extremely complex, we master them quickly, efficiently, and long before we can write. When we learn a foreign language as adults, however, things are rather different. As with our first language, there is an extent to which we can rely on our *implicit* sense of what is right and wrong. But beyond a certain point, it becomes useful to develop a more *explicit* awareness of the ways in which syntax works. One reason for doing this is so that we can appreciate some of the more subtle meanings which are expressed by different types of word order.

Consider, for example, the following:

> *Sie hat dir eine Karte zum Geburtstag geschickt.*
> *Hat sie dir eine Karte zum Geburtstag geschickt?*
> *Ich weiß, dass sie dir eine Karte zum Geburtstag geschickt hat.*

These three sentences are grammatically well-formed. Together, they also illustrate an aspect of word order which most foreigners must confront in the early stages of learning German: the position of the finite verb. In the first sentence, we can see that the finite verb *hat* is in second position, whereas the past participle *geschickt* is in final position. In the second example, the finite verb and the pronoun *sie* have been reversed in order to form a question. In the third sentence, by contrast, the word order has changed much more radically. This is because the use of the subordinating conjunction *dass* means that the finite verb *hat* must now take final position.

In these three examples, we can say that the position of the verb is *syntactically* defined. In other words, there are rules of syntax which state in which part of the sentence the various verb forms must occur. This type of word order is known in linguistics as **syntactic ordering** or grammatical word order. Now take a look at the following:

> *Zum Geburtstag hat sie dir eine Karte geschickt.*
> *Sie hat dir zum Geburtstag eine Karte geschickt.*
> *Eine Karte hat sie dir zum Geburtstag geschickt.*

These sentences are also syntactically well-formed, although their grammaticality is perhaps not as obvious as in the previous three examples. We could say that the sentences are correct, but that they would not necessarily be appropriate in every situation or context. We are beginning to see therefore that word order is not always a straightforward question of right or wrong: in these sentences, the syntax depends on which part of the sentence you particularly wish to emphasise. This type of word order is known in linguistics as **pragmatic ordering** or communicative word order.

In this chapter, we shall take a closer look at both syntactic and pragmatic ordering. We will then be able to explore some of the nuances of meaning which can be expressed through these different types of word order, and also make some important comparisons between German and English. But before we do this, it will be necessary to introduce some of the grammatical terminology which is needed in order to describe sentences in more detail.

7.1   Describing and analysing sentences

In order to understand the ways in which sentences are constructed, it is essential to break them down into smaller units. Consider:

> *die ein liest Studentin Buch heute interessantes.
> *heute die Studentin liest ein interessantes Buch.

Each of these sentences is grammatically ill-formed. But there is an important difference in the type of mistake which is being made. In the first sentence, every single aspect of the word order has been mixed up in a way which renders the statement virtually incomprehensible. The second sentence, by comparison, illustrates a typical error made by English-speaking learners of German – the order of the subject *die Studentin* and the finite verb *liest* has not been reversed after the adverb *heute*. This sentence is also incorrect, but would almost certainly be understood by a native German speaker. This is because the four main grammatical **constituents** *heute, die Studentin, liest,* and *ein interessantes Buch* have not been separated. Constituents are those units of syntax which normally occur together. They may consist of one word (*heute* or *liest*), two words (*die Studentin*), three words (*ein interessantes Buch*) or more (*ein sehr interessantes und informatives Buch*).

We are beginning to see that the crucial difference between the two sentences above relates to the distinction between words, on the one hand, and constituents, on the other. We can therefore say that the first sentence is an example of wholly incorrect *word order*. This kind of word order is of little relevance to the study of syntax, since it would not make sense in any language. The second sentence, by comparison, is an example of incorrect *ordering of constituents*. This is of interest to syntacticians because the order is wrong in German, but would be correct in many other languages, e.g. English. This may seem like a rather trivial distinction to make, but it is nonetheless important. Thus, when we look at sentences in this chapter, and compare the structures of German and English, it is not really the order of the individual words we are interested in, but the order in which the various grammatical constituents must occur.

7.1.1   The constituents of German sentences

The study of syntax can be very complex, and there are many different ways of describing sentences and their constituents. Here we will look at only the very simplest model of analysis. Accordingly, we can say that every German sentence may contain up to five basic grammatical constituents. These are:

- Subject
- Verb
- Object
- Complement
- Adverbial

We will now look at some examples of these different types of constituent.

SUBJECT

The **subject** of a sentence is the person or thing performing the action on the verb. It is often made up of a determiner plus a noun:

Die Studentin	liest.
Subject	Verb
(Det + N)	(V)

However, the subject can also be a proper noun (i.e. a name):

Angelika	liest.
Subject	Verb
(N)	(V)

a personal pronoun:

Sie	liest.
Subject	Verb
(Pro)	(V)

or an impersonal pronoun:

Es	regnet.
Subject	Verb
(Pro)	(V)

Recall how in section 5.2.2 we saw that the subjects of verbs must always occur in the nominative or *subject* case.

VERB

Verbs describe the actions or events which are taking place in a sentence. Verbs can also be divided into infinitives (e.g. *lesen*) or finite forms which mark person and number (e.g. *lese* or *lest*). Finite verbs usually occur together with (i.e. next to) their subjects in German, and these two constituents must then agree in terms of person and number:

Ich	*lese.*
Subject	Verb
(Pro)	(V)
1st person singular	1st person singular

Ihr	*lest.*
Subject	Verb
(Pro)	(V)
2nd person plural	2nd person plural

These types of constructions are also known as **declarative** statements since they are *declaring* information.

Sometimes a sentence may consist of a verb without a subject: *Mach!, Geh sofort!, Sag bloß!* These kinds of constructions are known as **imperative** statements, a term which is derived from the Latin *imperativus* meaning 'command'. However, not all imperatives occur without a subject. In the polite form of the 2nd person, the subject *Sie* still occurs with its finite verb: *Machen Sie!, Gehen Sie sofort!, Sagen Sie bloß!*

OBJECT

Objects are those people or things affected by the action which is performed by the subject of the verb. There are a number of different types of object in German sentences. As we saw in section 6.2.2 on declension, an object may be *directly* affected by the action performed by the subject. In such cases, the object is known as a direct object or **accusative object**:

Der Mann	schreibt	*einen Brief.*
Subject	Verb	Accusative Object
(Det+N)	(V)	(Det+N)

Sometimes, an object is only *indirectly* affected by the action of the verb. In these cases, it is known as an indirect object or **dative object**:

Der Mann	schreibt	*der Frau*	einen Brief.
Subject	Verb	Dative Object	Accusative Object
(Det+N)	(V)	(Det+N)	(Det+N)

Alternatively, an object may be a **genitive object**, although this kind of construction is typical of only fairly formal usage:

Sie	bedarf	*meines Buchs.*
Subject	Verb	Genitive Object
(Pro)	(V)	(Det+N)

A second type of object is the so-called **prepositional object**. This is where the prepositions and the verb together dictate whether the object will take the accusative or dative case:

Ich	denke	*an die Arbeit.*
Subject	Verb	Accusative Prepositional Object
(Pro)	(V)	(Prep+Det+N)

Ich	rechne	*mit deiner Hilfe.*
Subject	Verb	Dative Prepositional Object
(Pro)	(V)	(Prep+Det+N)

Every time you learn a new verb in German, note the kind of object which must accompany it, and any relevant prepositions and cases which are required. If you fail to do this, you are likely to find it very difficult to use the verb correctly in future. (For a detailed description of the use of objects, verbs, and prepositions, see Durrell (1991), Chapters 18 and 20, and the accompanying exercises in Durrell, Kohl and Loftus (1993).)

COMPLEMENT

After the verbs *sein* and *werden*, a so-called **complement** may occur. For example:

Das Wetter	ist	*schön.*		Er	wurde	*rot.*
Subject	Verb	Complement		Subject	Verb	Complement
(Det+N)	(V)	(Adj)		(Pro)	(V)	(Adj)

Das Haus	war	*sehr groß.*
Subject	Verb	Complement
(Det+N)	(V)	(Adv+Adj)

In these sentences, the complement is an adjective (*schön, rot*) or an **adjectival phrase** (*sehr groß*), which is describing the subject of the verb. Note how in such cases there are no endings on the adjectives. This is because German adjectives are only inflected when they occur *before* the noun, e.g. *schönes Wetter* or *großes Haus*. In this respect, German differs from other languages such as French and Spanish which inflect their adjectives both before and after the noun.

A complement may also consist of a noun:

Meine Mutter	ist	*Lehrerin.*		Mein Vater	wurde	*Arzt.*
Subject	Verb	Complement		Subject	Verb	Complement
(Det+N)	(V)	(N)		(Det+N)	(V)	(N)

The nouns *Lehrerin* and *Arzt* may look like objects here, but this is not in fact the case. This is because the subjects, *meine Mutter* and *mein Vater,* are not actually performing any action on the complements, *Lehrerin* and *Arzt.* Instead, the subjects are being described by the complements. The nouns here are therefore functioning in a similar way to the adjectives in the earlier examples *das Wetter ist schön, er wurde rot* and *das Haus war sehr groß.*

Note also that because noun complements are not objects, they must occur in the subject or nominative case, and *not* the accusative case. This can be seen clearly in the following examples where the complement is not a straightforward noun, but a **noun phrase**:

Meine Mutter	ist	*eine sehr gute Lehrerin.*
Subject	Verb	Complement
(Det+N)	(V)	(Det+Adv+Adj+N)

Mein Vater	wurde	*ein sehr guter Arzt.*
Subject	Verb	Complement
(Det+N)	(V)	(Det+Adv+Adj+N)

ADVERBIALS

Many sentences also contain **adverbials**. An adverbial is any kind of structure which gives us more information about the verb. In the following example, the adverbial consists of a single adverb:

Vorgestern	las	ich	das Buch.
Adverbial	Verb	Subject	Accusative Object
(Adv)	(V)	(Pro)	(Det+N)

Whereas in the next sentence, the adverbial is made up of an **adverbial phrase**, that is to say, more than one word which together function like an adverb:

Jeden Freitag	spiele	ich	Karten.
Adverbial	Verb	Subject	Accusative Object
(Det+N)	(V)	(S)	(N)

Finally, adverbials sometimes consist of a **prepositional phrase**, i.e. a phrase containing a preposition, for example:

Sie	kam	*ohne Geld.*
Subject	Verb	Adverbial
(Pro)	(V)	(Prep+N)

7.1.2   The ordering of constituents

Now that we have broken down sentences into different types of constituent, we can begin to say something about the *order* in which these constituents normally occur.

The most frequent kind of ordering in German is SVO or SVC, i.e. a subject and a finite verb followed by an object or a complement. For example:

Sie	schickt	eine Karte.
Subject	Verb	Object
(Pro)	(V)	(Det+N)

Sie	ist	sehr hilfsbereit.
Subject	Verb	Complement
(Pro)	(V)	(Adv+Adj)

This SVO/SVC pattern is also typical of English:

She	sends	a card.		She	is	very helpful.
Subject	Verb	Object		Subject	Verb	Complement
(Pro)	(V)	(Det+N)		(Pro)	(V)	(Adv+Adj)

In German, however, the object or complement may also occur in initial position, resulting in an OVS or CVS structure:

Eine Karte	schickt	sie.		*Sehr hilfsbereit*	ist	sie.
Object	Verb	Subject		Complement	Verb	Subject
(Det+N)	(V)	(Pro)		(Adv+Adj)	(V)	(Pro)

But this is not normally possible in English, except perhaps in very stylised, literary usage. Note also that in English, the order of the subject and finite verb would not be reversed (as in German), therefore resulting in an OSV or CSV structure:

*A card	she	sends.		*Very helpful	she	is.
Object	Subject	Verb		Complement	Subject	Verb
(Det+N)	(Pro)	(V)		(Adv+Adj)	(Pro)	(V)

We shall return to these kinds of structures in section 7.3.

Finally, the position of adverbials within a sentence is fairly flexible, although they do tend to stay close to the main verb:

Ich	las	*gestern*	ein Buch.	*Gestern*	las	ich	ein Buch.
Subject	Verb	Adverbial	Object	Adverbial	Verb	Subject	Object
(Pro)	(V)	(Adv)	(Det+N)	(Adv)	(V)	(Pro)	(Det+N)

If there is more than one adverbial, these are normally ordered according to the principle of time, manner, place:

Er	fährt	*morgen*	*mit dem Zug*	*nach London.*
Subject	Verb	Adverbial	Adverbial	Adverbial
(Pro)	(V)	(Adv of time)	(Adv of manner)	(Adv of place)

This rule is often taught to foreign learners of German and is a useful guide to the ordering of adverbials. Having said this, we shall see in section 7.3 how there may be good reasons for not adhering to this pattern, especially when we want to place extra emphasis on one particular adverbial.

7.1.3   Sentences and clauses

So far, we have talked about constituents and the position of constituents within sentences. Now consider the following:

Susanne	fuhr	am Montag.
Subject	Verb	Adverbial
(N)	(V)	(Prep+Det+N)

This is an example of a **simple sentence**. It is simple because it is made up of only one **clause**. A clause is a structure which contains its own subject and finite verb. Of course, sentences frequently consist of more than one clause. For example:

Susanne	fuhr	am Montag	und	Peter	blieb	bis Dienstag.
Subject	Verb	Adverbial		Subject	Verb	Adverbial
(N)	(V)	(Prep+Det+N)	(Conj)	(N)	(V)	(Prep+N)
CLAUSE 1				CLAUSE 2		

or

Susanne	fuhr	am Montag,	weil	sie	am Dienstag	arbeiten musste.
Subject	Verb	Adverbial		Subject	Adverbial	Verbs
(N)	(V)	(Prep+Det+N)	(Conj)	(Pro)	(Prep+Det+N)	(V1+V2)
CLAUSE 1				CLAUSE 2		

Sentences such as these, which contain two (or more) clauses, are referred to as **complex sentences**.

In complex sentences, there are two main ways in which the individual clauses can be joined together. If the clauses are linked by **coordinating conjunctions** such as *und, aber, oder*, etc., then we can speak of two main clauses. For example:

Susanne	fuhr	am Montag	und	Peter	blieb	bis Dienstag.
Main Clause			Coordinating Conjunction	Main Clause		

In a sentence such as this, the two clauses are said to have equal status. This is because the information in the second clause is just as important as that which is contained in the first.

Alternatively, if the clauses are linked by **subordinating conjunctions** such as *weil, wenn, dass*, etc., then we can speak of a main clause and a **subordinate clause** (also known as a dependent clause):

Susanne	fuhr	am Montag,	weil	sie	am Dienstag	arbeiten musste.
Main Clause			Subordinating Conjunction	Subordinate Clause		

In this type of sentence, the two clauses have unequal status. This is because the subordinate clause is merely giving us extra information about the main clause. In other words, it is telling us *why Susanne went on Monday*.

Note, however, that a main clause must not necessarily be in first position within a German sentence which contains a subordinate clause. For example, the following structure is also possible:

Weil	sie	am Dienstag	arbeiten musste,	fuhr	Susanne	am Montag.
Subordinating Conjunction		Subordinate Clause			Main Clause	

We shall return to this kind of sentence in the next section. In the meantime, there are two points which can be made regarding main and subordinate clauses generally. First of all, notice how coordinating conjunctions such as *und, aber, oder* and subordinating conjunctions such as *weil, wenn, dass* have a different effect on the position of the finite verb which follows them. Thus, in main clauses the finite verb retains its original (i.e. second) position, whereas in subordinate clauses it occurs last. This is because the *position* of the verb is linked to its *status*. In other words, in a main clause, the verb is more important than in a subordinate clause, where it is therefore *subordinated* to final position. In this respect, we can see how the rules of syntax cannot ultimately be separated from the study of meaning or semantics.

This leads us to the second point. A similar distinction between coordination and subordination was discussed in section 6.3.2 on compounding. There we saw how compound words can also be described according to this principle of equal or unequal status. Thus, coordinating compounds were those which displayed equal meaning between the two components, e.g.:

> *Strumpfhose*   (socks which are also trousers = tights).
> *Schleswig-Holstein*   (a region consisting of *Schleswig* + *Holstein*)

These differed from subordinating compounds, where the second element of the compound was merely being described by the first, e.g.:

> *hellgrau*   (a grey which is light = light grey).
> *Milchkanne*   (a jug for milk   = milk jug)

It will become clear later in this chapter how this is not the only parallel which can be drawn between the grammar of individual words and the grammar of whole sentences. In this respect, we can see how the principles of syntax are closely tied up with those of morphology.

7.2   Syntactic ordering

From the examples discussed so far, it has become clear that the position of the verb is crucial to the structure of German clauses and sentences. In many ways, the verb is the most important constituent, around which everything else must fit. In this section, we shall be therefore focusing on the syntactic rules which govern the position in which verbs may or may not occur.

7.2.1 Position of verbs

Learners of German as a foreign language are often taught that the verb takes *second* position in a clause or sentence. Whilst this is a useful principle to bear in mind, the reality is slightly more complex. There are, in fact, three possible positions for the verb: first, second, and final.

VERBS IN FIRST POSITION

Probably the most common situation where verbs occur in first position is in commands containing **imperative** forms. For example:

Mach!
Verb
1

Mach	jetzt!
Verb	Adverbial
1	2

Mach	das	jetzt sofort!
Verb	Object	Adverbial
1	2	3

Verbs also occur in initial position in questions such as the following:

Kennst	du	meine Mutter?
Verb	Subject	Object
1	2	3

Ist	es	gut?
Verb	Subject	Complement
1	2	3

These questions are known as **yes–no interrogatives** because they can normally be answered with either 'yes' or 'no'.

VERBS IN SECOND POSITION

There are many different contexts in which the verb may occur in second position. The most common is in straightforward SVO/SVC constructions:

Sie	*haben*	keine Lust.
Subject	Verb	Object
1	2	3

Sie	*ist*	Sportlehrerin.
Subject	Verb	Complement
1	2	3

However, in the following clauses there are two verbs:

Sie	*haben*	keine Lust	*gehabt.*
Subject	Verb 1	Object	Verb 2
1	2	3	4

Sie	*ist*	Sportlehrerin	*gewesen.*
Subject	Verb 1	Complement	Verb 2
1	2	3	4

From these examples, we can see that it is not all verbs which occur in second position, only the *finite verb*, that is to say, the one which marks person and number. In these two cases, the finite verbs are the **auxiliary verbs** *haben* and *sein*, respectively. Auxiliary verbs are those which 'help' the main verb.

The finite verb also takes second position within main clauses which have been joined by a coordinating conjunction such as *und, aber, oder*:

Susanne	*fuhr*	am Montag	und	Peter	*blieb*	bis Dienstag.
Subject	Verb	Adverbial	Conj.	Subject	Verb	Adverbial
Main Clause				Main Clause		
1	2	3		1	2	3

Note, however, that if the same verb occurs in both clauses, then it is usually omitted the second time. Hence: *Susanne fuhr am Montag und Peter fuhr am Dienstag* becomes *Susanne fuhr am Montag und Peter am Dienstag*.

Another situation where the finite verb takes second position is when the clause begins with an adverbial:

Heute	*haben*	sie	keine Zeit.
Adverbial	Verb	Subject	Object
1	2	3	4

Jetzt	*ist*	sie	Ärtzin.
Adverbial	Verb	Subject	Complement
1	2	3	4

From these examples, we can see how, when an adverbial occurs in initial position, the subject must then move from *first* to *third* place so that the finite verb can retain its traditional *second* position. This is known as *inversion* of the subject and finite verb. There are a small number of English adverbs which also require this kind of inversion such as 'neither', 'nor' and 'so' as in: 'neither am I', 'nor do we', or 'so is he'.

Now look at the following examples, where the order of the subject and finite verb has similarly been reversed:

Letzte Woche	*sah*	ich	sie.
Adverbial	Verb	Subject	Object
1	2	3	4

Vor zwei Jahren im Herbst	*sah*	ich	sie.
Adverbial	Verb	Subject	Object
1	2	3	4

An adverbial may consist of more than one word. The important point here is that, irrespective of the number of words contained in the adverbial, the finite verb is still the second *constituent* which occurs. Again, we can see why it is important to think in terms of grammatical constituents as opposed to individual words when analysing clauses and sentences. The same applies to the following example:

Wenn ich Zeit habe,	*fahre*	ich	nach Italien.
Adverbial	Verb	Subject	Adverbial
1	2	3	4
Subordinate Clause	Main Clause		

This type of complex sentence is sometimes referred to as a 'verb, comma, verb' structure, e.g. *habe, fahre*. At first glance, the verb in the main clause, *fahre*, might not appear to be in second position. This is because the first constituent which occurs is a complete clause in its own right. However, it is also possible for subordinate clauses to have the same grammatical function as an adverbial. Hence, in syntactic terms, the above sentence is not unlike saying:

Morgen	*fahre*	ich	nach Italien.
Adverbial	Verb	Subject	Object
1	2	3	4

Note, however, that in such cases the adverbial is *not* followed by a comma – a mistake frequently made by English speakers when writing German. This may seem trivial but it is important to realise that punctuation is taken very seriously in German. This means that a comma after the adverb *morgen* in the above example has virtually the same status as an error of syntax.

Finally, another situation where verbs occupy second position is in questions such as the following:

Wo	*wohnen*	Sie?		Was	*macht*	Michael?
Adverbial	Verb	Subject		Adverbial	Verb	Subject
1	2	3		1	2	3

These types of sentences are known as **w-interrogatives** because the so-called **interrogative adverb** (or question word) usually begins with the letter 'w', e.g. *wo, was, warum, wann, welcher*. However, sometimes the English term 'wh-interrogative' (derived from *where, what, why, when, which*, etc.) is also used with reference to German. W-interrogatives differ from yes–no interrogatives in so far as a fuller answer is normally required, i.e. not just a simple 'yes' or 'no'.

VERBS IN FINAL POSITION

The finite verb usually occupies final position in subordinate clauses such as the following:

Ich	weiß,	dass	er	es	*macht.*
Subject	Verb		Subject	Object	Verb
1	2		1	2	3
Main Clause		Subordinating Conjunction	Subordinate Clause		

Note that where a subordinate clause contains more than one verb, it is still the finite verb which occurs last:

Ich	weiß,	dass	er	es	gemacht	*hat.*
Subject	Verb		Subject	Object	Verb 1	Verb 2
1	2		1	2	3	4
Main Clause		Subordinating Conjunction	Subordinate Clause			

One important exception to this rule is where there is a finite verb plus two infinitives at the end of the subordinate clause. In such cases, the finite verb occurs *before* the infinitives:

Ich	weiß,	dass	er	es	*hat*	machen	wollen.
Subject	Verb		Subject	Object	Verb 1	Verb 2	Verb 3
1	2		1	2	3	4	5
Main Clause		Subordinating Conjunction	Subordinate Clause				

Another situation where finite verbs are relegated to final position is in **relative clauses**, which are one particular type of subordinate clause:

Ich	habe	den Mann	heute	gesehen,	der	gestern	im Zug	*saß.*
Subject	Verb 1	Object	Adverbial	Verb 2	Subject	Adverbial	Adverbial	Verb
1	2	3	4	5	1	2	3	4
Main Clause					Relative Clause			

In this example, the relative clause has been introduced by the **relative pronoun**, *der*, which refers directly back to the noun, *der Mann*.

In the next two examples, the relative clause begins with the **relative adverbs** *wo* and *wann*, which refer back to the verbs *wissen* and *machen*, respectively:

Ich	habe	nicht	gewußt,	wo	er	*war.*
Subject	Verb 1	Adverbial	Verb 2	Adverbial	Subject	Verb
1	2	3	4	1	2	3
Main Clause				Relative Clause		

Sie	macht	es,	wann	sie	*will.*
Subject	Verb	Object	Adverbial	Subject	Verb
1	2	3	1	2	3
Main Clause			Relative Clause		

In all of these cases, the term *relative* is being used because the pronoun or adverb in question is not independent – it is *related* to a noun or verb which has already occurred in the main clause.

7.2.2   The verbal bracket

So far we have looked at some of the syntactic rules governing the position in which the finite verb may occur in German clauses and sentences. However, there is an important general principle of German syntax which applies to many of the examples we have analysed so far, and which is worth considering in more detail. Look at the following:

Hast	du	mein Buch	*gesehen?*
Verb 1	Subject	Object	Verb 2
1	2	3	4

Sind	Sie	letzte Woche	nach Wien	*gefahren?*
Verb 1	Subject	Adverbial	Adverbial	Verb 2
1	2	3	4	5

One of the things we can see from these examples is that when two verb forms occur in the same clause, one is placed at the beginning and one at the end of the clause. This is what is known in German syntax as the **verbal bracket** (*Satzklammer*) or verbal frame (*Satzrahmen*). It is as though the two verbs were 'bracketing off' or 'framing' the rest of the clause.

With this type of construction, we can further distinguish between an *opening bracket* (always a finite verb), a *closing bracket*, and the *central elements* which occur between the two:

OPENING BRACKET (FINITE VERB)	CENTRAL ELEMENTS	CLOSING BRACKET
[		]
Hast	du mein Buch	*gesehen?*
Sind	Sie letzte Woche nach Wien	*gefahren?*

Moreover, bracketing occurs not only with auxiliary verbs and main verbs as in the above examples, but also with a number of other verbal constructions in German.

Modal auxiliary + main verb:

OPENING BRACKET (FINITE VERB)	CENTRAL ELEMENTS	CLOSING BRACKET
[		]
Wollen	Sie das wirklich	*machen?*
Kannst	du dir das	*vorstellen?*

Verb + separable prefix:

OPENING BRACKET (FINITE VERB)	CENTRAL ELEMENTS	CLOSING BRACKET
[		]
Hören	Sie damit	*auf?*
Nimm	das bitte	*weg!*

Verb + object/complement:

OPENING BRACKET (FINITE VERB)	CENTRAL ELEMENTS	CLOSING BRACKET
[		]
Fährst	du jeden Tag	*Auto?*
Ist	sie	*Ärtzin?*

Of course, these are all examples where the finite verb occupies first position. But even where the verb takes second position, the principle of bracketing still applies. Having said this, one of the most important rules of German syntax is that only *one* constituent may occur before the verbal bracket begins, so that the finite verb can retain its traditional second place:

INITIAL ELEMENT	OPENING BRACKET (FINITE VERB)	CENTRAL ELEMENTS	CLOSING BRACKET
	[		]
Morgen	*wollen*	Sie das wirklich	*machen?*
In zehn Tagen	*kannst*	du dir das	*vorstellen?*
Nächstes Jahr	*hören*	Sie damit	*auf?*
Wenn ich gehe,	*nimm*	das bitte	*weg!*
Seit wann	*ist*	sie	*Ärtzin?*
Bitte	*nehmen*	Sie mir das nicht	*übel.*

When a verb occurs at the end of a subordinate clause, we can still speak of a closing bracket. This time, however, it is as though the finite verb in the main clause and the finite verb in the subordinate clause were acting together in order to frame the sentence:

INITIAL ELEMENT	OPENING BRACKET (FINITE VERB)	CENTRAL ELEMENTS	CLOSING BRACKET (FINITE VERB)
	[		]
Ich	*weiß,*	dass er es	*macht.*
Ich	*weiß,*	dass er es gemacht	*hat.*

The verbal bracket is one of the main principles of syntax which distinguishes German and English. It is for this reason that the ordering of verbs can initially seem rather unfamiliar to the English-speaking learner of German. However, there are still one or two examples where this type of construction occurs in English:

INITIAL ELEMENT	OPENING BRACKET (FINITE VERB)	CENTRAL ELEMENTS	CLOSING BRACKET
	[		]
I	*have*	a room	*booked.*
We	*have*	a table	*reserved.*

Finally, take a look at the following kinds of words which were discussed in Chapter 6 on morphology: *gespielt, gefahren, Gebirge*. Can you spot any similarity between the structure of these words and the verbal bracket in syntax?

The link is that, in each case, the root of the word is being bracketed by a circumfix, i.e. a prefix plus a suffix:

OPENING BRACKET (PREFIX)	CENTRAL ELEMENT (ROOT)	CLOSING BRACKET (SUFFIX)
[		]
ge+	spiel+	t
ge+	fahr+	en
Ge+	birg+	e

Thus, we can see how the principle of bracketing in German syntax is the equivalent of circumfixing in German morphology:

	OPENING BRACKET	CENTRAL ELEMENT/ROOT	CLOSING BRACKET
	[		]
Syntax	*Bist*	du nach Hause	*gefahren?*
Morphology	ge+	fahr+	en

7.3 Pragmatic ordering

Earlier, a distinction was made between syntactic and pragmatic ordering. Syntactic ordering is concerned with the grammatical rules which dictate where in a sentence the various constituents may or may not occur. In the following examples, we can see that the position of the finite verb is related to the fact that the first sentence is a declarative statement, whereas the second is an interrogative:

Sie *hat* dir das Buch geschenkt.
Hat sie dir das Buch geschenkt?

Pragmatic ordering, on the other hand, is concerned with a different aspect of syntax. In the following sentences, the word order varies because the speaker wishes to place special emphasis on one particular constituent:

> *Zum Geburtstag* hat sie dir ein Buch geschenkt.
> *Ein Buch* hat sie dir zum Geburtstag geschenkt.

Pragmatics is therefore the branch of linguistics which deals with language 'in action'. It is less concerned with the theoretical rules laid down by grammar books, and more interested in the way language works when it is used by real people in specific contexts. In Chapter 9, we shall be looking at pragmatics in much greater detail. Here, however, we shall concentrate on the ways in which pragmatic considerations affect German syntax.

7.3.1   Old information, new information

We have already seen how the rules of syntactic ordering mean that the position of the finite verb in a German clause or sentence is fairly fixed. The other constituents, however, are relatively flexible. Consider the following two statements:

> *Ich kaufe mir nächste Woche ein neues Fahrrad.*
> *Ich kaufe mir ein neues Fahrrad nächste Woche.*

Each of these sentences is grammatically correct, i.e. they both fulfil the requirements of syntactic ordering. But the difference is one of emphasis. In the first sentence, *das Fahrrad* is being stressed, whereas in the second, the fact that *das Fahrrad* will be bought *nächste Woche* is more important. There is a tendency to place those constituents we particularly wish to emphasise at the *end* of the clause or sentence.

In order to understand how pragmatic ordering works in German, it is essential to differentiate between the 'old' and the 'new' information in a given statement. But how can you tell which constituents are old and which are new in the two examples we have just looked at? In practice, everything depends upon the *context* in which these statements were uttered. So, for example, if the two sentences were answers to questions, then the questions would look very different:

> Q: *Was* kaufst du dir nächste Woche?
> A: Ich kaufe mir nächste Woche *ein neues Fahrrad*.
>
> Q: *Wann* kaufst du dir ein neues Fahrrad?
> A: Ich kaufe mir ein neues Fahrrad *nächste Woche*.

Now that we have the full context, we can distinguish more readily between the old and the new information in each case. Thus, in the first question and answer sequence, it is the 'bicycle' which is being mentioned for the first time. This compares to the second sequence where it is the time of purchase, i.e. 'next week', which constitutes the new information.

In pragmatic ordering, the old information (i.e. things which have already been mentioned) is referred to as the **theme** or **topic**. New information, on the other hand, is known as the **rheme** or **comment**. We can therefore reanalyse our two examples as follows:

THEME	RHEME
Ich kaufe mir nächste Woche	ein neues Fahrrad.
Ich kaufe mir ein neues Fahrrad	nächste Woche.

From these examples, we can also see how it is customary to place the new information or rheme *in final position*.

In practice, of course, it might not even be necessary to repeat the theme when answering questions such as these. Indeed, it would be much more natural to say:

> Q: Was kaufst du dir nächste Woche?
> A: *Ein neues Fahrrad.*
>
> Q: Wann kaufst du dir ein neues Fahrrad?
> A: *Nächste Woche.*

This is what is known in linguistics as **ellipsis**. Through elliptical usage, we are able to avoid the repetition of old, redundant information. In other words, we leave out – or ellipt – certain elements in order to speak more economically or effectively.

Now consider the following statement:

Ich	habe	meiner Freundin	ein Buch	zum Geburtstag	geschenkt.
Subject	Verb 1	Dative Object	Accusative Object	Adverbial	Verb 2

This sentence is an example of natural, ordinary word order. It appears so for two reasons: first, because it adheres to the basic pattern of SVO (plus other constituents); and second, because no one constituent is being singled out for special emphasis. This is what is known in syntax as **unmarked** word order. It is the kind of word order you would expect to find in grammar books for students of German.

There are, however, a number of ways in which it is possible to deviate from this pattern. German allows us to place an object of a sentence in initial position. For example:

Ein Buch	habe	ich	meiner Freundin	zum Geburtstag	geschenkt.
Accusative Object	Verb 1	Subject	Dative Object	Adverbial	Verb 2

or

Meiner Freundin	habe	ich	ein Buch	zum Geburtstag	geschenkt.
Dative Object	Verb 1	Subject	Accusative Object	Adverbial	Verb 2

We are now therefore dealing with an OVS structure as opposed to SVO. This is one example of what is known in syntax as **marked** word order.

One of the reasons why this type of marked order occurs is related to what was said earlier about old and new information. Thus, we saw how new information is normally placed in final position in a German clause or sentence. In the previous two examples, however, the rheme *ein Buch* or *meiner Freundin* has been placed first. This is what is known as a **foregrounded rheme**. A foregrounded rheme does not always have to be an object or a complement. In the following sentence, it is the adverbial, *zum Geburtstag*, which has been foregrounded in order to stress that the book was given as a *birthday* present:

FOREGROUNDED RHEME	THEME				
Zum Geburtstag	habe	ich	meiner Freundin	ein Buch	geschenkt.
Adverbial	Verb 1	Subject	Dative Object	Accusative Object	Verb 2

Finally, in the next example the foregrounded rheme is the past participle, *geschenkt*, stressing the book was given *as a present*:

FOREGROUNDED RHEME	THEME				
Geschenkt	habe	ich	meiner Freundin	ein Buch	zum Geburtstag.
Verb 2	Verb 1	Subject	Dative Object	Accusative Object	Adverbial

However, note that this last example is a case of *extremely marked* word order, not least because the structure does not conform to the syntactic principle of verbal bracketing. You would require a very special context indeed to use this kind of construction.

7.3.2   *The inflexibility of German word order?*

It is not uncommon to hear students protest that German word order is 'inflexible' or 'rigid' when compared to English. Let us explore the extent to which this claim is really justified by looking at some German sentences and their possible English equivalents. Consider, for example, the following:

1. *Ich habe meiner Freundin ein Buch zum Geburtstag geschenkt.*
   I gave my friend a book for her birthday.
   → unmarked word order in both languages.

2. *Zum Geburtstag habe ich meiner Freundin ein Buch geschenkt.*
   For her birthday, I gave my friend a book.
   → unmarked word order in both languages.

3. *Ein Buch habe ich meiner Freundin zum Geburtstag geschenkt.*
   *A book I gave my friend for her birthday.
   → foregrounded rheme (accusative object) in German.

4. *Meiner Freundin habe ich ein Buch zum Geburtstag geschenkt.*
   *My friend I gave a book for her birthday.
   → foregrounded rheme (dative object) in German.

5. *Geschenkt habe ich meiner Freundin ein Buch zum Geburtstag.*
   *Gave I my friend a book for her birthday.
   → foregrounded rheme (past participle) in German.

From these examples, we can see that there are five different ways of ordering the same constituents in German, whereas in English there are only two. How can this be so?

In sentence 5, a direct translation into English is not possible because the verb cannot be foregrounded in English. In examples 3 and 4, by contrast, we can appreciate the extremely important role played by case endings in German word order. Thus, there is enormous flexibility regarding the position of the subject, direct object, and indirect object in German because the case endings will always indicate how the constituents fit together syntactically. English, by comparison, does not mark cases in this way. It is therefore wholly dependent on word order (usually SVO/SVC) in order to demonstrate the grammatical function of each constituent. In other words, the subject *must* occur before the object(s), otherwise there will be confusion regarding who is doing what to whom. All of this provides us with a further example of the interrelationship between the structure of individual words, i.e. morphology, and the structure of whole sentences, i.e. syntax.

But if German allows us to do things we cannot do in English, does this mean that German is the more expressive of the two languages? The answer is no – or perhaps no, not necessarily. Take another look at sentences 3 to 5. How, when speaking English, could you convey the different types of emphasis which are created by foregrounding the rheme in German?

The answer is through intonation. Hence, you might pronounce these sentences in a way which stressed those constituents which are italicised as follows:

3. *Ein Buch habe ich meiner Freundin zum Geburtstag geschenkt.*
   I gave my friend *a book* for her birthday.
4. *Meiner Freundin habe ich ein Buch geschenkt zum Geburtstag.*
   I gave *my friend* a book for her birthday.

5. *Geschenkt habe ich meiner Freundin ein Buch zum Geburtstag.*
   I *gave* my friend a book for her birthday.

Thus, whereas German makes use of *word order* to stress different elements of a sentence, English often applies *intonation*.

In section 5.4.3, we looked at some of the intonational patterns of English which must be avoided when speaking German. One of the typical mistakes made by English speakers is to rely too heavily on intonation when trying to emphasise different parts of German sentences. This problem works both ways. Thus, when trying to transfer the very flexible patterns of German word order into English, it is sometimes necessary to change one's intonation. Of course, this only really applies with respect to the *spoken* language. Translating the above examples into *written* English would require different means, for example, the use of extra words or the perhaps even different orthographic conventions such as italics and underscoring.

It should be clear by now that many of the difficulties faced by English-speaking learners of German are not a question of the *inflexibility* of German word order, but its very *flexibility*. Occasionally, this flexibility is taken to extremes. So far, we have differentiated fairly clearly between syntactic and pragmatic ordering, but it is worth noting that even here there are areas of conflict. Sometimes, the possibilities for variation in German word order are so great, that pragmatic ordering begins to impinge upon the rules of syntactic ordering. Consider the following statements:

> *Ich habe Glück gehabt in meinen Prüfungen.*
> *Ich musste gehen wegen meinen Kopfschmerzen.*

These sentences break one of the basic rules of syntactic ordering: that of the verbal bracket (*Satzklammer*). This is because, in each case, central elements are occurring *outside of the verbal bracket*, a process known as ***Ausklammerung***:

INITIAL ELEMENT	OPENING BRACKET (FINITE VERB)	CLOSING BRACKET	CENTRAL ELEMENTS
	[	]	
Ich	habe	Glück gehabt	*in meinen Prüfungen.*
Ich	musste	gehen	*wegen meinen Kopfschmerzen.*

Ausklammerung, like most variation in German word order, is occurring here for pragmatic reasons. In this case, the adverbials, *in meinen Prüfungen* and *wegen meinen Kopfschmerzen*, are being placed in final position for extra emphasis. This is a typical feature of everyday spoken usage, although it is still fairly uncommon in written German. One possibility is that this kind of structure marks the beginning of the end of verbal bracketing, and a move towards the kind of word order more typical of English. On the other hand, it is equally likely that this is just a further example of the extreme flexibility which characterises German syntax.

Sources and recommended reading

- For an introduction to German syntax, see Chapter 5 of Fox (1990) and Chapter 8 of Russ (1994).
- Durrell (1992) provides an accessible summary of German grammar. See Chapter 5 for more information on the verbal bracket.
- See Durrell (1991) for detailed explanations of grammar and word order in German, and Durrell, Kohl and Loftus (1993) for self-study exercises.
- Kürschner (1989), Chapter 7, provides a good summary of syntax (in German).
- For general introductions to English syntax, see Chapter 16 of Crystal (1997) and Chapter 3 of Fromkin and Rodman (1993).
- Both Hurford (1994) and Wright and Hope (1996) contain detailed descriptions of English grammatical structures.

Exercises

1. Match the appropriate syntactic terms in Column A with the definitions in Column B.

COLUMN A	COLUMN B
1. verbal bracket	(a) It contains more than one clause.
2. constituent	(b) It surrounds the central elements of a German clause.
3. foregrounded rheme	(c) It sends the finite verb to the end of a German clause.
4. *Ausklammerung*	(d) The old information in a sentence.
5. theme	(e) It occurs when information is omitted to avoid unnecessary repetition.
6. subordinating conjunction	(f) One half of a complex sentence joined by *und* or *aber*.
7. ellipsis	(g) It occurs when new information is placed at the beginning of a clause or sentence.
8. main clause	(h) It occurs when central elements are placed outside the verbal bracket.
9. complex sentence	(i) It could be an adverb, a prepositional phrase or even a subordinate clause.
10. adverbial	(j) It consists of one or more words which belong together in a clause.

2. State whether the italicised phrases are objects (O) or complements (C) of the finite verb. In the case of objects, state whether they are accusative (AO) or dative (DO).

> *Example:*   Sie hat *eine sehr gute Ärztin.* (AO)
> Sie ist *eine sehr gute Ärztin.* (C)

1. Ich finde *es* nicht gut.
2. Er wollte immer *Lehrer* werden.
3. Hast du *Lust*?
4. Können Sie *die Arbeit* morgen machen?
5. Seid Ihr *Engländer*?
6. Sie wurden *sehr unglücklich.*
7. Sie bekamen *viel Geld* dafür.
8. Wir haben *ihr einen Brief* geschrieben.
9. Wir waren *ziemlich enttäuscht.*
10. *Mir* waren sie *sehr unsympathisch.*

3. Break down the sentences below into the following five types of constituent:

- Subject
- Verb (V1, V2, etc., if there is more than one verb)
- Object (Accusative Object/Dative Object)
- Complement
- Adverbial

Then say whether each constituent is a noun (N), pronoun (Pro), Determiner (Det), Verb (V), Preposition (Prep), Adjective (Adj), or Adverb (Adv).

> *Example:*   Heute ist das Wetter sehr schön.

Heute	ist	das Wetter	sehr schön.
Adverbial	Verb	Subject	Complement
(Adv)	(V)	(Det+N)	(Adv+Adj)

1. Es ist neu.
2. Wo wohnen Sie?
3. Ich mache es jetzt.
4. Sie ist eine sehr gute Schauspielerin.
5. Ich fahre Auto.
6. Sie hat dir das Buch vor zwei Wochen gekauft.
7. Hat sie es dir geschenkt?
8. Ich kann diese Frage nicht beantworten.
9. Diese Frage kann ich beantworten.
10. Mir gefällt das Buch.

4. Read, and make sure that you understand, the following passage. Then indicate whether the italicised phrases are subjects (S), objects (O), complements (C), or adverbials (A). In the case of objects, state whether they are accusative (AO), dative (DO), genitive (GO) or prepositional objects in the accusative (APO) or dative (DPO) case.

Wir ____ haben *schon im Sommer* ____ *einen Brief*____ *an das Wohnungsvermittlungsbüro Wippel und Co.*____ geschrieben: 'Sehr geehrte Herren! *Wir*____ sind *zwei Studentinnen*____, achtzehn und einundzwanzig Jahre alt, und *wir*____ werden *ab 1. Oktober dieses Jahres* ____ *in Wien* ____ leben. *Wir*____bitten *Sie*____, *uns*____ mitzuteilen, ob *Sie*____ *uns*____ beim Finden einer passenden Wohngelegenheit behilflich sein wollen. *Es*____ handelt sich *um zwei große, helle Zimmer*____, zentralgeheizt, evtl. Balkon, mit Telefon, in verkehrsgünstiger Grünlage, Bad und Küche, in Untermiete zu studentischem Preis. *In Erwartung Ihrer Nachricht* ____ grüßen *wir*____ *Sie*____ *mit vorzüglicher Hochachtung* ____.' Und *wir*____ haben *das Briefpapier* ___ aus dem Geschäft von Lores Vater verwendet, damit *sie*____ sehen, daß *wir*____ *aus gutem Haus*____ sind. Aber *das Vermittlungsbüro*____ hat *nicht* ____ geantwortet, und *jetzt* ____ sitzen *wir*____ *bei der Familie Krebich* ____.*

Source: *Der Mann fürs Leben* by Brigitte Schwaiger, Rororo, 1993

5. Read, and make sure you understand, the following film review from the youth magazine, *Bravo*.

FLIRTING WITH DISASTER
Abgefahrene Komödie

Der 30jährige Insektenforscher Mel, der bei Adoptiveltern aufgewachsen ist, will endlich seine leiblichen Eltern kennenlernen. Er beauftragt eine Detektei, seine Mutter und seinen Vater ausfindig zu machen. (1) *Bald erhält Mel die Nachricht, daß seine Eltern gefunden wurden.* (2) *Zusammen mit seinem kleinen Sohn und seiner Ehefrau Nancy, die von diesem Vorhaben nicht sehr begeistert ist, fährt Mel los.* (3) *Doch die beiden ersten Adressen erweisen sich als Computerfehler. Erst beim dritten Mal klappt es. Endlich steht Mel seinen Eltern Mary und Richard gegenüber.* (4) *Beide sind Künstler und leben als total ausgeflippte Hippies in einer Kleinstadt in New Mexico.* (5) *Mel lernt auch seinen schrägen Bruder Lonnie kennen.* Lonnie setzt alles daran, um Mel schnell wieder aus dem Haus zu haben. Die Situation spitzt sich zu, als der entsetzte Mel erfährt, daß sein Vater vor 20 Jahren wegen Drogenmißbrauch im Gefängnis gesessen hat. Gefühlsstarke und witzige Familienkomödie, frei ab 12 Jahren.

Source: *Bravo*, 27.6.96

Now describe the five sentences in italics indicated using the following terms where relevant:

- simple sentence
- complex sentence
- main clause
- subordinate clause
- relative clause
- coordinating conjunction
- subordinating conjunction

*Example: Der 30jährige Insektenforscher Mel, der bei Adoptiveltern auf-
gewachsen ist, will endlich seine leiblichen Eltern kennenlernen* can
be described as follows:

Complex sentence. Main clause: *Der 30jährige Insektenforscher
Mel will endlich seine leiblichen Eltern kennenlernen.* Relative
clause embedded within the main clause: *der bei Adoptiveltern
aufgewachsen ist.*

8

The meaning of German words

In Chapter 6, we saw how linguists traditionally explore words into two main areas: *grammar* and *meaning*. Morphology is concerned with the grammar of words. Here we now turn to the meaning of words, the branch of linguistics known as **semantics**.

Whenever we acquire a new word in a foreign language, it is not only the form of that word which must be learned (i.e. its pronunciation, grammar, and spelling), but also the meaning. Having said this, how do we actually learn meaning? Let us take the example of *Hund*. If you are a native speaker of German, and are hearing the word *Hund* for the first time, you will probably learn its meaning by association with a furry animal which barks. Foreign learners of a language can also acquire meaning in this way. Frequently, however, they try to make comparisons with their mother tongue, i.e., they hear a word such as *Hund* and want to know its English translation. They then measure their understanding of a new word in terms of whether or not they have found a semantic equivalent in their own language. This is perfectly natural thing to do, but it is not without its problems.

In many cases, finding semantic equivalents for words in German and English is easy: the translation of *Hund* is clearly 'dog'. Similarly, a German phrase such as *vor die Hunde gehen* is readily comprehensible because it draws on a similar image to the English expression 'to go to the dogs'. But what exactly is *kalter Hund*? A 'cold dog'? The opposite of a 'hot dog' perhaps? The answer is neither, and no amount of searching for an English equivalent will help you. Even the Oxford–Duden German–English dictionary cannot provide a direct translation. Instead, it describes or paraphrases *kalter Hund* as a colloquial term for 'a gateau consisting of layers of biscuit and chocolate-flavoured filling'!

We are beginning to see that the ways in which we learn meaning and, by implication, the study of semantics, is not always straightforward. One reason for this is because meaning draws on areas of knowledge which might appear to be 'outside' of the system of language itself. For example, understanding words is often a question of experience. If you have eaten something called *kalter Hund* at some point, then you will have no difficulty comprehending the term. Similarly, a familiarity with the culture of the country will help you acquire new vocabulary more easily. Thus, if you know a lot about the German-speaking countries, you are more likely to understand (and remember) the term *kalter Hund,* even if you have never experienced the pleasure of actually eating one.

Because meaning is so closely linked to concepts such as experience and culture, the study of semantics is a fascinating way of gaining insights into the world-view of the people who speak a particular language. By analysing the vocabulary or **lexicon** of a language, it is possible to learn a great deal about the way in which speakers perceive and structure their surroundings. Yet semantics has traditionally been neglected by linguistics because some scholars have felt that meaning, experience, and culture are too 'vague' to be studied in a systematic way. As a result, semantics tends to have been dealt with by philosophers, while linguists have concentrated on those aspects of language which are more stable and predictable.

It is not difficult to see why linguists should have preferred to study some aspects of language more than others. It is relatively uncomplicated to describe the phonemes and morphemes of a language in so far as these are unlikely to change significantly over a short period of time. Stable linguistic elements such as these constitute what is known in linguistics as a **closed set**. Words and their meanings, by comparison, are much less predictable. New words are constantly being created or loaned from other languages and, to complicate matters further, words which already exist may even begin to mean something else. Unlike phonemes and morphemes, therefore, the lexicon of a language constitutes what is termed an **open set**.

Having said this, it is not true that the meanings of words are completely unstructured simply because they are subject to fluctuation and change. In this chapter, we shall look at some of the ways in which the vocabulary of German is organised, and then make some comparisons with English. Before we do so, however, we will need to consider some of the more general problems associated with finding a suitable definition of meaning.

8.1   Problems with meaning

We have already seen how, for many learners of foreign languages, understanding the meaning of a word is often a question of finding a semantic equivalent or translation. However, when young children are learning to speak for the first time, they do not use dictionaries or compare the meanings of words with those of another language. Clearly, therefore, meaning cannot be a question of simply translating from one language to another. But, if not, what is it? In this section, we shall try to answer this question by looking at some of the different definitions of meaning which have been proposed.

8.1.1 *Where is meaning?*

Let us begin by asking what might seem to be a rather strange question: 'Where is meaning?' In other words, which part of language actually contains meaning? There are at least four possible answers:

- pronunciation
- writing
- words
- sentences

We will now look at each of these definitions individually.

PRONUNCIATION

Is it possible that the meaning of a word is somehow related to its pronunciation? Consider the following pairs of English and German words:

> bear/bare
> *Leere/Lehre* (emptiness/teaching)

The two words in each of these pairs are pronounced in exactly the same way. However, each word means something quite different. Pairs of words such as these are known in linguistics as **homophones**. Because it is possible for two words to have the same pronunciation but different meanings, we can see that the meaning of a word cannot really be contained in its sounds. If this were the case, every single word of a given language would have to be pronounced differently.

Having said this, there is one particular type of word where sounds *are* related to meaning. Consider the following:

> swish/slosh
> *knattern/rasseln* (to clatter/rattle)

These are examples of what is known as **onomatopoeia**. In onomatopoeic words, the sounds themselves are attempting to mimic that which is being described – a process which is nicely captured by German term, *Lautmalerei*, literally: 'painting with sounds'. One group of sounds commonly used in this way are so-called **sibilants** such as /s/, /z/, /ʒ/, /ç/, /ts/, and /ʃ/. These are often employed to imitate running water, for example, or the hissing of a snake.

WRITING

Is it possible that meaning is somehow linked to orthography, i.e. the way in which words are written? Consider the following English and German examples. What do they mean?

wind
überholen

In each case, there are two possibilities. 'Wind' (pronounced [wɪnd]) can mean 'air-flow', e.g. 'there's a lot of wind today'. Alternatively, 'wind' (pronounced [waɪnd]) describes a 'movement', e.g. 'I must wind up the clock'. Similarly, *'überholen* (first syllable stressed) is a separable verb meaning 'to keel over', as in *das Schiff holte über*. This compares to *über'holen* (third syllable stressed), which is an inseparable verb meaning 'to overtake', as in *ich überholte das andere Auto*.

Words such as these, which are written the same but have different meanings are known as **homographs**. From these examples, we can see that meaning cannot be linked to orthography otherwise every single word in a language would have to be spelled differently.

WORDS

Is it possible that the meaning of a word is somehow connected to the object to which it refers? This may seem a rather perplexing question, but consider the following:

(a)   (b)

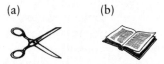

We would probably have no difficulty agreeing that picture (a) represents a pair of scissors and (b) a book. In linguistics, the words 'scissors' and 'book' are called the **signifier**. By contrast, the objects to which they refer, and which are represented visually by the images above, are known as the **signified**.

But is there any real reason why these objects *must* be referred to as 'scissors' and 'book'? Imagine, for example, that they had been labelled as follows:

(a) BOOK   (b) SCISSORS

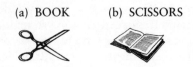

Even though this might seem rather strange, surely the English language would not cease to function simply because these two objects had been given different names? We would merely call a book 'scissors', and a pair of scissors would be known as a 'book'. Similarly, we all know that as soon as we begin to learn a foreign language, different words (or signifiers) are used to describe the same objects (or signifieds). Hence, the object for reading which we have been discussing here is known as a 'book' in English, whereas in German it is referred to as *Buch*, and in French as *livre*.

It was the Swiss linguist Ferdinand de Saussure (1857–1913) who stressed the importance of this phenomenon, which he described as *the arbitrary relationship between the signifier and the signified*. He argued that there is no real link between a given word and the object to which it refers. By implication, this means that meaning is not ultimately related to *words* themselves.

SENTENCES

If the meaning of words cannot be found in pronunciation, writing, or the words themselves, maybe it is necessary to look at larger units of language. Perhaps meaning becomes apparent when words occur in whole phrases or sentences? This was certainly the case with the earlier examples of 'wind' and *überholen*, but what about the following two German phrases?:

> *Da liegt der Hund begraben.*
> (Literally: that's where the dog is buried.)
> *Dort sagen sich Fuchs und Hase 'gute Nacht'.*
> (Literally: that's where the fox and the hare say 'good night'.)

These kinds of phrases are known as **idioms**, and no amount of translating the individual words into English will help you to predict the meaning of the whole sentence. In fact, the first idiom means: 'that's the root of the problem', whereas the second suggests: 'it's in the middle of nowhere'.

A similar problem applies to the following examples:

> *Er ist ein richtiger Elefant.*
> *Sie ist ein richtiger Affe.*

Here, the words *Elefant* and *Affe* are not to be understood literally – they are **metaphors**. Each animal symbolises a particular quality which is then being transferred to the human beings in question. In order to understand these sentences, you therefore need to know that elephants are often considered to be clumsy, and that monkeys are a bit crazy or stupid. Interestingly, many people associate the use of metaphors with only very literary language. To a certain extent, this is not surprising since they are indeed an important tool in more creative forms of writing. However, from the examples we have looked at, we can see that metaphors are also very much a part of the way we use language in everyday situations.

In conclusion, idioms and metaphors demonstrate how the meaning of a sentence may consist of more than the sum of its parts. In order to understand some sentences, therefore, you will need to know more than just the meaning of the individual words of which they are comprised.

8.1.2   *What is meaning?*

It should be clear by now that it is not really possible to locate meaning in any one particular area of the language system. In other words, meaning is not exclusively linked to sounds, writing, individual words or even whole sentences. Is it therefore possible that we have been asking the wrong question? Perhaps it would be more useful to ask: '*What* is meaning?'

One answer to this question is that meaning refers to an *object*. To go back to an earlier example, we can say that the signifier 'scissors' refers to an object with which paper or other types of materials can be cut. The signifier 'book', on the other hand, designates a number of printed pages bound together along one side and which can be read.

However, not all words refer to tangible objects such as scissors and books. For example, how would you define 'ghosts'? Most people would claim never to have seen a real ghost, but we can still talk about them quite easily. And what about so-called abstract nouns such as 'fear' or 'injustice'? We all think we know what they mean, but we cannot buy them at the local shop. Perhaps it is therefore better to say that words refer to *concepts* rather than simply to objects.

So far we have only looked at nouns. But what about other classes of word such as prepositions or adverbs? Clearly, these kinds of words do not refer to objects, so again the term 'concept' might seem more useful. But now try to think of the concepts associated with the preposition 'below' or the adverb 'quickly'. How do you actually *imagine* a concept? One of the things we often do is to create a mental picture which illustrates the concept. So, for example, we might think of a cat sitting under a table in order to describe 'below'. Or, in the case of 'quickly', we might visualise a fast car. But if this is true, then there is a problem: if we need to refer to objects in order to explain concepts, what, ultimately, is the difference between an object and a concept?

The most appropriate way forward is to say that every word has a **referent**, i.e. an object or concept to which it *refers*. But here we have a different kind of problem. For example, if a number of different people hear the word *car*, will each person necessarily think of the same object? Surely, some might picture a Mini whereas others will think of a Mercedes. However, this is not so serious because Minis and Mercedes are simply different types of cars. The issue becomes more acute when we are dealing with abstract nouns. Thus, the word 'fear' can conjure up very different referents in the minds of individuals. For one person, 'fear' might be symbolised by a spider whereas for another it is the thought of being alone. Definitions of 'injustice' can be even more controversial. For the boss of Company X, this might mean receiving only a £100,000 bonus when the boss of Company Y is getting £150,000. For the employees of those companies, however, having to manage with a pay freeze in the same financial year might appear to be a better example of 'injustice'.

The problem, it seems, is that we can never really be certain that we are all using the same words for the same referents. There is always the very real possibility that different people are using different words to describe the same thing – or even the same words for different things. Moreover, how can we ever really be sure that other people mean the same as we do? We are beginning to see why the study of meaning has often been considered a branch of philosophy rather than linguistics.

There is an interesting experiment which can be carried out in order to illustrate this point. Fig. 8.1 contains pictures of five objects. First of all, a group of native English speakers were asked how they would refer to each of the five objects. Then a group of native German speakers were asked to do the same.

Fig. 8.1 Chairs
(Adapted from Crystal, 1997: 102)

Here are their various replies:

OBJECT	ENGLISH	GERMAN
(a)	cushion, seat, sofa, couch, chair, sofa-bed	Sessel, Polster, Sofa, Couch, Sofabett, Sitzelement
(b)	chair	Stuhl, Sessel
(c)	chair, seat	Sessel, Stuhl, Hocker
(d)	chair, dining chair	Stuhl, Sessel
(e)	armchair, sofa	Sessel, Klubsessel, Fauteuil, Lehnstuhl

This experiment reveals two things: first of all, the English native speakers were largely unable to agree on exactly which word to use in order to describe each object, and the answers given by the German native speakers were equally varied. This provides a further illustration of the point made by Saussure regarding the arbitrary relationship between the signifier and the signified. This is because if the relationship between words and their referents were fixed, then there could only be one possible term for each of the five objects in English, and one in German – or, strictly speaking, only five words altogether, since if the relationship were entirely fixed there would only be one world language.

Second, the fact that the English and German speakers could not agree among themselves on what to call these objects has implications for anyone trying to learn German. Because there is often no fixed relationship between the signifier and the signified in any one single language, it is clearly very difficult to find perfect translations between, say, English and German, which will be appropriate in every context. For example, learners of German are usually taught that the word for 'chair' is *der Stuhl,* and that an 'armchair' is *der Sessel.* But in Austria *der Sessel* is in fact a 'chair' whereas *das Fauteuil* is used for 'armchair'.

This takes us back to what was said earlier about the lack of semantic equivalence between different languages. One of the reasons why there are not always clear translations between, say, English and German is because of the variation which exists within each individual language. In the case of *Stuhl/Sessel,* we can see how variation in usage between Germany and Austria leads to a lack of semantic equivalence with English. Likewise, differences between British and American English will present German-speaking learners of English with similar problems.

All of this uncertainty regarding meaning might sound very frustrating for anyone trying to learn a foreign language. You may well ask whether it is ever possible to learn new vocabulary. In fact, you might even begin to wonder how languages function at all. Fortunately, however, there is one very simple solution to the problem of defining meaning. This can be summed up in a famous quotation from the Austrian philosopher, Ludwig Wittgenstein (1889–1951):

'The meaning of a word is in its use in the language.'

By this, Wittgenstein was drawing attention to the fact that words do, of course, make sense. However, their meanings only really become clear in the specific contexts in which they are being used. To go back to the pictures in Fig. 8.1, we can see that, in practice, there would be no difficulty knowing which word to use for which object. Take object (a), for example. Many of those asked could not decide whether this was a sofa-bed or couch. But in a real-life situation, this dilemma would probably not arise. Were the informants to see that particular object in the context of a bedroom or a sitting room, then they would have immediately known which word to use. Moreover, how often are most of us asked to find five different names for five different types of chair? There are clearly many situations where we can just say 'chair' and be perfectly understood.

We have begun to see how the meaning of words cannot really be separated from the **context** in which they are used. In Chapter 6 on syntax, we also looked at the ways in which word order can vary according to the specific situation in which a sentence is being uttered. In section 8.2.4 and in Chapters 9 and 10, we shall go into the relationship between context and meaning in even greater detail.

8.2   The structure of meaning

So far in this chapter, we have tried to define the meaning of words in terms of their referents, that is, the objects and concepts to which they refer. As we have seen, however, such an approach is not without its problems. This is because the relationship between words and their referents is not always predictable, and the different contexts in which the same words are used often leads to variations in meaning. To study meaning in this way, it would probably be necessary to analyse every single word of a language in every single context in which it might occur – something which is clearly not possible. It is for this kind of reason that linguists have tried to find an alternative approach to the study of meaning.

In semantics, an important distinction is made between what is known as **reference** and **sense relations**. Reference explores the meanings of words in relation to their referents. Sense relations, on the other hand, looks at the ways in which the meanings of words are structured *vis-à-vis* one another. Let us look at a specific example in order to illustrate what is meant by this. Consider the following lexical items:

black, red, white, yellow, brown, ruby, blue, scarlet

These words are clearly related to one another. They form what is known in linguistics as a **semantic field**, i.e. a group of words which has some aspect of meaning in common. In this case, the semantic property which the words share is 'colour'. However, the sense relations which obtain within this group of colours are not identical. So, for example, the relationship between 'red/yellow/blue' is not the same as between 'red/ruby/scarlet'. Likewise, 'ruby' and 'scarlet' are structured in a different way to 'black' and 'white'.

Depending on whether we analyse this group of colours in terms of reference or sense relations, we can pose rather different questions about their meanings. If we study their reference, we might ask: 'What is red?' or 'What is black?' In other words: 'What types of colours do we refer to as red or black?' Such questions are, however, concerned with perceptions of the physical world, and are therefore very difficult to answer from the point of view of a linguist. If, on the other hand, we study the sense relations between these words, we would be more likely to ask: 'What is the relationship between black and white?' or 'Is the status of red, scarlet, and ruby equal?' This approach gives us a much more tangible way of analysing meaning. It also allows us to make comparisons between the semantic structures of different languages. This, in turn, can provide us with insights into the ways in which speakers of certain languages perceive the world which surrounds them, allowing us to explore the ways in which those perceptions may be similar or different to our own.

In this section, we shall be looking at the following different types of sense relations:

synonymy	–	sameness of meaning
hyponymy	–	inclusion of meaning
incompatibility	–	exclusion of meaning
antonymy	–	opposition of meaning
homonymy/polysemy	–	multiplicity of meaning

8.2.1　Synonymy

Synonymy is one of the most familiar types of sense relation, and is concerned with the way in which certain words appear to mean the same as others. We probably all think we know what **synonyms** are, and most of us have at some point used dictionaries of synonyms such as *Roget's Thesaurus*. However, once you begin to analyse this particular sense relation more closely, the idea of 'sameness' of meaning is not as clear as it might initially appear. Let us begin by looking at some examples of German synonyms:

> *Sonnabend/Samstag*
> *Linguistik/Sprachwissenschaft*
> *Apfelsine/Orange*
> *Metzger/Schlachter/Fleischer/Fleischhacker*

The above words would seem to be clear examples of synonymy. But to be absolutely sure that they mean the same thing, there is a simple test that can be carried out:

> *Es ist Sonnabend aber nicht Samstag.*
> *Sie studiert Linguistik aber keine Sprachwissenschaft.*
> *Das ist eine Apfelsine aber keine Orange.*
> *Er ist Metzger aber kein Schlachter/Fleischer/Fleischhacker.*

In these examples, we have constructed sentences which try to show that '*a* is not equal to *b*'. However, the sentences do not make sense because '*a is* equal to *b*'. We can therefore safely conclude that, in each case, the words constitute synonyms.

By comparison, the pairs of words underlined in the following sentences are not synonymous. Hence, when the same test is applied, the sentences still make sense (even if they do sound rather strange):

> *Es ist <u>Sonnabend</u> aber nicht <u>Sonntag</u>.*
> *Sie studiert <u>Linguistik</u> aber keine <u>Biologie</u>.*
> *Das ist eine <u>Apfelsine</u> aber keine <u>Banane</u>.*
> *Er ist <u>Metzger</u> aber kein <u>Elektriker</u>.*

Sometimes, relationships of synonymy are more subtle. Consider, for example, the words *Frau* and *Dame*. These clearly have the same referent i.e. 'adult female' but the test for synonymy does not quite work:

> *Sie ist eine Frau aber keine Dame.*
> *Sie ist eine Dame aber keine Frau.*

In this case, it is possible to be a *Frau* (woman) without being a *Dame* (lady), but it is not possible to be a *Dame* without being a *Frau*. There is therefore a different relationship of synonymy here involving *inclusion* of meaning, which we shall explore further in the next section. In the meantime, we must conclude that *Frau* and *Dame* cannot be considered *absolute* synonyms but that they are certainly *near* synonyms.

Now look at the following three words, all of which mean 'to die':

> *sterben, entschlafen, krepieren.*

Again, what we find here is that the referent is the same, but that there is a different relationship of inclusion. You cannot, for example, say:

> *Er ist entschlafen aber nicht gestorben.*
> *Sie ist krepiert aber nicht gestorben.*

whereas you could theoretically say (even if they do sound very strange):

Er ist gestorben aber nicht entschlafen.
Sie ist gestorben aber nicht krepiert.

However, a further difference between these three words relates to the contexts in which it would be appropriate to use them. Thus, *sterben* is the neutral term for 'die' whereas *entschlafen* is highly euphemistic and would be more akin to the English 'pass away'. *Krepieren* is either used for animals or, colloquially, to describe humans dying in an animal-like state, e.g. 'to snuff it'. Clearly, therefore, the following sentences would not normally be stylistically appropriate:

*Meine beste Freundin ist gestern Nacht krepiert.
*Meine Katze ist überfahren worden und ist entschlafen.

Where the meanings of words differ in this way, semantics makes a crucial distinction between **denotation** and **connotation**. Denotation refers to the referent or what the word actually means, in this case, 'die'. Connotation, on the other hand, refers to the additional meanings carried by a word when it is used in a particular context, in this case, whether it conveys respect or sorrow, etc. This distinction has important implications for anyone trying to learn new vocabulary in a foreign language. This is because understanding the possible connotations of a word is just as important as learning its denotation. Thus, although they are in one sense synonymous, using *entschlafen* and *krepieren* in the wrong contexts could have very serious consequences.

We are beginning to see how even words which look like synonyms are not necessarily interchangeable when we try to use them in practice. Another situation where this applies is with foreign loans and their German equivalents:

Telefon – *Fernsprecher*
Computer – *Rechner*

Facts – *Tatsachen*
PR – *Öffentlichkeitsarbeit*

Again, these words constitute four pairs of synonyms. However, while their denotation might be the same, their connotations vary. In the first two cases, it is the foreign words *Telefon* and *Computer* which are more common, whereas the German terms *Fernsprecher* and *Rechner* would probably be used in technical contexts, perhaps by people who work with telephones or computers. In the second two examples, the reverse is true. The German *Tatsachen* and *Öffentlichkeitsarbeit* are the unmarked terms, whereas the English loans *Facts* and *PR* would be more likely to be used by journalists or marketing managers. The words may therefore carry connotations associated with those particular groups of speakers.

But there is another reason why foreign words are not necessarily synonymous with their German equivalents. Consider the following example: *klug – clever*. It might seem as though these two words mean the same thing. But foreign loans are often false friends. It is important to realise that when one language borrows from another, it does so for a particular reason: to introduce shades of meaning which cannot be conveyed by existing words. Thus, why should German incorporate the English word *clever* into its lexicon if this is going to be totally synonymous with a German word which already exists such as *klug*? It follows then that the English loan 'clever' will have different connotations to the German word *klug*. While it certainly still means 'clever', it also has the additional sense of 'sly', 'witty' or 'smart'. Clearly, native speakers of English must be doubly careful when employing such loans in German. This is because the connotations of an English word will not necessarily the same when used in English and German.

Another reason why potential synonyms may be used differently relates to regional variation within a language. To go back to the earlier example of *Metzger/Schlachter/Fleischer/Fleischhacker,* we can say that all of these words are roughly the equivalent of 'butcher' in English. However, you would be unlikely to find a *Fleischhacker* in northern Germany or a *Schlachter* or *Fleischer* in southern Germany, Switzerland, and Austria. Other examples of regional variation in the use of potential synonyms are *Sonnabend/Samstag, Apfelsine/Orange,* and *Stuhl/Sessel,* the first term in each pair being more common in the north, the second in the south.

Finally, it is not only foreign loans and regional variation which may affect potential synonymy but also the historical context in which words may have been used. Consider, for example, the following pair of words: *Euthanasie – Sterbehilfe*. In terms of their denotation, these words are synonymous: they both refer to 'euthanasia', the act of killing people painlessly usually to relieve them from a terminal illness. However, they are not interchangeable in German. This is because the first term, *Euthanasie*, was used by the National Socialists to denote a programme of mass extermination of those people whom the regime considered to be unworthy of life, most notably, those with some kind of physical or mental disability. Ever since that time *Euthanasie* has carried with it the connotations of that particular policy. Needless to say, all discussions of euthanasia are still especially problematical in Germany, but where the practice is discussed, say, in a medical context, the term *Sterbehilfe* tends to be used. This one simple example illustrates how it is unlikely that you will understand the connotations of words if you do not know the contexts in which they are used or have been used in the past. This is why it is ultimately not possible to learn a language without reference to the history and politics of the countries in which it is spoken.

8.2.2 Hyponymy

We have already explored a number of reasons why even words which are technically synonymous tend to mean different things when used in practice.

Frequently, this is because words have the same denotation but different connotations as in the examples of:

Frau, Dame
sterben, entschlafen, krepieren

However, these two groups of words are not merely synonyms (or near synonyms), they also illustrate an additional kind of sense relation. Thus, we said that these sentences do not make sense:

*Sie ist eine Dame aber keine Frau.
*Er ist entschlafen aber nicht gestorben.
*Sie ist krepiert aber nicht gestorben.

whereas the following were theoretically possible, even if they sound very strange (whereby the last two are more marked than the first):

Sie ist eine Frau aber keine Dame.
Er ist gestorben aber nicht entschlafen.
Sie ist gestorben aber nicht krepiert.

What we are dealing with here is the sense relation known as **hyponymy**. Whereas synonymy is concerned with sameness of meaning, hyponymy is about *inclusion* of meaning. In other words, all *Damen* are *Frauen,* though not all *Frauen* are *Damen.* Similarly, all 'acts of dying' come under the heading *sterben,* whereas not every death can be referred to as *entschlafen* or *krepieren.* This relationship can also be expressed in the form of tree diagrams:

In each of these cases, we can differentiate between two types of lexical item. The word which heads the tree is known as the **superordinate term**. The words included under that heading are known as **hyponyms**. In the above examples, we can therefore say that *Frau* and *sterben* are the superordinate terms, whereas *Dame* and *entschlafen/krepieren* are the hyponyms.

However, a word is not always simply a hyponym *or* a superordinate term. Sometimes, it can be both. Take a look at the following tree diagram:

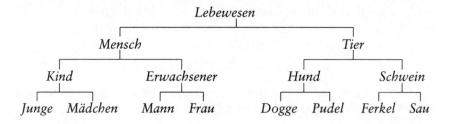

There are two main points which can be made on the basis of this diagram. First of all, we can observe how some words within this group function simultaneously as superordinates and hyponyms e.g. *Mensch, Tier, Kind, Erwachsener, Hund,* and *Schwein.*

Second, we can also see that some words share a similar status within the hierarchy e.g.:

> *Mensch/Tier*
> *Kind/Erwachsener/Hund/Schwein*
> *Junge/Mädchen/Mann/Frau/Dogge/Pudel/Ferkel/Sau*

These words, which occur on the same level within the diagram, are said to be **co-hyponyms** in relation to one another.

Relationships of hyponymy are not, however, always as logically structured as the examples we have looked at so far. Sometimes, there are **lexical gaps**. In the following cases, one word functions as both the hyponym *and* the superordinate:

There are two ways of looking at this. On the one hand, we could say that there is no specific term for a female cat or a male dog, and this is why the superordinate term *Katze* and *Hund* is used. Or we could take the opposite view and argue that there is no superordinate term for cat and dog, and that the hyponyms *Katze* and *Hund* have therefore been elevated to the status of superordinate.

But at least in the case of cats and dogs, there is actually both a superordinate and a hyponym available – even if they are the same. In the following example, there is a very definite lexical gap where the superordinate is concerned. Thus, while there is a term available to describe different types of 'movement', there is no single word which denotes 'the act of being stationary':

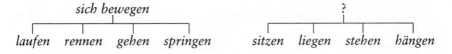

8.2.3   Incompatibility and antonymy

In the previous section, we saw how *sameness* of meaning is sometimes related to *inclusion* of meaning. In this section, we shall see how inclusion is also related to *exclusion* of meaning, and how exclusion sometimes leads to *opposition* of meaning. In order to explore how this is so, we need take a look at some more co-hyponyms, that is, words which share the same superordinate term. Consider the following:

In this example, there is no conflict of meaning between the co-hyponyms *Musiker* and *Tourist*. It is perfectly possible to be a musician and a tourist at the same time. We can therefore say that the relationship between the two words is one of **compatibility**.

Now take a look at the following:

Here the relationship between the co-hyponyms is different. Because it is not possible for a piece of furniture to be a *Tisch* and a *Bett* at the same time, we can say that there is conflict of meaning. Thus, the relationship between the two words is one of **incompatibility**.

While we can certainly say that *Tisch* is not the same as *Bett*, what we cannot say is that the two are opposites. *Tisch* and *Bett* are simply two types of furniture which could be taken from a long list of alternatives. The only thing they really have in common is the fact that they share the same superordinate term, *Möbelstück*.

Sometimes, however, incompatibility does lead to opposition of meaning as in the following case:

Schwein
Eber   Sau

This time, we can say that the two co-hyponyms *are* mutually exclusive. If an adult pig is not an *Eber* (boar), then it must ordinarily be a *Sau* (sow). The sense relation between these two words is therefore one of opposition or **antonymy**.

However, not all antonyms are characterised by the same type of opposition. There are at least three different ways in which this particular sense relation functions. Consider, first of all, the following pair of words:

wahr – falsch

In this case, we can say that 'what is not *a* is necessarily *b*'. So, for example, if something is *nicht wahr*, then it must be *falsch*, or if something is *nicht falsch*, then it must be *wahr*. Opposites such as these are known as **complementaries** or **complementary pairs**. They are probably the closest thing to true antonyms in a language. One important feature of complementaries is that it is not possible to grade them: something cannot be **wahrer* or **sehr falsch*. For this reason, complementaries are also sometimes referred to as **non-gradable antonyms**.

Non-gradable antonyms compare to the second group of opposites, which are known as **gradable antonyms**:

> *lang – kurz*
> *groß – klein*

Here the relationship of opposition is different. Just because something is not *lang* does not necessarily mean that it is *kurz*. Similarly, something which is not *groß* does not have to be *klein*. As their name suggests, gradable antonyms can be graded: it is therefore possible to speak of *länger, kürzer, nicht sehr groß, sehr klein*, etc. Rather than see these types of words as total opposites, it is probably better to think of them in terms of a continuum with a variety of intermediary stages.

Finally, the third group of antonyms are so-called **relational opposites** or **converse terms**, for example:

> *kaufen/verkaufen*
> *Lehrer/Schüler*

These types of antonyms display symmetry in their meaning. Thus, if *a* buys something from *b*, then *b* has necessarily sold something to *a*. Just as in English, nouns which are relational opposites in German often employ the suffix *-er* in order to indicate this relationship.

Understanding which type of antonym is being used can often help when formulating certain types of sentences. It is important to realise that not all antonyms can be used when constructing questions. With complementaries, it is possible to form so-called 'yes–no interrogatives' (see 7.2.1). You can therefore ask:

> *Ist es wahr?*
> *War sie anwesend?*

However, complementaries cannot be used in 'w-interrogatives':

> **Wie wahr ist es?*
> **Wie anwesend war sie?*

By comparison, it is possible to form w-interrogatives with gradable antonyms, although you still need to know which of the pair will be used:

Wie lang ist es? (NOT *Wie kurz?*)
Wie groß ist es? (NOT *Wie klein?*)

From these examples, we can say that *lang* and *groß* constitute the unmarked terms, whereas *kurz* and *klein* are marked. Whilst it is nonetheless possible to ask *Wie kurz ist es?* or *Wie klein ist es?*, you would need a special context in which to do so. Furthermore, note that it is customary for the unmarked term to be the one which indicates the greater size, for example, *Wie breit?* (as opposed to *Wie eng?*) or *Wie schwer?* (as opposed to *Wie leicht?*).

8.2.4   Polysemy, homonymy and collocation

In this section we will look at some further types of sense relations where words display a *multiplicity* of meanings. Consider the following sentences:

Er setzte sich auf die Bank.
Er ging in die Bank, um Geld zu holen.

In these examples, the word *Bank* has two quite distinct meanings. In the first sentence, it is being used in the sense of a 'bench', whereas in the second, it is a 'financial institution'. When two words have the same pronunciation (and often the same spelling) but *clearly different* meanings, this is known as **homonymy**. Homonyms include homophones (same pronunciation, different meaning) and homographs (same spelling, different meaning) which were discussed in 8.1.1. An English homonym would be the word 'bat' as in 'the animal', 'the stick' or 'to bat one's eyelids'.

In theory, of course, homonyms could lead to **ambiguity** or vagueness of meaning in language. In practice, however, this is not normally the case because the context tends to clarify in which sense the word is being used. Thus, we can deduce which meaning of *Bank* is intended in the above sentences since it is not customary to sit on a financial institution, and it is not normally possible to fetch money from a bench!

Now look at the following:

Shakespeare war ein großer Dramatiker.
Ich trinke ein großes Bier.

In these two sentences, the word *groß* also has more than one meaning. But this time, the different meanings are quite close to one another, i.e. they both indicate 'size', either metaphorically or literally. When the same word has *different but related* meanings, this is known in linguistics as **polysemy**. An example of polysemy in English would be the word 'face', which could mean the face of a person, a building or a clock. With polysemy, there is less potential for ambiguity than with homonymy precisely because the different meanings are quite similar. Where there might be confusion, however, the context will clarify in which sense the word is being used.

Homonymy and polysemy present enormous difficulties for both compilers and users of dictionaries. How lexicographers deal with these problems will depend on the type of dictionary they are editing and the needs of its users. For example, where homonymy is concerned, bilingual dictionaries tend to number and then translate the words separately. Thus, under *Bank,* you would probably find two entries as follows:

> *Bank*[1] = bench
> *Bank*[2] = bank, financial institution

By contrast, in the case of polysemy the possible translations tend to be listed, and an attempt is made to indicate the different contexts in which the word can be used:

> *groß* = big, large (*house, window, room, etc.*), large (*pack, size, can, etc.*); great (*length, person, etc.*); tall (*person*) etc.

This leads us to a further point about the way in which different words will be used in different contexts. If someone were to ask you for the English translation of *groß,* you would probably reply: 'big'. Indeed, this is the first word listed in the possible translations above. Yet in the context of the phrases we have already discussed, a different English adjective is clearly needed, e.g:

> *ein großer Dramatiker* = a *great* dramatist
> *ein großes Bier* = a *large* beer

It is part of your knowledge about English which tells you which adjectives of size can be used with the two nouns 'dramatist' and 'beer'. You therefore know that the adjective 'great' will be used in conjunction with 'dramatist', whereas 'beer' will be accompanied by 'large'. The way in which some words typically occur together with others is known in linguistics as **collocation** or the 'company words keep'. When speaking your native language, you can generally rely upon your instinct to tell you which collocations are appropriate. However, because words do not always keep the same company in different languages, this is precisely the kind of instinctive knowledge which you tend not to have in the early stages of learning a foreign language.

Let us continue to use the example of 'beer' to explore this point further. An English speaker will generally be familiar with the company this word keeps. So, for example, you might order a 'half' or a 'pint'. Furthermore, you can describe beer as 'cold, warm, gassy, flat, bitter, mild', etc. However, in the German-speaking countries beer is brewed differently. It also tastes different and is served in glasses of different shapes and sizes to its English counterpart. As a result, the word *Bier* keeps rather different company to 'beer'.

But how can you find about the type of collocations which typically occur in German? Unfortunately, it is not normally within the remit of bilingual dictionaries to present you with this kind of information. This is where a different kind of reference book is useful such as the *Duden Stilwörterbuch*. If you look up the word *Bier*, this book will tell you that the following adjectives can occur *after* the noun:

> Das Bier ist frisch, gut, gepflegt, süffig, bitter, abgestanden, schal
> Beer is fresh, good, choice, drinkable, bitter, flat, stale

and that the following adjectives are typically used *before* the noun:

> helles, dunkles, einfaches, starkes Bier
> light, dark, simple, strong beer

It will also indicate which verbs tend to be used in conjunction with the noun:

> Bier brauen, zapfen, ausschenken
> to brew, tap, pour beer

From these examples, we can see a further reason why it is not always easy to find exact semantic equivalents between different languages. Because the culture of beer and beer-drinking is different in the German-speaking countries, the company *Bier* keeps in German sometimes varies from the company which is typically kept by its English counterpart 'beer'. This is why it sounds odd, for example, to speak of 'fresh' or 'choice' beer in English or *flaches* or *mildes Bier* in German. All of this brings us back to the point discussed in the introduction to this chapter, namely, that the meanings of words are closely related to the culture in which they are used. So the ability to find the appropriate collocations for German words tends to be closely related to your own knowledge and experience of that culture.

Here, we have looked at homonymy and polysemy in order to illustrate the ways in which the meanings of words cannot really be separated from the contexts in which they are used. Similarly, by studying collocation or the company words keep, we have seen how the varying contexts in which words occur in different languages sometimes leads to a lack of semantic equivalence between those languages. But what are the practical consequences of all this for a student who is attempting to learn new vocabulary in a foreign language?

Many students try to memorise new vocabulary by compiling lists of words alongside their English translations. In the early stages of acquiring a foreign language this is probably quite useful, for example, when learning the 'days of the week'. But for advanced students, this is unlikely to constitute an adequate method. This is because, as we have seen from the example of homonymy and polysemy, the meaning of words is rarely identical from one context to the next. If you therefore remove a word from the context in which it occurs, you necessarily lose much of its meaning. Furthermore, acquiring new vocabulary is not simply a question of understanding meaning in a passive sense. You also want to learn words so that you can use them actively in the future. Again, therefore, if you write down individual German words which are removed from their original context, then you will be forfeiting the all-important collocations (and connotations) which are so crucial for the next time you try to use that word yourself.

In conclusion, a much more effective way of learning vocabulary is to read texts, writing the translations/explanations of those words you do not understand in the margins. Then, instead of re-reading an abstract list of vocabulary, you should re-read the text itself, referring to the notes you have made. In this way, you will not only be building your vocabulary, but also learning how to use words in the contexts in which they naturally occur *in German* – as opposed to the contexts in which they might occur in English.

Sources and recommended reading

- For an introduction to German semantics, see Fox (1990), Chapter 6.
- Russ (1994), Chapter 10, deals with the structure of German vocabulary and outlines current changes, especially the influence of English.
- Clyne (1995), Chapter 8, summarises recent Anglo-American influence on German vocabulary.
- Durrell (1992), Chapter 2, looks at German words and their meanings and has a section on easily confused German and English words.
- Kürschner (1989), Chapter 2, provides a summary of semantic issues (in German).
- Chapter 4 of Linke *et al.* (1994) deals with semantics (in German).
- For a general introduction to semantics, see Chapter 17 of Crystal (1997) and Chapter 4 of Fromkin and Rodman (1993).

Exercises

1. Match the terms in Column A with their appropriate definitions in Column B.

COLUMN A	COLUMN B
1. Homophones	(a) The company words typically keep.
2. Antonyms	(b) Inclusion of meaning.
3. Polysemy	(c) Words which have the same or similar meanings.
4. Connotation	(d) Different words with the same pronunciation.
5. Synonyms	(e) Words which are written and/or pronounced in the same way.
6. Homographs	(f) Words which have opposite meanings.
7. Collocation	(g) A word as opposed to its referent.
8. Homonyms	(h) When the same word has different but related meanings.
9. Signifier	(i) The extra meaning(s) which a word gains when used in context.
10. Hyponymy	(j) Different words which are written in the same way.

2. Underline the superordinate term in the following groups of words:
   1. schreiten, sich bewegen, schlendern, spazieren
   2. Rock, Hose, Kleidung, Krawatte, Schuh
   3. Tropfen, Pillen, Tabletten, Arzneimittel
   4. Hund, Haustier, Katze, Hamster, Kaninchen
   5. Schach, Damen, Spiel, Mensch ärgere Dich nicht, Karten
   6. Bruder, Onkel, Großvater, Vetter, Verwandter
   7. Finger, Körperteil, Arm, Bein, Auge
   8. Tisch, Möbelstück, Sessel, Lampe, Schrank
   9. Blumenkohl, Gemüse, Bohnen, Kartoffeln, Erbsen
   10. hinrichten, töten, ermorden, erschießen

3. Draw five tree diagrams which describe the relationships of hyponymy between the following groups of words.
   1. Naturwissenschaft/Biologie/Geisteswissenschaft/Chemie/Soziologie/ Germanistik/Psychologie/Physik/Wissenschaft/Sozialwissenschaft/ Romanistik
   2. Trommel/Schlagzeug/Musikinstrument/Geige/Blasinstrument/ Saiteninstrument/Kontrabass/Querflöte/Posaune

3. Schlafcouch/Stehlampe/Möbelstück/Bett/Hallogenlampe/
Sitzgelegenheit/Beleuchtung/Hocker/Sessel/Schlafgelegenheit/
Schlafcouch

4. Insekt/Pferd/Kaninchen/Lebewesen/Fisch/Tier/Hund/Ameise/
Kabeljau/Forelle/Käfer/Biene

5. Kuchen/Obst/Brot/Keks/Gemüse/Banane/Gurke/Lebensmittel/
Getränke/Backwaren/Orangensaft/Mineralwasser/Milch/Erdbeere

4. State whether the following pairs of words are complementaries,
gradable antonyms or relational opposites. Bear in mind that, in some
cases, the answers may not necessarily be clear-cut.

1. jung/alt	6. Leben/Tod
2. neu/alt	7. sinnvoll/sinnlos
3. männlich/weiblich	8. borgen/leihen
4. Schüler/Lehrer	9. wachen/schlafen
5. dick/dünn	10. geben/nehmen

5. State whether the following pairs of words are homophones (same
pronunciation) or homographs (same spelling) or both.

	WORD A	WORD B	SENSE RELATION
1.	Rock (Kleidung)	Rock (Musik)	Homophones and homographs
2.	Montage (erste Tage der Woche)	Montage (das Montieren)	
3.	Birne (Frucht)	Birne (Leuchtkörper)	
4.	umfahren (zu Fall bringen)	umfahren (um . . . herumfahren)	
5.	arm (finanziell)	Arm (Körperteil)	
6.	Bank (Sitzgelegenheit)	Bank (Geldinstitut)	
7.	Pferd (Tier)	Pferd (Schachfigur)	
8.	Bremse (beim Auto)	Bremse (Stechfliege)	
9.	kosten (wert sein)	kosten (probieren)	
10.	Beete (Blumenbeete)	Bete (rote Bete)	

USING GERMAN IN THE REAL WORLD

9

Meaning in context

In Chapter 8, we looked at the meaning of German words. First, we explored the general relationship between words and meaning. Then we considered how meaning is structured within groups of words, that is to say, in terms of similarity, inclusion, opposition, etc.

One of the things which became clear was the fact that it is not always possible to understand a sentence merely by analysing the individual words it contains. This is particularly true of idioms such as *Wo sich Fuchs und Hase gute Nacht sagen* or metaphors such as *Sie ist ein richtiger Affe*. We saw how familiarity with all the words which make up such sentences will not necessarily guarantee your grasping the overall meaning: in order to understand idioms and metaphors, you need to draw upon additional knowledge or experience, which is *outside* of the language system itself.

In this chapter, we shall be pursuing this point further. Consider, for example, the statement *Mir ist kalt*. If you analyse this sentence simply in terms of the individual words it contains, then it means 'I am cold'. However, there are many situations in which it could mean something rather different. For example, if it is snowing and you have just entered somebody's house, by saying *Mir ist kalt,* you might in fact be asking for a hot drink. Alternatively, you could be sitting in a draughty room, and by pointing out that you are cold, you might be making a polite request for a window to be closed. Once again, in order to understand what is really meant, you need to look *outside* of the language system and consider what is going on around you at the precise moment when the statement is uttered. In other words, the real *meaning* of language only emerges when you take into account the *context* in which it is being used.

Here, we shall be looking at two areas of linguistics which deal specifically with meaning in context. We shall begin with **pragmatics**. The term 'pragmatics' is derived from the Greek *pragma* meaning 'act'. This branch of linguistics is therefore particularly concerned with the way in which language use is often the equivalent of concrete *act*ion. For example, if someone begins a sentence with *Ich verspreche* or *Ich wette*, then everything which follows those words will be of consequence in the real world. If the promise is broken, someone will be angry or disappointed. If the bet is won, someone will have incurred a debt. In addition, pragmatics looks at examples like *Mir ist kalt* in order to show how the same statement can mean different things in different contexts.

In the second half of this chapter, we turn to **text analysis**. Like pragmatics, this branch of linguistics also deals with meaning in context. Unlike pragmatics, however, it tends to focus on longer stretches of languages, i.e. whole texts rather than isolated phrases or sentences. Text analysis is particularly concerned with the way in which groups of sentences must be ordered if they are going to form texts which appear logical. For example, the following does not make sense:

> *Dann bin ich ins Bett gegangen. Zuerst habe ich ein Glas Wein getrunken.*

The problem with these two statements is obvious: normally we would expect the action which took place *zuerst* to appear first, followed by the sentence beginning with *dann*. There are many such rules governing the links which must be made between different sentences in order to produce well-structured texts. Sometimes, however, the necessary links are not made explicit. As a result, we are forced to make them ourselves. Clearly, this is not something which is always easy for learners of foreign languages. The aim of this section is therefore to give students some guidance on what to look for in order to make sense of German texts they may encounter in future.

For the sake of clarity, the chapter is divided in such a way that the section on pragmatics will be discussing primarily examples of *spoken* German. This compares to the section on text analysis where we will be dealing mainly with *written* texts. However, it is important to point out at this juncture that the issues described in both parts are relevant to both types of language.

9.1   Pragmatics: language in action

Pragmatics is concerned with the way in which meaning works in real-life contexts. But before we explore this point further, it will be necessary to make one important terminological distinction. Consider the following:

1. *Ich habe es schon getan.*
2. *Machen Sie jetzt bitte die Tür zu.*
3. *Raus jetzt!*
4. *Nein, das nicht!*

Of these statements, only 1 and 2 constitute syntactically well-formed clauses or sentences. By comparison, 3 and 4 are grammatically incomplete.

In Chapter 7 on syntax, we saw how the terms 'clause' and 'sentence' have very specific implications in so far as both normally contain at least one finite verb.

However, it is important to note that pragmatics does not limit itself to the study of perfectly formed clauses and sentences – it is interested in the meaning of *anything* we might say or write in a particular context. For this reason, it is customary to refer to **utterances**. Note then, that all four of the above examples can be described as utterances, and that all are equally meaningful from the point of view of pragmatics.

9.1.1 *Performing with language*

Speaking is not simply a way of passing the time. Nor is it just a way of communicating information to other people. In many cases, saying something is much more like *doing* something. It was the British philosopher J. L. Austin (1911–60) who first coined the term **speech act**, and tried to show how using language is often the equivalent of real action. Let us look at some examples in German to see what he meant by this:

1. *Ich verspreche, dass ich es machen werde.*
2. *Ich taufe dieses Kind auf den Namen „Rebecca".*
3. *Ich wette zehn Mark, dass er nicht kommt.*

If we utter statements such as these, we will be doing more than simply speaking – we will be *performing* an action. These kinds of statements are therefore known as **performative utterances**.

One important point about performatives is that the action which is being performed is not complete until the statement has actually been uttered. In other words, a promise is not made until the speaker has said the words *Ich verspreche;* a baptism has not taken place until someone declares *Ich taufe;* and a bet only begins when someone has said *Ich wette.* In these three examples, we can also see that the action is being performed by the verbs *versprechen, taufen* and *wetten.* These can therefore be described as **performative verbs**.

Now compare the performative utterances above to the following statements:

1. *Ich werde es machen.*
2. *Dieses Kind heißt Rebecca.*
3. *Er kommt nicht.*

With utterances such as these, we will not be performing an action. Instead, we will simply be making an assertion or *constatation*. These types of statements are therefore known as **constative utterances**.

Understanding the difference between constative and performative utterances is crucial if we are to use language appropriately. This is because if someone makes a constative statement, then it is perfectly acceptable to question the truth value of what has been said. For example:

> A: *Dieses Kind heißt Rebecca.*
> B: *Nein, das glaube ich nicht. Es heißt Susanne.*

However, you cannot normally question the truth value of a performative utterance. In pragmatic terms, then, the following sequence is not possible:

> A: *Ich taufe dieses Kind auf den Namen „Rebecca".*
> B: **Nein, das glaube ich nicht. Es heißt Susanne.*

One thing we can begin to appreciate with the help of this last example is that it is perfectly possible to say something which is *grammatically correct, but pragmatically inappropriate.* This is an important distinction, not least because learners of foreign languages do not always realise that they may have said something which was correct, grammatically speaking, but which was not quite the right thing to say in a particular context.

9.1.2   Classifying speech acts

The distinction between performative and constative utterances is a useful one, but in practice speech acts are rather more complex. A later version of speech act theory therefore took a somewhat different approach. This time the emphasis was placed on the different *perspectives* from which speech acts can be analysed:

- The **locutionary act** refers to the simple act of speaking or communicating. This is similar to the idea of the constative utterance.
- The **illocutionary act** refers to the way in which an *action* takes place because of something which has been said by the speaker. Such acts might include telling a joke or threatening someone. This is similar to the notion of a performative utterance.
- The **perlocutionary act** refers to the *effect* which the statement has on the listener. This might include being amused or feeling threatened. By including the perlocutionary act, this later version of speech act theory is therefore taking into account the perspective of the listener, and not just the speaker.

It is important to realise, however, that the so-called force of the illocutionary act and the effect of the perlocutionary act do not always coincide. For example, if someone tells you a joke, you might not necessarily laugh. Alternatively, if someone threatens you, you might not feel afraid. It is easy to see how such discrepancies can have very real consequences. Not laughing at someone's joke may cause offence. Similarly, by not recognising a threat, you may put yourself in danger. Once again, therefore, we can see how your ability to function properly when speaking a foreign language will not just depend on your understanding what has been said, and giving an answer which is grammatically correct. If someone says something, you need to know how to react *appropriately*.

According to this slightly different approach to speech act theory, there have been many attempts to classify the various types of illocutionary act which may occur. Probably the most influential suggestion was made by J. R. Searle, who differentiated between the following five categories:

1. **Representatives.** Here the speaker is committing himself or herself to the truth of a proposition by using such verbs as *glauben* (to believe), *vermuten* (to suppose), *annehmen* (to assume), *bezweifeln* (to doubt), etc.
2. **Directives.** In such cases, the speaker is trying to get the listener to take some form of action with the use of such verbs as *fragen* (to ask), *bestehen* (to insist), *bitten* (to request), *befehlen* (to command), etc.
3. **Commissives.** Here, the speaker is making a commitment to some form of action which has already occurred or which may occur in the future e.g. *versprechen* (to promise), *garantieren* (to guarantee), *schwören* (to swear), etc.
4. **Expressives.** In these cases, the speaker is expressing an attitude towards something as in *Ich gratuliere!* (Congratulations!), *Ich danke dir!* (Thank you!), *Herzlich willkommen!* (Welcome!), etc.
5. **Declaratives.** Here the speaker actually makes a concrete change to the real world through an utterance e.g. *Ich trete zurück* (I resign), *Ich taufe* (I baptise), *Sie sind gefeuert* (You're fired), etc. In practice, it is extremely difficult, or even impossible, to reverse declaratives.

(Adapted from Crystal, 1997: 121)

In the discussion of performative and constative utterances in section 9.1.1, we saw how an important distinction between the two was that it is not normally possible to question the truth value of performatives. Thus, if someone says *Ich danke dir*, it is inappropriate to reply *Ich glaube es nicht*. However, this assumption also requires a little refinement. This is because for speech acts to be successful they must also satisfy a set of criteria which are known as **felicity conditions.** For example, if someone utters the words *Ich taufe*, the speech act will only be valid if that person has the necessary *authority*, i.e. is a priest. Similarly, the act must be executed in the correct manner – the priest must know exactly when in the ceremony the words are to be uttered. If they are spoken too early or too late, then the baptism is likely to be invalid.

Another important felicity condition is that of *sincerity*. Thus, if someone makes a promise to you, it is not normally appropriate to say that you don't believe them. However, if that person has made several promises to you in the past, all of which have been broken, then it is possible that the condition of sincerity will not be fulfilled. As a result, the speech act may be invalidated. This is a further example of the way in which the force of the illocutionary act (= intention of the speaker) and the effect of the perlocutionary act (= reaction of the addressee) do not always coincide.

Finally, there is one particular type of speech act which is extremely common in everyday language usage. Consider the following:

1. *Mach' die Tür bitte zu.*
2. *Warum machst du die Tür nicht zu?*
3. *Mir ist kalt.*

In terms of their grammatical structure, these three utterances are quite different: 1 is an imperative or command, 2 is an interrogative or question, whereas 3 is a declarative statement. Yet, from the point of view of pragmatics, it is possible to imagine circumstances in which each of these utterances might fulfil the same function. For example, all three could in fact mean: 'close the door!' even if it is only 1 which says so explicitly. In this context, we can describe utterances 2 and 3 as **indirect speech acts** – the speakers are saying one thing, but meaning another.

People often use indirect speech acts in order to avoid appearing too abrupt or rude. For example, it is often more polite to say that you are cold, than to instruct someone to close the door. But at the same time it is an important part of our linguistic competence to understand the real illocutionary force of indirect speech acts and to respond appropriately. In order to see what is meant by this, consider the following responses to utterances 2 and 3:

2. A: *Warum machst du die Tür nicht zu?*
   B: **Weil ich keine Lust habe!*

3. A: *Mir ist kalt.*
   B: **Mir auch!*

Once again, we are faced here with statements which are grammatically correct, but highly inappropriate in pragmatic terms. It is not difficult to see the potential for humour when we give unsuitable responses such as these. But in the real world, it is important to appreciate that a failure to react appropriately to indirect speech acts can have very serious consequences indeed. This, in turn, can lead to all kinds of cross-cultural misunderstandings between speakers of different languages. This is because if we give the kinds of responses illustrated above, other people may consider us impolite, stupid, or quite simply insane!

9.1.3   *Implied meaning*

The study of indirect speech acts emphasises a point made in Chapter 8 on semantics: frequently, the meaning of what we say is not directly contained in the words we are actually using. Thus, when someone says *Mir ist kalt,* we may need to think a little further. If we are competent communicators, we will know that this utterance may in fact be a request to close the door or turn up the heating.

Indirect speech acts are not the only examples of situations where the meaning may lie *outside* of the utterance itself. Consider, for example, the use of *sie, hier* and *morgen* in following:

1. *Sie wohnt in Heidelberg.*
2. *Hier ist es sehr schön.*
3. *Morgen gehe ich zur Universität.*

In order to understand these statements fully, you need to know who *sie* is, where *hier* is, and when *morgen* is. This information is not contained in the words themselves – it can only be found by looking elsewhere, i.e. to the context in which the utterances were made.

These three examples illustrate a phenomenon known in linguistics as **deixis** (pronounced: [daɪksɪs]). This is a term which is derived from the Greek *deiknunai* meaning 'to point' or 'show'. Thus, deictic structures consist of a word or phrase which is *pointing* towards something outside of the utterance itself. There are three main ways in which this can happen.

1. **Personal deixis** occurs when pronouns are used to refer to people or objects:

   Sie wohnt in Heidelberg.
   Der Film hat ihr gut gefallen.
   Dein Buch liegt auf dem Tisch.

2. **Spatial deixis** points to places:

   Hier ist es sehr schön.
   Dort fahre ich nicht mehr hin.
   Komm her!

3. **Temporal deixis** refers to time:

   Morgen gehe ich zur Universität.
   Gestern bin ich nach London gefahren.
   Dann ging es mir besser.

The important point about deictic structures is that their meaning changes according to the specific context in which they are being used. For example, in *Morgen gehe ich zur Universität*, the adverb *morgen* could refer to any day of the week. Thus, if today is *Montag*, then *morgen* means *Dienstag*. But if today is *Mittwoch*, then *morgen* will be *Donnerstag*.

Another example where meaning depends very much on the context in which an utterance is made is with so-called **presuppositions**. Consider, for example, the following:

1. *Es war meine Freundin, die das gesagt hat.*
2. *Ich wusste nicht, dass Andreas gestorben ist.*
3. *Meine Schwester hat den Job bekommen.*

These three utterances only make sense in relation to information which has been supplied previously. In 1 we need to be aware of the fact that 'something has been said'; in 2 we need to know who 'Andreas' is; and in 3 we need to know that 'there was a job for which my sister applied'. Having said this, presuppositions are also partly implying information. In other words, we can also deduce from 1 that something has been said, from 2 that there was someone called Andreas, and from 3 that there was a job for which my sister applied.

The fact that presuppositions not only *presuppose* but also *imply* information is one reason why their use is strictly controlled in legal contexts. In court, for example, a lawyer is not allowed to ask a defendant: 'Have you stopped stealing cigarettes now?' This is because the presupposition implied in the question is that the defendant has stolen cigarettes before. In such situations, it can be very difficult for the jury to ascertain whether that presupposition is true, i.e. did the defendant really steal cigarettes before? Moreover, it is virtually impossible for the defendant to reply without appearing to accept the truth value of the original utterance. It does not matter whether he or she answers 'yes' or 'no' – the very fact that the question is answered implies that the presupposition has been accepted.

Finally, closely related to presuppositions are so-called **implicatures**. These describe situations where we can make practical assumptions on the basis of what has been said. Thus, if someone utters the statement *Ich habe zwei Pferde,* the implicature is that they have *only* two horses. It would be unlikely that they have more, or fewer than two (unless they are deliberately trying to deceive us). Similarly, consider the following sequence:

A: *Kann ich bitte dein Telefon benutzen?*
B: *Es ist in der Küche.*

B's response to A's request is an indirect speech act which does not explicitly state that A may use the telephone. But by saying 'it's in the kitchen', the implicature is that permission to use the telephone has, in fact, been granted.

Indirect speech acts, deixis, presuppositions, and implicatures all demonstrate how the real meaning of an utterance only becomes clear when you consider the context in which it is made. In other words, meaning can be *implicit* as well as *explicit*. Here, we have considered only isolated utterances in order to explore this point. But in the next section, we shall see how the same principle also applies to longer sequences of language usage.

9.2   Text analysis

In Chapters 4, 5, 6, and 7, we looked at some of the structures of the German language. In Chapters 4 and 5, we discussed sounds. Then, in Chapters 6 and 7, we moved on to grammar – first, the grammar of words, then the grammar of sentences. You may have noticed that there was a certain logical progression here in the sense that each unit of analysis was 'larger' than the one before. But the description of language structure does not stop here. This is because, most of the time, speaking or writing requires the use of many different sentences. It follows, therefore, that anyone who wishes to achieve genuine competence in a foreign language needs to know something about the way in which language works at a level which is 'beyond the sentence', i.e. in whole texts.

Most people use the word **text** to refer to a piece of *written* language, for example, in the sense of 'textbook' or 'set text'. In linguistics, however, the term is used slightly differently. Thus, when we talk about a text here, we will be referring to any stretch of language which consists of *more than one sentence –* whether written *or* spoken. Having said this, there are some instances where it is possible to imagine whole 'texts' which consist of only one sentence or even single words, such as road signs or menus, although we shall not be looking at these kinds of texts in this section. Moreover, some linguists differentiate between a text and a **discourse**. They use 'text' in the sense of what *one* writer/speaker says, and 'discourse' to refer to interaction between *two or more* writers/speakers. For the sake of simplicity, however, we will not be adhering to this distinction here, and will only be referring to 'texts'.

In Chapter 7 on syntax, we saw how, when words are joined together to form a sentence, there are certain rules which govern the order in which those words may occur. If a sentence breaks the rules of word order, we normally say that it is *ungrammatical*. By analogy, when we link sentences together to form a text, they cannot be placed in random order. However, we do not refer to a poorly constructed text as ungrammatical: we say that it is *incoherent*.

The study of **coherence**, then, is concerned with finding out what make texts hang together. It explores the reasons why some texts appear logical and orderly, whilst others seem illogical and disjointed. In the following three sections, we shall be looking at a number of factors which affect textual coherence.

9.2.1   Cohesive devices

One of the most important elements of textual coherence are so-called **cohesive devices**. These are like the 'glue' which is needed to hold together the various sentences within a text. In this section, we shall begin by looking at seven such devices, and exploring the different ways in which these can help a text to become coherent.

CONJUNCTIVE TIES

Conjunctive ties are those features of a text which help to forge links between different sentences. Consider, for example, the following:

1. *Sabine ist um 9 Uhr gefahren. Jürgen blieb jedoch bis zum Ende.*
2. *Schließlich geht es um sehr viel Geld.*

Here the words *jedoch* and *schließlich* link the sentences in which they occur to information which has been stated previously. For example, in 1, the fact that Jürgen stayed until the end is contrasted with Sabine's departure at 9 o'clock. In 2, the use of *schließlich* implies that money is not the only factor which has been mentioned – a number of other points have been discussed prior to this statement.

If the term 'conjunctive' sounds familiar, this is because we have already observed a similar principle with reference to syntax. In section 7.1.2 we talked about coordinating conjunctions such as *und, aber* and *oder,* and subordinating conjunctions such as *weil, wenn* and *dass.* We then looked at the different ways in which these conjunctions link simple sentences (one clause only) to form complex sentences (two or more clauses). What we can now see is that conjunctive ties perform the same function with respect to sentences and texts. In other words, conjunctive ties hold two or more sentences together in a way which helps a text seem logical and coherent.

COREFERENCE

Conjunctive ties involve the linking of ideas between sentences in a very general way. **Coreference** is based on a similar principle but is more specific. It occurs where one feature (often a pronoun) can only be understood with *direct reference* to another. There are two types of coreference. The first is **anaphora**. This is when a word refers *backwards,* i.e. to something which has been stated previously. For example:

<u>Deutsche</u> fahren gern in Urlaub. <u>Sie</u> sind sehr reisefreudig.
←

Here we can see that *Sie* refers back to *Deutsche*. Another way of saying this is that two words share the same referent, hence the term *co*reference.

Cataphora is the opposite of anaphora. This time there is a *forward* reference, i.e. to something which has not yet been mentioned. For example, in the following, *er* refers to *der Mann*:

Das ist <u>er</u>. Das ist <u>der Mann</u>, der mein Geld gestohlen hat.
→

Coreference is not unlike the principle of deixis which was discussed in section 9.1.3. However, there is one crucial difference: with anaphora and cataphora the feature which is being referred to is contained *within the text*. This contrasts with deixis where, although the person, place, or time referred to can sometimes be found within the text, it is frequently necessary to look *outside of the text* to the context of the utterance generally.

REPETITION

As its name suggests, **repetition** occurs when the same feature is used more than once:

> *Klaus kam an. Klaus war sauer.*

In longer texts, repetition can be a very helpful way of demonstrating that different ideas are related to one another. It is therefore a useful device for creating thematic continuity and, by implication, coherence. In short texts such as this one, however, it would probably be more common to use the anaphoric *er* in the second sentence. Thus, repetition may be occurring here for extra emphasis or even humour.

SUBSTITUTION

Substitution refers to the way in which one feature stands in place of another:

> A: *Hast du einen Bleistift?*
> B: *Nein, ich habe <u>keinen</u>.*
> A: *Glaubst du wir sind pünktlich da?*
> B: *Ich glaube <u>ja</u>.*
> A: *Ich fahre nächste Woche nach Griechenland. <u>Das</u> mache ich jedes Jahr.*

Substitution is one way of avoiding unnecessary repetition. Note how, in the first example, the relationship between *Bleistift* and *keinen* is also anaphoric.

ELLIPSIS

Ellipsis occurs when a feature is omitted or *ellipted*. Like substitution, it is another way of preventing repetition:

> A: *Wo steht dein Wagen?*
> B: ∧ *Auf der Straße.*

Note how in such cases the symbol ∧ can be used to indicate a missing element.

COMPARISON

Comparison, as its name implies, refers to cases where one expression is *compared* to another:

> *Der letzte Urlaub war schlimm. Aber dieser war <u>noch schlimmer</u>.*
> *Deine roten Schuhe gefallen mir. Aber die Blauen finde ich <u>besser</u>.*

LEXICAL COHESION

Finally, a useful way of holding a text together is through **lexical cohesion.** This occurs where certain words are related to one another in terms of meaning. Consider the following:

1. *Der <u>Arbeitgeber</u> von Birgit war unzufrieden, weil sie immer zu spät zur Arbeit kam. Birgit sagte: 'Mein <u>Chef</u> ist sehr streng'.*
2. *Die <u>Blumen</u> waren sehr schön. Am Besten fand ich die <u>Tulpen</u>.*
3. *100 <u>Menschen</u> sind gestorben. Davon waren 36 <u>Männer</u> und 64 <u>Frauen</u>.*

In these examples, we can see that lexical cohesion is based on the sense relations of synonymy, hyponymy, and antonymy which were discussed in Chapter 8. Thus, in 1 the relationship between *Arbeitgeber* and *Chef* is one of synonymy. In 2 *Tulpe* is a hyponym of *Blume*. Finally, in example 3 *Männer* and *Frauen* are hyponyms of *Menschen* as well as co-hyponyms and antonyms in relation to one another.

A further kind of lexical cohesion occurs when words from the same *semantic field* are used within a text. For example, a text about animals might mention many different types of animal – the reader will then mentally group these words together in order to achieve an overall sense of thematic coherence or unity.

Knowing how to interpret cohesive devices is clearly important if we are going to understand the overall meaning of texts. Similarly, an ability to use such devices will be helpful when trying to construct coherent texts of our own – irrespective of whether this is in our mother tongue or a foreign language.

Having said this, different languages do not always employ the same kinds of cohesive devices in the same situations. Consider, for example, the following English passage together with its German translation:

> The interdependence between a company's business activities, market conditions, and IT *implementation* strategies are clearly apparent. The manner of *implementation* depends on the type of technology, the available expertise, and the timing.

> Die Interdependenzen zwischen Geschäftstätigkeit des Unternehmens, den Marktgegebenheiten und den *Einsatz*strategien von Informationstechnologien sind klar zu erkennen. Ein kompetenter *Einsatz* ist DABEI abhängig von der Art der Technologie, des Know-hows, und vom richtigen Zeitpunkt.
> (*Source:* Salkie, 1995: 109)

Here the English text gels perfectly well due to a single cohesive device: the repetition of 'implementation'. In German, however, the repetition of *Einsatz* alone is insufficient to make the text cohere. German therefore requires extra help in the form of the conjunctive tie *dabei*.

Another cohesive device which is used differently in German and English is ellipsis. Thus, in the following examples, German prefers an elliptical structure whereas English adds the noun substitute 'one':

> *der Große* – the big *one*
> *Jene* – that *one*
> *mein Neues* – my new *one*

When reading German texts in future, try to spot your own examples of situations where usage varies between the two languages.

9.2.2 *Thematic progression and relevance of ideas*

We have already seen how cohesive devices can be used in order to make a stretch of language cohere. But now take a look at the following text:

> Eine Woche hat sieben *Tage*. Jeden *Tag* gehe ich *im Park* spazieren. *Dort* gefällt es mir sehr *gut*. Das Essen war *auch gut*. *Aber* Schwimmen ist *besser*.

What this passage illustrates is that even if a text contains all the appropriate cohesive devices, this will not necessarily guarantee that it will make sense. Clearly, therefore, coherence is more than just a question of making the right structural links between words and sentences. For a text to be coherent, the ideas which are being presented need to follow some kind of *thematic progression*. In addition, they must be organised in such a way that the reader can understand their *relevance*.

So how do texts develop thematic progression? In what order must ideas be expressed if they are going to appear relevant to one another? It is in fact very difficult to specify rules which will account for all texts, not least because there are so many different types of text. However, one structure which has been proposed is the so-called **Background, Problem, Solution, and Evaluation (BPSE)** pattern. This states that many texts can be approached as a series of answers to the following questions:

1. What is the BACKGROUND to the text? What time, place, people, etc. are going to be involved? What do we need to know in order to be able to understand the information which will follow in the next part of the text, i.e. the 'problem'?
2. What is the PROBLEM that arises out of the situation described in the background section? What is this text principally about? What need, dilemma, puzzle, obstacle or lack is addressed here? Note that in this section *das Problem* or related words may well occur.

3. What is the SOLUTION to this problem? How were the needs met, the dilemma resolved, the puzzle solved, the obstacle overcome, or the lack remedied? In this section, it is not uncommon to find *die Lösung* or related words.

4. Finally, how is this solution EVALUATED? What comments are made on the solution which is being proposed? For example, is this a good way of solving the problem? If there is more than one possible solution, which one is best?

(Adapted from Salkie, 1995: 91)

Let us now examine an authentic German text in order to see how this pattern might work in practice. The passage '*Weniger Drogentote. Grund zur Entwarnung?*' is taken from the magazine *TV Hören und Sehen,* and was intended as an introduction to a television documentary on drug abuse.

Weniger Drogentote
Grund zur Entwarnung?

Leben mit der Droge: Rausch, Gift, Krankheit, Armut, Angst. Wie viele Menschen im Teufelskreis der Sucht leben, ist ungewiß. Gezählt werden nur die Toten. Und die Zahl der Rauschgifttoten – über neunzig Prozent davon waren Heroinkonsumenten – ist 1995 weiter gesunken. Womit sich ein Trend der vergangenen Jahre fortsetzt. Grund zur Entwarnung?

'Der Konsum von Heroin scheint sich ein wenig zu verringern,' so Hamburgs Drogenbeauftragter Horst Bossong. 'Gleichzeitig sehen wir aber eine beträchtliche Zahl von Abhängigen, die in einer exzessiven Weise alle möglichen Drogen durcheinander konsumieren und psychisch wie sozial ziemlich verwahrlost sind.' Vom gesellschaftlichen Leben ausgeschlossen, sehen sie einer düsteren Zukunkft ohne Perspektive entgegen.

Mit ungeahnten gesundheitlichen Folgeschäden muß die wachsende Zahl der Ecstasy- und Amphetamin-Konsumenten rechnen. Diese 'Party-Drogen' gewinnen in erschreckendem Ausmaß an Attraktivität, sind aus der Techno-Szene kaum mehr wegzudenken.

Wer durch den trügerischen Rausch in die Abhängigkeit gerät, kann sich selten allein aus dem Sumpf retten. Wie stehen heute die Chancen, wieder clean zu werden? 'Die therapeutische Versorgung hat sich in Deutschland qualitativ und quantitativ erheblich verbessert,' berichtet Horst Bossong. 'Es gibt ein breites Spektrum an Hilfsangeboten, wodurch sich die Chancen erhöhen, aus dem Teufelskreis der Sucht herauszukommen.'

Eine anerkannte Therapie: die Methadonbehandlung. Etwa 20 000 Süchtige werden zur Zeit bundesweit mit dem Drogenersatzstoff behandelt. Wesentlich mehr Abhängige aber wollen in das Methadon-Programm aufgenommen werden. Doch ein rigides Regelwerk (NUB) legt fest, wann Krankenkassen verpflichtet sind zu zahlen. Nur Extremfälle (z.B. Aids-Kranke) haben Chancen. Horst Bossong: 'Eine unhaltbare Richtlinie. Je früher im Suchtverlauf eine Methadonsubstitution begonnen wird, desto wirksamer kann sie die Gesundheit der Heroinabhängigen schützen und ihre Heilung fördern.'

(Source: TV Hören und Sehen, 27, 28.6.96)

We can now begin to explore how the BPSE structure works in this text.

Background:

Weniger Drogentote
Grund zur Entwarnung?

Leben mit der Droge: Rausch, Gift, Krankheit, Armut, Angst. Wie viele Menschen im Teufelskreis der Sucht leben, ist ungewiß. Gezählt werden nur die Toten. Und die Zahl der Rauschgifttoten – über neunzig Prozent davon waren Heroinkonsumenten – ist 1995 weiter gesunken. Womit sich ein Trend der vergangenen Jahre fortsetzt. Grund zur Entwarnung?

'Der Konsum von Heroin scheint sich ein wenig zu verringern,' so Hamburgs Drogenbeauftragter Horst Bossong.

The title, the first paragraph, and the first line of the second paragraph provide the background information which we will need in order to understand this text. The topic of the text is drugs and their consequences. We are told that it is not known how many people actually take drugs because statistics only measure deaths. However, there were fewer drug-related fatalities in 1995 – 90 per cent of which were linked to heroin – and this continues a trend set in previous years. We are then asked a question which will be answered later in the text: is this a sign that we can stop worrying about drugs? In addition, we are introduced to an expert who will also appear later: Horst Bossong, a drugs advisor from Hamburg. He gives us some further background information, telling us that the consumption of heroin has decreased slightly.

Problem:

'Gleichzeitig sehen wir aber eine beträchtliche Zahl von Abhängigen, die in einer exzessiven Weise alle möglichen Drogen durcheinander konsumieren und psychisch wie sozial ziemlich verwahrlost sind.' Vom gesellschaftlichen Leben ausgeschlossen, sehen sie einer düsteren Zukunkft ohne Perspektive entgegen.

Mit ungeahnten gesundheitlichen Folgeschäden muß die wachsende Zahl der Ecstasy- und Amphetamin-Konsumenten rechnen. Diese 'Party-Drogen' gewinnen in erschreckendem Ausmaß an Attraktivität, sind aus der Techno-Szene kaum mehr wegzudenken.

Here we are provided with an answer to the question posed in the background section: no, we cannot stop worrying about drugs. This is because, notwithstanding the apparent decrease in drugs-related deaths and heroin consumption, there appears to be a new problem – the increasing number of addicts who take a mixture of drugs. These people suffer a variety of social and psychological consequences. There will also be unforeseen health problems for the growing number of ecstasy and amphetamine users, the so-called 'party drugs', which have become a permanent feature of the techno-scene.

Solution:

Wer durch den trügerischen Rausch in die Abhängigkeit gerät, kann sich selten allein aus dem Sumpf retten. Wie stehen heute die Chancen, wieder clean zu werden? 'Die therapeutische Versorgung hat sich in Deutschland qualitativ und quantitativ erheblich verbessert,' berichtet Horst Bossong. 'Es gibt ein breites Spektrum an Hilfsangeboten, wodurch sich die Chancen erhöhen, aus dem Teufelskreis der Sucht herauszukommen.'

Eine anerkannte Therapie: die Methadonbehandlung. Etwa 20 000 Süchtige werden zur Zeit bundesweit mit dem Drogenersatzstoff behandelt.

We are now introduced to some possible solutions to this problem. These are prefaced by the question: what is the likelihood that addicts will be able to stop taking drugs? Horst Bossong provides a partial answer by pointing out that there have been considerable improvements in the quantity and quality of treatment provided in Germany. There are many different ways in which addicts can receive help – one of the main forms of therapy is the use of the heroin substitute, methadone. At present, approximately 20 000 addicts are receiving such treatment in the Federal Republic.

Evaluation:

Wesentlich mehr Abhängige aber wollen in das Methadon-Programm aufgenommen werden. Doch ein rigides Regelwerk (NUB) legt fest, wann Krankenkassen verpflichtet sind zu zahlen. Nur Extremfälle (z.B. Aids-Kranke) haben Chancen. Horst Bossong: 'Eine unhaltbare Richtlinie. Je früher im Suchtverlauf eine Methadonsubstitution begonnen wird, desto wirksamer kann sie die Gesundheit der Heroinabhängigen schützen und ihre Heilung fördern.'

Despite the fact that solutions are clearly available, the evaluation part of the text tells us why these are not as effective as they could be: it seems that too few addicts are able to participate in a programme of methadone treatment. The main difficulty appears to lie with the health insurance companies, who operate according to very strict guidelines, providing funding for only extremely serious cases such as AIDS sufferers. Bossong evaluates this shortfall by pointing out how such a policy is untenable. This is because the earlier heroin addicts are put onto a methadone programme, the greater the likelihood of successful treatment.

9.2.3   Omission of information

Many texts are characterised by the kind of BPSE structure which has just been outlined. Having said this, some texts vary the order in which the different elements are presented. For example, newspaper articles often try to attract their readers' attention by stating the solution first, before giving the background, problem, more details of the solution, and an evaluation. This then results in an SBPSE structure. Alternatively, it is not uncommon to find texts which present background information, a problem, an interim solution and evaluation, followed by more background information, and/or a further problem.

But not only do texts *vary* the order in which they present the BPSE pattern, some actually *omit* one or more of these elements. Consider, for example, a hypothetical advertisement for socks. The *background* to buying a pair of socks is that you have two feet, and the *problem* is that your feet get cold. However, the advertisement does not need to state this. It assumes that you are only really interested in the *solution* (buying a pair of socks) and the *evaluation* (how good are the socks made by company X?). Thus, such an advertisement might consist of a simple SE structure.

When a text omits information in this way, we can say that *presuppositions* are being made of the kind we looked at in section 9.1.3 on implied meaning. There we saw how if someone says *Meine Schwester hat den Job bekommen*, then it is presupposed that you knew there was a job for which my sister applied. What we are now seeing is that whole texts also make presuppositions. In other words, they often assume that you are already in possession of certain pieces of information *before* you begin reading.

TEXT ANALYSIS IN PRACTICE

Let us now look at another authentic German text in order to see how presuppositions work in practice. The passage *'Sozialdemokraten. Für eine "linke Regierung" mit der PDS'* is taken from the weekly German news magazine *Focus*. Do not worry if it does not initially appear coherent – the text has been chosen precisely because it expects the reader to share a very high number of presuppositions. The subsequent discussion will clarify what these are, and consider why they are not being spelled out more explicitly.

SOZIALDEMOKRATEN
Für eine "linke Regierung" mit der PDS

Der Bochumer SPD-Bundestagsabgeordnete Christoph Zöpel, der im Wahlkampf 1994 mit der Forderung nach einem allgemeinen Tempolimit Schlagzeilen machte, meldet sich wieder zu Wort: Im PDS-Blatt 'Neues Deutschland' sprach er sich als erster prominenter Genosse für Rot-Grün mit PDS-Unterstützung in Bonn aus. 'Wenn die Situation entsteht, daß die linken Parteien zusammen mehr als 50 Prozent haben,' so Zöpel, 'dann ist es an ihnen, eine linke Regierung möglich zu machen.' Die 'Dresdener Erklärung', in der sich die SPD noch gegen eine Zusammenarbeit mit der PDS ausgesprochen hatte, gilt für ihn nicht mehr: 'Nach Sachsen-Anhalt sind prinzipielle Einwände vom Tisch.'

(*Source: Focus*, 27, 1.7.96)

It is often suggested that the key to working out the BPSE structure of a text is to begin by identifying the *problem*. This is because once you know what the problem is, it is easier to understand how the other ideas fit together. But like our imaginary sock advert, this text fails to state the problem. Instead, it assumes you already know what this is, and that you are simply interested in the background, solution, and evaluation. Let us take a look at the actual structure of the text before we consider what the problem is, and why it is missing.

Background:

SOZIALDEMOKRATEN

Für eine 'linke Regierung' mit der PDS

Der Bochumer SPD-Bundestagsabgeordnete Christoph Zöpel, der im Wahlkampf 1994 mit der Forderung nach einem allgemeinen Tempolimit Schlagzeilen machte, meldet sich wieder zu Wort: Im PDS-Blatt 'Neues Deutschland' sprach er sich als erster prominenter Genosse für Rot-Grün mit PDS-Unterstützung in Bonn aus.

The title provides us with some initial background information. It tells us that the article is about the Social Democrats, and that there will be a discussion of a 'left-wing government' with the PDS. We are then introduced to the main character of the text, Christoph Zöpel, who is the member of the German parliament representing Bochum. We are told that Zöpel made the headlines during the 1994 election campaign when he declared himself in favour of a speed limit. We are then informed that Zöpel has made a statement in *Neues Deutschland*. He is thereby the first prominent member of the SPD to speak out publicly in favour of 'a red-green coalition in Bonn with PDS support'.

Solution:

'Wenn die Situation entsteht, daß die linken Parteien zusammen mehr als 50 Prozent haben', so Zöpel, 'dann ist es an ihnen, eine linke Regierung möglich zu machen.'

The second sentence presents us with the solution to the problem. If a situation arises whereby the left-wing parties together obtain more than 50 per cent of the vote, then Zöpel believes it is up to those parties to form a 'left-wing' government.

Evaluation:

Die 'Dresdener Erklärung', in der sich die SPD noch gegen eine Zusammenarbeit mit der PDS ausgesprochen hatte, gilt für ihn nicht mehr: 'Nach Sachsen-Anhalt sind prinzipielle Einwände vom Tisch.'

We are now told that Zöpel does not see why the so-called 'Dresden declaration' should prevent cooperation between the SPD and PDS. This declaration had originally stated the SPD's opposition to such cooperation, but Zöpel no longer believes this is relevant given the situation in Sachsen-Anhalt.

Even with the explanation offered so far, it is still possible that this text may seem somewhat incoherent to certain readers. Yet we can reasonably assume that it is perfectly coherent to the German readership for which it was intended. This is because the magazine *Focus* would be unlikely to publish an article which it does not consider its readers to be capable of understanding. So how can a text be coherent to some readers but not others?

Let us first of all look at some of the missing additional background information, in other words, the kind of general knowledge which this text presupposes. The list is not intended to be complete, so you may be able to identify other points.

FURTHER BACKGROUND INFORMATION

- *Sozialdemokraten* = SPD (*Sozialdemokratische Partei Deutschlands*)
  'Social Democratic Party of Germany'. This is the major centre–left party in the former West Germany and in the unified, post-1990 Germany.
- *PDS* (*Partei des Demokratischen Sozialismus*)
  'Party of Democratic Socialism'. This is the successor to the SED (*Sozialistische Einheitspartei Deutschlands* or Socialist Unity Party of Germany), which was the ruling party in East Germany.
- *Links*
  'Left' or 'left-wing'. This is an umbrella term often used to describe the political orientation of the SPD, the Greens, and the PDS. It is also being used in *linke Parteien/linke Regierung*.
- *der Bundestag*
  The German lower house of parliament (the upper house = *der Bundesrat*).
- *das Tempolimit*
  'Speed limit'. You need to be aware that there is no speed limit on German motorways, although there have been many attempts to establish one.
- *'Neues Deutschland'*
  Literally 'New Germany'. A German newspaper. *Neues Deutschland* was originally the main daily newspaper in East Germany and organ of the SED.
- *Genosse*
  'Comrade'. This is a term often used to denote East Germans, generally, or East German politicians, specifically. Here it is probably being used ironically to refer to members of the SPD.

- *Rot-Grün*
  Red is the colour of the SPD, and green is the colour of the Greens. Here, the term *Rot-Grün* refers to the idea of a coalition between the SPD and the Greens.
- *Bonn*
  At the time the article was written, seat of the *Bundestag* (which has since moved to Berlin).
- *Sachsen-Anhalt*
  One of the so-called *neue Bundesländer*, i.e. a state which was formerly part of East Germany. At the time the article was written, there was a red–green coalition with PDS support in Sachsen-Anhalt.
- *Bochum*
  Town in North-Rhine Westphalia, one of the *alte Bundesländer*, in the former West Germany.
- *50 Prozent*
  The percentage of votes which would automatically secure a majority in the *Bundestag*.

From this brief analysis, we can see that the reader needs to be in possession of a considerable amount of background knowledge in order to understand this article. But why is so much seemingly vital information being omitted? Moreover, how can a text make so many presuppositions and still be coherent for its intended readership?

The answer is that a magazine such as *Focus* is aimed at readers who are more than likely to be familiar with all of the points listed above. The author of the text does not therefore wish to explain background information which can be taken for granted. There are two main reasons for this. First of all, to repeat such information would take up unnecessary space, and this is meant to be a short news feature. Second, such repetition would run the risk of not only boring, but also offending the intended readership. This is because *Focus* readers are already fully aware, for example, that *Neues Deutschland* was the main East German newspaper and that red is the colour of the SPD, etc.

The same point applies to the reason why the 'problem' part of the text is not explicitly stated. Generally speaking, *Focus* readers will know what is happening on the political scene. This is information which they will have acquired from newspapers, television and radio, and quite probably from earlier editions of *Focus*. It therefore assumed that they know what the 'problem' is, and that their only real concern is to discover the *very latest* in a long line of developments. Now that some of the main terms have been explained, we can outline that problem – or indeed *problems*.

THE MISSING PROBLEMS

The text was written in June 1996, two years prior to the next Federal elections which were to take place in 1998. At that time, there had been a centre–right coalition government in the Federal Republic of Germany since 1982. This spanned both the eight years in West Germany prior to unification (1982–90) and the six years following unification (1990–96). The coalition, led by Helmut Kohl, was formed by the Christian Democratic Union (CDU), its Bavarian sister party, the Christian Social Union (CSU), and the Free Democratic Party (FDP).

Between 1982 and 1996, the SPD was obliged to consider various coalitions strategies should it wish to obtain a majority in the *Bundestag* in future elections. There were many discussions of alliances with the Greens, but there was also talk of a 'grand coalition' with the CDU/CSU. (Both possibilities had been tried out in some of the regional parliaments.) But in the case of a possible red–green coalition, should a sufficient majority still not be secured, then the two parties would have to consider forming a further alliance with the PDS. For many members of the SPD, this was politically problematic given the close relationship between the present PDS and the SED, the former ruling party in East Germany. Indeed, the SPD had previously stated in their 'Dresden Declaration' that they would *not* be prepared to form an alliance with the PDS. However, this was contradicted by later developments in Sachsen-Anhalt where there was in fact such a coalition at regional level.

In summary, therefore, the missing problems are:

- What kind of alliances should the SPD form if it did not secure an overall majority in the next election?
- Assuming the SPD could not form a majority government of its own, what would happen if a coalition with the Greens still failed to provide the requisite 50 per cent of votes?
- What was the position of the SPD with regard to the PDS and, by implication, to the former East German state?

The article is then presenting the background, solution, and evaluation to these problems as seen by one SPD member, Christoph Zöpel. Because of the situation in Sachsen-Anhalt, where there was already a red–green coalition with PDS support, Zöpel does not see why the SPD could not, in principle, work with the PDS following the election in 1998. Intriguingly, the fact that there was to be an election in 1998 is not mentioned at all – again, the reader is either expected to know this or at least be able to deduce it from the text itself.

COHERENCE AND LANGUAGE LEARNING

What does the analysis of the text *Sozialdemokraten Für eine 'linke Regierung' mit der PDS* tell us about textual coherence in more general terms? In sections 9.2.1 and 9.2.2 we looked at features of texts which typically lead to coherence, for example, cohesive devices, thematic progression, and relevance of ideas. We saw how texts which do not make appropriate use of such mechanisms may fail to cohere as a result. However, the important point about the features analysed was that they were all contained *within the text*.

By contrast, what we can see here is that coherence is not necessarily something which can be established exclusively within the text: *external factors* also play an important role. This is because coherence is at least partly the product of *interaction* between writers and readers. For a text to seem coherent, it is essential that the same kinds of presuppositions are shared by both parties. If, however, the writer presupposes background knowledge which the reader does not possess, then there will be a problem. In such a case, the text is likely to appear incoherent to that reader.

What this also shows us is that coherence is not simply a question of correct or incorrect textual structure. This is because it is perfectly feasible for a text to be coherent for one reader but not another. It is also possible for a text to be *more* or *less coherent* depending on the *extent* to which the individual reader shares the same presuppositions as the author. In other words, it is possible for the reader to share some, but not all, of the presuppositions.

Finally, what does all this mean for anyone trying to learn German? Have you ever experienced the following situation – perhaps when asked to translate a German passage into English?

- you read the German text;
- you look up in a dictionary all the unfamiliar words;
- you now understand most or all of the individual words;
- yet still the text does not make sense in any general way.

If this sounds familiar, the study of coherence can provide a possible explanation. What has often happened in such cases is that **cultural presuppositions** have been made by the writer of the text – based on information which you, the reader, do not share. Of course, this is not necessarily your 'fault'. It is simply the case that most texts are intended for a native-speaker audience. This means that writers assume that readers will know certain things about the country or countries where the language in question is spoken. The text we have just analysed, for example, presupposes that you are familiar with the German political system (*Bundestag, 50 Prozent, SPD, PDS, die Grünen*), several place names (*Bonn, Sachsen-Anhalt*), the fact that there was to be an election in 1998, and much more besides.

We are beginning to see, then, how learning a foreign language is not just about memorising vocabulary and grammar. It is also about working your way into a position where you share at least some of the same cultural presuppositions as native speakers. Thus, the more you know about the history, geography, politics, economics, and literature of the German-speaking countries, the more likely you are to understand the German *language*. This is because much of the German you read or hear will automatically assume that you are in possession of this kind of background information. If you are not, then you find yourself in the position described above: you understand the individual words, but the text as a whole does not make sense. To go back to the title of this chapter: coherence can only be achieved when the *meanings* of words have a *context* in which they can be understood.

Sources and recommended reading

- Fox (1990), Chapter 7, contains an introduction to the principles of German pragmatics and text analysis.
- Davies (1997), Chapter 5, deals with cohesion and coherence in German from the point of view of student essay writing.
- Chapters 5 and 6 in Linke *et al.* (1994) cover pragmatics and text linguistics (in German).
- Salkie (1995) is a very accessible introduction to principles of text and discourse analysis in English.
- Crystal (1997), Chapters 20 and 21, provide a good summary of text/discourse analysis and pragmatics.
- Chapter 4 on semantics in Fromkin and Rodman (1993) also includes a discussion of discourse meaning and pragmatics.

Exercises

1. Write the letters C or P in order to indicate whether the following utterances are constatives or performatives.

    1. Ich wette fünfzig Mark, dass er das nicht tut.
    2. Ich gratuliere dir zum Geburtstag!
    3. Dieses Schiff heißt 'Prinzessin Alexandra'.
    4. Das gefällt mir nicht.
    5. Ich schwöre, dass ich es nicht getan habe.
    6. Ich habe dafür bezahlt.
    7. Morgen fahre ich nicht nach Berlin.
    8. Ich warne dich: so etwas gefällt mir nicht.
    9. Du bist gefeuert!
    10. Ich bestehe darauf, dass du jetzt vorbeikommst.

2. By ticking the appropriate box, classify the following verbs according to the kind of illocutionary act which they would introduce. If in doubt, refer back to section 9.1.2 (p. 227).

VERB	REPRESENTATIVE	DIRECTIVE	COMMISSIVE	EXPRESSIVE	DECLARATIVE
1. schwören					
2. vermuten					
3. glauben					
4. befehlen					
5. gratulieren					
6. versprechen					
7. fragen					
8. taufen					
9. bitten					
10. danken					

3. The following utterances all contain some form of presupposition. State in English what that presupposition is.

> *Example:* Utterance: *Machst du bitte das Fenster zu?*
> Presupposition: The window is open.

1. Jürgen ist nicht mehr so traurig.
2. Dieses Mal wird er schon pünktlich ankommen.
3. Heutzutage ist es nicht mehr so schwierig, ins Ausland zu fahren.
4. Die Unzufriedenheit der Spanier wächst.
5. Es war Peter, der das gesagt hat.
6. Das vereinte Deutschland.
7. Bring dein Fahrrad ins Haus.
8. Ich bin auch Einzelkind.
9. Er hat jetzt zum vierten Mal geheiratet.
10. Würdest du bitte deine Sachen vom Tisch räumen?

4. Fairy tales for children are normally told in a strictly chronological fashion. Using your knowledge of cohesive devices and the ways in which texts must follow some kind of thematic progression, re-order the following phrases into a coherent passage. (When you have finished, you will need to change the punctuation and capital letters.)

- traurig dachte er an seine Eltern
- plötzlich aber hörte er von weitem ein lustiges Singen
- er fühlte sich sehr alleine und sehnte sich nach Gesellschaft
- der hatte in den ersten milden Frühlingstagen sein Ränzlein geschnürt* und sich auf Wanderschaft begeben
- nachdem er von Vater und Mutter recht herzlich Abschied genommen hatte
- es war einmal ein fröhlicher Müllersbursch**
- am Abend des ersten Tages seiner Wanderschaft kam er in einen tiefen, dunklen Wald

* Er hat sein Ränzlein geschnürt = he fastened his little rucksack.
** Ein fröhlicher Müllersbursch = a jolly young miller.

5. Read the following newspaper article, then work out which parts describe the background, problem, solution, and evaluation. (Remember that the text need not follow the BPSE order exactly and that some parts may be omitted.)

Gehaltsausbau

Um der Forderung nach einer Gehaltsvorauszahlung Nachdruck zu verleihen, hat der Copilot eines Airbusses den Bordcomputer ausgebaut. 323 Passagiere saßen deshalb am Sonntag acht Stunden auf dem Flughafen Berlin-Tegel fest. Nach Angaben der 'Holiday Airlines' wollten sie in den türkischen Ferienort Antalya fliegen. Eine Sprecherin der türkischen Fluggesellschaft sagt, der 33jährige Copilot habe gefordert, sein Arbeitgeber möge ihm sein Gehalt bis Ende der Saison im voraus zahlen. Als er dies nicht erhielt, baute er den Bordcomputer aus und steckte ihn in seine Tasche. Erst Stunden später wurde der geklaute Bordcomputer bei ihm entdeckt und wieder in den Airbus eingebaut. Der Copilot wurde entlassen.

(*Source: Frankfurter Rundschau*, 19.6.96)

6. Read the following film review taken from the magazine *Bravo*, then answer the subsequent questions.

FLIRTING WITH DISASTER

Abgefahrene Komödie

(1) Der 30jährige Insektenforscher Mel, der bei Adoptiveltern aufgewachsen ist, will endlich seine leiblichen Eltern kennenlernen. (2) Er beauftragt eine Detektei, seine Mutter und seinen Vater ausfindig zu machen. (3) Bald erhält Mel die Nachricht, daß seine Eltern gefunden wurden. (4) Zusammen mit seinem kleinen Sohn und seiner Ehefrau Nancy, die von diesem Vorhaben nicht sehr begeistert ist, fährt Mel los. (5) Doch die beiden ersten Adressen erweisen sich als Computerfehler. (6) Erst beim dritten Mal klappt es: Endlich steht Mel seinen Eltern Mary und Richard gegenüber. (7) Beide sind Künstler und leben als total ausgeflippte Hippies in einer Kleinstadt in New Mexico. (8) Mel lernt auch seinen schrägen Bruder Lonnie kennen. (9) Lonnie setzt alles daran, um Mel schnell wieder aus dem Haus zu haben. (10) Die Situation spitzt sich zu, als der entsetzte Mel erfährt, daß sein Vater vor 20 Jahren wegen Drogenmißbrauch im Gefängnis gesessen hat. (11) Gefühlsstarke und witzige Familienkomödie, frei ab 12 Jahren.

(*Source: Bravo*, 27.6.96)

1. To whom does the second *der* in sentence 1 refer? What kind of cohesive device is this?
2. Describe the various sense relations between *Adoptiveltern/leibliche Eltern/Eltern/Mutter/Vater* (sentences 1, 2 and 3).
3. Is the use of *die* (sentence 4) anaphoric or cataphoric?

4. To which phrase in sentence 5 does *beim dritten Mal* in sentence 6 refer, thereby creating coherence between the two?
5. Is the use of *vor 20 Jahren* in sentence 10 deictic or anaphoric?
6. What is noticeable about the grammatical structure of sentence 11?
7. The text contains many words from the same semantic field, which help it to cohere lexically. Identify the semantic field and give examples of the relevant words.

|10|

Variation in German

In the early stages of learning a foreign language, it is easy to believe that all we need to do is to master the rules of grammar, learn some vocabulary, and try to pronounce everything such that native speakers will hopefully understand us. These tasks keep us fairly well occupied until we spend some time in a country where the language is spoken. There we often realise that things are not as simple as we might have thought, since native speakers do not always seem to use the kind of language we have been learning. Frequently, they appear to break the rules of grammar we have so arduously internalised; they use words in ways we have not encountered before; and, most noticeably perhaps, their pronunciation of those words does not always coincide with the pronunciation we have been taught.

What the foreign language learner finds in such situations is known in linguistics as **variation**. By this, we mean that the vocabulary, grammar, and pronunciation of any language will vary according to who is communicating with whom, in what situation, and on what topic. By contrast, the kind of language we learn in the classroom is, of necessity, more uniform. This is because most teaching and learning is based on what is considered to be the **standard** variety of the foreign language in question.

In all modern societies it is, of course, essential to have standard languages. This is because people from different regions of a country must be able to communicate with one another, both in speech and in writing. Also, foreign learners of the language need to know which variety will be most widely accepted and understood. But it is important to remember that standard German was developed primarily on the basis of the *written* language. Also, the norms of standard pronunciation (in Germany, at least) are based on regional dialects found in the *north* of the country. Thus, there always was, and probably always will be, considerable variation in the way German is used. In other words, people do not always speak the language as they would write it nor, when speaking, do they necessarily conform to the north German model of standard pronunciation.

It is not only German which is subject to such variation. It is a characteristic of all living languages that they are used differently by different people in different situations. Consider, for example, the following: your best friend, your favourite film star, and the Prime Minister. Do they all speak in exactly the same way? Is their pronunciation identical? Do they use the same kinds of vocabulary? The answer to these questions is clearly 'no'. This is because the language used by these people will vary according to their country/region of origin, social class, age, profession, and many other factors. In linguistics, the way in which people use language differently according to the social groups to which they belong is known as **variation according to user**.

Now try to think of the way in which *you* would speak to the following people in your own language: your best friend, a prospective employer, or a famous person. Would the way you speak to these people be identical? Now imagine you were writing a letter to each of them. Would you use the same kind of language in each letter? And would the way you write to these people be the same as the way you would address them face-to-face? Again the answer is clearly 'no'. This is because most language users realise that they need to adapt their language according to the medium of communication (e.g. spoken or written) and the level of formality of the situation in which they find themselves. In linguistics, the way in which people use language differently in different situations is known as **variation according to use**.

In Chapter 9, we talked about the kinds of knowledge which advanced learners of a foreign language must have if they are to use that language not just correctly but also appropriately. It should be clear by now that learning German is more than just a question of getting the pronunciation and grammar right, or memorising large amounts of vocabulary. In this chapter, we shall see how it is also essential to understand something about when and why native speakers *vary* their use of German. Similarly, learners need to know how to adapt their own usage in order to enable them to produce the right kind of German in the right place at the right time.

The branch of linguistics most directly concerned with variation is known as **sociolinguistics**. Sociolinguists are interested both in *how* people vary their language and *why*. In this chapter, we shall be exploring each of these aspects of variation, looking at the ways in which the use of German can differ, but also the underlying reasons for these differences.

10.1   Variation according to user

Consider speaking, in your own language, to someone you have never met before on the telephone. What kind of information will you be able to deduce about that person simply by listening to the way they speak? Can you tell which country or region they come from? Can you gain an impression of their social class background? Would you be able to make assumptions regarding their level of education or even their intelligence? In all probability, by the time the phone call is over, you will have a pretty clear mental picture of what that person is like.

Should you ever meet the person to whom you were speaking on the telephone, the chances are that he or she will bear little resemblance to the person you had imagined. This is because the judgements we make are frequently tainted by prejudice and stereotypes, and all too often are simply wrong. But none of this prevents us from making such judgements in the first place. It is a natural feature of human behaviour that we constantly evaluate other people in order to find out who they are and what they are like. We then process this information (albeit subconsciously) so as to gauge how we should behave towards them and how we expect them to behave towards us. In order to do this, we use *linguistic cues* in much the same way that most of us form an opinion about people by the clothes they are wearing.

Native speakers possess a considerable amount of social and cultural knowledge about their own language. This is knowledge which they have acquired through growing up and living within a culture where that language is used. They tend therefore to know what kinds of judgements are commonly made about their language, and which features of pronunciation, vocabulary, and grammar carry the relevant messages. Consider, for example, the following the ways of pronouncing the English words 'far' and 'house':

'far' [fɑr]   versus 'far' [fɑ]
'*h*ouse' [haʊs] versus 'ouse'[aʊs]

Most native speakers of English will be able to infer some kind of information from the presence or absence of [r] in the word 'far', for example, whether the speaker is from the USA or Britain, or even from which particular part of Britain. Similarly, h-dropping might signal that the language being used is of a fairly casual register.

Inexperienced foreign learners of a language will not normally be in a position to process what they hear in this manner. In this section, therefore, we shall be looking at some of the ways in which German varies according to the people who use it, and consider how such variation might be interpreted by native speakers of German. We shall begin by looking at geographical/regional differences, before turning to social class, age, and ethnicity.

10.1.1   Geography

The most obvious kind of information we can glean from the speech of other people is their region or country of origin. We do this primarily on the basis of pronunciation, but also because of differences in vocabulary and grammar. Linguists make an important distinction in this regard. If it is only pronunciation which varies, it is customary to speak of **accent**. If there are differences in vocabulary, grammar, *and* pronunciation, then we are dealing with **dialect**. Since British English was standardised comparatively early, regional variation tends to be limited to pronunciation, and is primarily a question of accent. In the German-speaking countries, however, where standardisation occurred much later, it is still possible to find many traditional dialects where pronunciation, vocabulary, and grammar all differ markedly from the standard language. The study of the distribution and use of dialects is known as **dialectology**.

TRADITIONAL GERMAN DIALECTS AND REGIONAL
COLLOQUIAL LANGUAGES

Traditional German dialects can still be classified more or less in terms of the historical divisions discussed in Chapter 2. In other words, the German-speaking countries can be divided into three broad areas, each of which contains a number of different dialects (*see* Fig. 10.1 and Table 10.1). Above

Fig. 10.1 Traditional German dialects

the Benrath Line in the northern part of Germany, Low German dialects (*Niederdeutsch*) are still found, which were not affected by the High German (second) sound shift. Between the Benrath and Germersheim Lines, Central German dialects (*Mitteldeutsch*) are spoken, which were only partially affected by the High German sound shift. Finally, below the Germersheim Line, that is, in southern Germany, Switzerland, and Austria, Upper German dialects (*Oberdeutsch*) are spoken, which display all the features of the High German shift. (The lines on maps which divide different dialect areas are known as **isoglosses**.)

Although dialect continues to function as an extremely important marker of regional and social identity in Germany, traditional dialects have been in general decline during the past 200 years or so (see 2.3.1). There are three main reasons for this. First, dialects have been much derided since the nineteenth century due to the higher prestige increasingly afforded to standard usage. Second, mass migration and urbanisation in the nineteenth and twentieth centuries meant that many people have moved away from

Table 10.1   Traditional German dialects

NIEDERDEUTSCH (not affected by High German sound shift)	Westniederdeutsch	Schleswigsch / Holsteinisch / Nordniedersächsisch / Westfälisch / Ostfälisch
	Ostniederdeutsch	Mecklenburgisch / Märkisch
MITTELDEUTSCH (partially affected by High German sound shift, e.g. *Appel* not *Apfel*)	Westmitteldeutsch (*pund*)	Ripuarisch (*dat, dorp*) / Moselfränkisch (*dat, dorf*) / Rheinfränkisch (*das, dorf*) / Hessisch (*das, dorf*)
	Ostmitteldeutsch (*fund*)	Thüringsch / Obersächsisch
OBERDEUTSCH (fully affected by High German sound shift)	Oberfränkisch	Südfränkisch / Ostfränkisch
	Bairisch	Nordbairisch / Mittelbairisch / Südbairisch
	Alemannisch	Schwäbisch / Niederalemannisch / Hochalemannisch

(Adapted from Stedje, 1989: 190)

their traditional dialect-speaking areas (typically from villages to towns). Third, the influence of the media, education, and tourism has meant that all speakers are now in more or less continuous contact with the standard language.

As a result of these changes new forms of language have gradually gained in importance during the twentieth century, which are often referred to as regional colloquial languages (*regionale Umgangssprachen*). These varieties are probably closer to the standard language than to the traditional dialects, but still contain features of vocabulary and pronunciation (especially intonation) which are recognisably typical of certain areas. Examples of such colloquial languages are to be found in Baden-Württemberg, and in and around Berlin.

Finally, even though it is possible to talk about 'traditional German dialects', 'regional colloquial languages', and 'standard German' as though they were quite separate, it is important to emphasise that these are *not* discrete varieties. On the contrary, most speakers vary their usage between these different styles of German in quite subtle – and sometimes less subtle – ways. It is therefore helpful to think of regional variation in German as a continuum. Having said this, the reasons why speakers move up and down this continuum are not simply a question of regional origin, but are closely linked to social class status, and to the formality of the situation in which speakers find themselves at any given time.

DIALECT AND STANDARD IN GERMANY, SWITZERLAND, AND AUSTRIA

The relationship between standard language and dialect usage is not the same in all the German-speaking countries. Yet the standard varieties of German found in Switzerland and Austria are often classified as 'dialects' of *Binnendeutsch*, i.e. the German used in the Federal Republic of Germany. This is misleading because both Switzerland and Austria have their own standardised versions of German, namely, Swiss Standard/High German and Austrian Standard German, as well as a number of indigenous regional dialects.

There are probably two main reasons why the standard varieties of Switzerland and Austria tend to be misclassified as dialects of *Binnendeutsch*. First, Germany is the largest of the German-speaking countries, and is therefore often perceived to be the home of the 'real' standard. Second, for obvious geographical reasons, the standard varieties of Switzerland and Austria are closely related to the regional dialects which are spoken in the south of Germany, particularly in Baden-Württemberg and Bavaria, respectively.

To avoid misunderstandings, many linguists prefer the term **national variety** of German when discussing the different standard languages used in Germany, Switzerland, and Austria. Moreover, any language which has more than one recognised standard form can be described as **pluricentric**.

English is probably the clearest example of a pluricentric language since there are so many different standards, for example, in England, Scotland, Wales, Ireland, the United States, Canada, Australia, India, and South Africa. But it is equally possible to refer to German as a pluricentric language with differing norms in Germany, Switzerland, and Austria.

GEOGRAPHICAL VARIANTS OF GERMAN

What then are the main linguistics features typical of the different parts of the German-speaking areas? Clearly, there is insufficient space here to describe the precise differences between all the regional and national varieties. However, it will still be possible to mention a few features which are generally considered typical of certain areas such as the north and centre of Germany, and south Germany, Austria, and Switzerland. Tables 10.2, 10.3 and 10.4 outline some of the main phonological, lexical, and morpho-syntactic variants found in German, i.e. differences in pronunciation, vocabulary, and grammar.

Table 10.2 Phonological variants

Area	Word	Standard pronunciation	Regional pronunciation
NORTH	*Pfund*	[p͡fʊnt]	Word-initial [p͡f] often pronounced as [f], e.g. *funt* [fʊnt].
	Rat *grob*	[ʀɑt] [gʀɔp]	Long vowels often pronounced short in monosyllabic words, e.g. *ratt* [ʀat] and *gropp* [gʀɔp].
	nicht	[nɪçt]	Final [t] often deleted, e.g. *nich* [nɪç].
NORTH + CENTRE	*dreißig* *Zeug*	[dʀaɪsɪk] [tsɔɪk]	Final [k] pronounced as [ç], e.g. [dʀaɪsɪç] and [tsɔɪç].
	rot	–	[R] pronounced as uvular roll (see 4.2.4 and 4.4.2).
	geht *gemacht*	[get] [gəmaxt]	Salient-initial [g] pronounced as [j], e.g. *jeht* [jet] and *jemacht* [jəmaxt] (especially Berlin and Cologne).
CENTRE + SOUTH	*ich* *mich*	[ɪç] [mɪç]	*ch* often pronounced like *sch*, e.g. *isch* [ɪʃ] and *misch* [mɪʃ].
	lachen *Lampen*	[laxən] [lampən]	Word-final [n] often lost, e.g. *lache* [laxə] and *Lampe* [lampə].
	packen/backen *Tier/dir* *Garten/Karten*	[pakən]/[bakən] [tiɐ]/[diɐ] [gartən]/[kartən]	Distinction between voiced and voiceless plosives/fricatives lost, a process known as **lenition**. Hence: *bagge*→[bagə], *dia* → [diɐ], *Garde*→[gardə]. (Meaning of words becomes clear in context.)
	Brüder *schön*	[brydɐ] [ʃøn]	[y] and [ø] pronounced as [i] and [e], respectively, e.g. *Brieder* [bridɐ], *scheen* [ʃen].

Table 10.2 (continued)

Area	Word	Standard pronunciation	Regional pronunciation
	Wasser *schlafen*	[vasɐ] [ʃlafən]	[a] pronounced as [ɔ], e.g. *Wosser* [vɔsɐ] and *schlofen* [ʃlɔfən].
	heute *Leute*	[hɔɪtə] [lɔɪtə]	Word-final schwa often lost, e.g. *heut* [hɔɪt] and *Leut* [lɔɪt].
	nicht	[nɪçt]	Pronounced *net* [nɛt] or *nit* [nɪt].
SOUTH	*China*	[çina]	[ç] pronounced as [k], e.g. *Kina* [kina].
	rot	—	[r] pronounced as alveolar roll (see 4.2.4 and 4.4.2).
	gemacht *bestellt*	[gəmaxt] [bəʃtɛlt]	Schwa often deleted in prefixes, e.g. *gmacht* [gmɔxt], *bstellt* [bʃtɛlt].
	sagen *lesen*	[zɑgən] [lezən]	Salient-initial [z] often pronounced as [s], e.g. *sagen* [sɔgən] and *lesen* [lesən].
	beste *Wespe* (SW)	[bɛstə] [vɛspə]	[st] and [sp] pronounced as [ʃt] and [ʃp], e.g. *beschte* [bɛʃtə] and *Weschpe* [vɛʃpə].
	Kaffee *Tabak*	[ˈkafe] [ˈtabak]	Word stress on final syllable, e.g. *Ka'ffee* [kaˈfe] and *Ta'bak* [taˈbak].

(Adapted from Durrell, 1992: 14–15)

Table 10.3 Lexical variants

Area	Standard variant	Regional variant	English
NORTH	*Abendessen* *sehen* *der Fleischer* *das Butterbrot*	*Abendbrot* *kucken/kieken* *der Schlachter* *die Stulle*	supper to look/see butcher sandwich
CENTRE + SOUTH	*zu Hause* *nicht wahr?* *der Fleischer* *der Rotkohl* *der Tischler*	*daheim* *gell?* *der Metzger* *das Rotkraut (C)/* *das Blaukraut (S)* *der Schreiner*	at home . . . isn't it/aren't they, etc.? butcher red cabbage carpenter/joiner
SOUTH	*immer* *sehr* *der Junge* *die Kartoffel* *die Straße* *schnell* *der Schrank* *das Mädchen*	*alleweil (SE)* *arg* *der Bub* *der Erdapfel (SE)* *die Gasse (SE)* *geschwind* *der Kasten* *das Mädel/Mädle*	always very boy potato street quick(ly) cupboard girl

Area	Standard variant	Regional variant	English
	nicht mehr	*nimmer*	no longer
	die Apfelsine	*die Orange*	orange
	die Sahne	*der Rahm*	cream
	arbeiten	*schaffen (SW)*	to work
	sehen	*schauen*	to see/look
	das Brötchen	*die Semmel (SE)* *der Wecken (SW)*	bread roll

(Adapted from Durrell, 1992: 20–2)

Table 10.4   Morpho-syntactic variants

Area	Standard	Regional	Description
NORTH	*ich habe begonnen* *ich habe angefangen*	*ich bin begonnen* *ich bin angefangen*	*sein* not *haben* in past perfect of *beginnen* and *anfangen*.
	er hat mich gesehen	*er hat mir gesehen*	Variable use of accusative and dative.
	die Doktor *die Onkel* *die Wagen*	*die Doktors* *die Onkels* *die Wagens*	*-s* sometimes used to form plural nouns.
CENTRE + SOUTH	*gedacht* *gewinkt*	*gedenkt* *gewunken*	Use of different past participles.
	das Auto, das da steht	*das Auto, wo da steht*	*wo* used as relative pronoun.
SOUTH	*ich habe gelegen* *ich habe gesessen* *ich habe gestanden*	*ich bin gelegen* *ich bin gesessen* *ich bin gestanden*	*sein* used in past perfect of *liegen, sitzen, stehen*.
	sie fuhr *er sagte* *sie lachten*	*sie ist gefahren* *er hat gesagt* *sie haben gelacht*	No imperfect tense (see also 10.2.3).
	mit den Büchern	*mit den Bücher* *mit die Bücher (SE)*	No *-n* in dative plural/no dative form of definite article.
	die Wagen *die Stücke* *die Stiefel*	*die Wägen* *die Stücker* *die Stiefeln*	Different plural forms.
	die Butter *das Radio* *die Gewalt* *die Schokolade* *die Kartoffel*	*der Butter* *der Radio* *der Gewalt* *der Schokolad* *der Kartoffel*	Variation in gender of nouns.
	er schläft *sie läßt*	*er schlaft* *sie laßt*	No umlaut in 3rd person present forms.

(Adapted from Durrell, 1992: 16–17)

10.1.2   Social class

The use of German, like most other languages, is closely related to the social class status of its speakers. Nevertheless, it is extremely difficult to find a satisfactory definition of social class in modern, industrial societies. Class could be based on a number of factors such as occupation, income, education, or place of residence.

Whatever the problems of defining social class, it is still possible to say that the relationship between class and language usage depends very much on the historical status of the standard variety in question. In Britain, for example, there has been a long tradition of a standard accent known as **Received Pronunciation (RP)**. This is the accent of the *English* middle and upper classes, and is closely linked to institutions such as the royal family, public schools, and the BBC. Traditionally, the high social prestige afforded to RP has been accompanied by considerable prejudice towards non-standard and regional varieties of English, typically used by working-class speakers. In many cases, this has meant that a command of the standard language has been one of the prerequisites for access to certain high-status professions although this is undoubtedly changing.

Because of the relatively late standardisation of German, the relationship between social class and standard/dialect usage is probably less fixed in Germany than in Britain. Also, the national institutions which continue to uphold the prestige of RP do not exist as such in Germany. The period in which Germany was united under a single monarch was brief (1871–1918), and prior to that the Prussian monarchy often preferred to speak French (see 2.2.3). Similarly, Germany has never really had a class-based system of private education through which the prestige of the standard has been promoted. Nonetheless, the media and state schools have played no small part in the dissemination of standard German throughout the twentieth century.

On the basis of these historical differences, there are two main comparisons which can be made between social class status and use of the standard language in Germany and Britain. First, there is undoubtedly a correlation between social class and standard usage in Germany in so far as regional dialects tend to be used more by working-class speakers than by the middle and upper classes. But, at the same time, regional forms of language are often used by German speakers of a *higher* social class status than would normally be the case in England. This is particularly common in southern Germany, especially Bavaria and Baden-Württemberg, where dialect is perceived as an extremely positive expression of regional identity. Consequently, it is not unusual to hear well-educated and influential south Germans on television or radio using very marked forms of dialect. In this respect, the status of regional varieties in southern Germany is probably more akin to that of the national varieties of English used in Ireland, Scotland, and Wales.

The second difference between Britain and Germany relates to the notion of the continuum, discussed in the previous section on geographical variation. It is probably true to say that, irrespective of social class, Germans from dialect-speaking areas are much more inclined to move up and down the continuum between standard language and dialect than would be the case with English speakers (who probably have fewer varieties to choose from in the first place). For example, as a foreigner, it is not uncommon to find oneself in mid-conversation with a south German using standard German, who then turns to a member of his or her family and says something in broad dialect. This is a phenomenon known in linguistics as *code switching* (see also 3.1.8). However, the reasons why speakers code switch are extremely complex, and also relate to the medium of communication and level of formality of the situation in question.

10.1.3   Age

Many changes take place in our lives as we grow from childhood to adulthood. The most obvious differences are physical, but these are usually accompanied by shifts in social behaviour, and this includes the way we use language. Our language changes in order to meet the needs of our social environment. Thus, the speech patterns typically used by a 5 year-old are no longer appropriate forty years later.

Age clearly affects all human beings, but it is the language of one particular group – youth – which has attracted most attention in socio-linguistics. There are many reasons why young people might want (or need) to use language differently from adults (and children). Adolescence is typically a time where there is intensive contact with other people of the same age, for example, through education or leisure activities. It also constitutes a stage in life when young people begin to mark out an identity for themselves which is separate from that of their elders. Using different forms of language is one way of signalling such independence from, and even rejection of, the adult world. Nevertheless, it is very difficult to make any real generalisations about the kind of language used by young people. As far as German is concerned, for example, it has been noted that there are probably as many different types of youth language – or *Jugendsprache* – as there are young Germans. (See Schlobinski (1995) from which examples of youth language are also taken.)

A typical claim regarding youth language in Germany is that it contains a high number of English loans, e.g. *cool, Sound, Power,* or words derived from English, such as *speedig* (zappy), or *poppig* (trendy). Similarly, young people are thought to make extensive use of onomatopoeia, or so-called 'sound words'. This *Päng-Sprache*, as it is sometimes known in German, includes exclamations such as *ächz, würg,* and *hechel,* expressing relief, dislike, and exhaustion, respectively.

But while it may be true that there is a strong element of English and onomatopoeia in the speech of young Germans, these forms are also typically found in the media. Thus, magazines such as *Bravo* read by young people all draw on what might be termed *Jugendsprache* so as to increase their sales appeal to that age group. Ultimately, it becomes difficult to say which styles of language are genuinely typical of young people, and which are simply created artificially by marketing managers and journalists in order to sell their products.

However, there is probably one generalisation which can be made about young people's use of language, that is, their tendency to be extremely creative. It seems that young people frequently take ideas from advertising, films, and pop music, turning them around for humorous effect. For example, a 007 film might be spoofed when someone says in a James Bond-type voice *Mein Name ist Hinz. Hans Hinz!* Alternatively, the well-known quiz show on German TV *Der große Preis* (The Big Prize) might be referred to as *Der große Scheiß* (The Big Shit)! Clearly, the use of **expletives** (swear words) also plays an important part in the German spoken by many young people, as is the case with many other languages.

10.1.4   Ethnicity

Variation in a language is not only the product of geographical, class, or age divisions in society, it may also come about as the result of population movements or immigration. In the Federal Republic of Germany, there are some 4 million migrant workers – or *Gastarbeiter* as they are often euphemistically known – who were invited by the former West German government to help fill the labour shortfall between the 1950s and 1970s. These workers came mainly from Italy, Spain, Greece, Turkey, Portugal, and the former Yugoslavia. Although some have since returned to their country of origin, many have stayed with their families, who now form the second and third generations. The largest single group of migrant workers living in Germany today is of Turkish origin (approximately 1.5 million).

Many sociolinguistic studies of so-called *Gastarbeiterdeutsch (GAD)* were undertaken from the late 1960s onwards, focusing on the language of the first generation of migrant workers in what was then West Germany. Here are some examples of the type of structures which were found to be fairly typical:

ich auch bisschen mehr trinken
I also little bit more drink

ich nur in Deutschland gehe
have gone only to Germany

deine Sohn Espania wieder bleibe
your son has stayed again in Spain

er jetzt Wohnung schaffe
now is working he at home

ich drei Jahre hier arbeite
I three years here work
(From: Barbour and Stevenson, 1990: 195–204)

One of the features of language usage which fascinated linguists studying *Gastarbeiterdeutsch* were the similarities in the type of mistake made in German by speakers of different first languages. So, for example, the sentences above are all characterised by the misplacement of the verb at the end of the clause. But the five statements were produced by native speakers of Serbo-Croatian, Italian, Spanish, Greek, and Turkish, respectively. One might expect such mistakes to have been directly transferred from those other languages, yet only Serbo-Croatian and Turkish actually have the kind of word order pattern which requires the verb to be placed in final position in such phrases.

Now consider the following sentences:

gestern du immer Schnaps trinken, ja?
yesterday you always drink schnaps, yes?

Komm, Foto machen (= röntgen)
Come on, make photo (= x-ray)
(From: Barbour and Stevenson, 1990: 202)

These types of structures might also appear to be typical of *Gastarbeiterdeutsch*. However, they were not uttered by non-native speakers but by Germans. This suggests two things. First, it seems that both native and non-native speakers have similar ways of simplifying the German they are using, for example, by placing the verb at the end of the clause and using infinitives to avoid the necessary finite verb endings. Second, it could also be argued that native speakers do not help immigrants to learn German properly by using this kind of **foreigner talk**. On the contrary, speaking German in this way is extremely unhelpful to non-natives, who need to hear authentic German as the basis for their own language learning.

Much of what has been written about the language of migrant workers has tended to stress their poor proficiency in German and the problems of miscommunication which arise between native and non-native speakers. Yet many immigrants have achieved native speaker competence in German, especially those belonging to the second and third generations. Having said this, these younger generations still face a number of difficulties, which are often different to those encountered by their parents and grandparents. Most children of migrant workers grow up speaking two languages: that of the family used in the home and the German which they learn at school and elsewhere. This, in turn, can lead to ongoing doubts surrounding personal and social identity. For example, does the bilingual daughter of Turkish migrant workers growing up in Germany consider herself to be Turkish or German? Or is it possible, as some writers have suggested, to develop a kind of hybrid identity, with different types of allegiance to the two countries and languages? These are the kinds of questions now being explored by researchers looking at language and cultural identity among the third generation children of migrant workers in Germany.

10.2   Variation according to use: register

So far, we have looked at some of the reasons why different groups of speakers vary their use of German. We now turn to a discussion of variation not according to *user*, but *use*. This concerns the ways in which people vary their language according to the medium of communication they adopt (e.g. speaking or writing) and the level of formality of the situation in which they are communicating (e.g. formal or informal). Together, these two factors leads to differences of **register**. We can therefore speak of various types of register, for example, spoken versus written, formal versus informal etc.

In section 10.1 on language *users*, there was an obvious tendency to concentrate on speech because this was the medium of communication most affected by geographical and social variation. But in the case of language *use*, writing also becomes important. We shall begin therefore by looking at the main ways in which language varies according to whether someone is speaking or writing.

10.2.1   Speech and writing

Whenever we want to communicate with someone, the medium we choose will always have a direct impact on the kind of language we use. So, for example, our language will vary depending on whether we are speaking or writing, giving a lecture, or sending a fax message.

Before considering some of the main ways in which language differs according to the medium of communication, it is worth asking why people must vary their language in the first place. Why can't they simply use the same language irrespective of the medium of communication? The reason lies primarily in the **physical distance** which exists between the addresser and the addressee – collectively known as the **participants**. Take the following sentence, for example: *Angelika sagt, sie hat es nicht.* As a written statement, this is highly ambiguous. To whom does the *sie* refer – to Angelika or another person? And what exactly is the missing *es*?

Now consider the possibilities which are open to you if you utter this sentence in a face-to-face encounter, that is, where the participants can see and hear one another. For example, by pointing towards Angelika or some other person, you could make it clear who the *sie* is. You could even change your intonation to this end. Moreover, you and your addressee might be standing in front of a library shelf where there is a gap between two books. If so, it will be self-evident that the *es* to which you are referring is *das Buch*.

When writing, none of these means are available to you. For example, you cannot use body language or intonation to point to people or objects in your immediate environment. Because of the physical distance between you and your addressee(s), the *context* of your message will not be as explicit. This means that if you are going to write the above sentence, you will need to create the context for the reader. You must make sure that you state clearly to whom the *sie* refers, and also indicate the exact nature of the missing object *es*. You might therefore need to write: *Angelika sagt, Petra hat das Buch nicht* or *Angelika sagt, sie selbst hat das Buch nicht*. In addition, the subjunctive mood would be more usual in writing, hence, the following type of construction might be used: *Angelika sagt, Petra habe das Buch nicht* or *Angelika sagt, sie selbst habe das Buch nicht*.

This question of context and the physical distance between participants takes us back to a point explored in Chapter 9. In section 9.2.3, we saw how writers of texts often assume that readers are in possession of certain types of information – they make presuppositions about what readers know. If, however, the reader does not share the same presuppositions as the writer, the result is a text which is incoherent. We can now see that the same principle applies to speech. But it is also becoming clear that speech and writing often require *different* linguistic strategies in order to make their messages cohere.

One linguistic feature which functions differently in speech and writing is *deixis*. In section 9.1.3 on implied meaning, we saw how personal deixis is used to refer to people and objects (e.g. 'him/her'), spatial deixis to refer to places (e.g. 'here/there'), and temporal deixis to refer to moments in time (e.g. 'now/then'). In speech, the fact that participants can normally see one another means that the referents of deictic structures are usually clear. As we saw in the earlier example, *Angelika sagt, sie hat es nicht*, if you are speaking, then you can use body language and intonation in order to clarify to whom or what the pronouns *sie* and *es* refer. In writing, however, this is not possible. The referents of such pronouns must therefore be made explicit. One way of doing this is to avoid the use of deixis altogether, and refer to the people and objects in question by name, e.g. *Angelika, Petra*, and *das Buch*.

Another difference between spoken and written language is the level of *spontaneity*. Speaking is a much more spontaneous activity than writing. Consider, for example, the following excerpt from a discussion where Peter, Tom, and Regine are talking about Peter's plans to give up his job (*kündigen*), and spend six months in Belgium:

(..) signals a pause
= signals an interruption

Tom: Und du hast jetzt Lust zu kündigen?
Peter: Ja, Lust=
Tom: =wegen der Arbeit?
Peter: Ja, wegen der Arbeit, ich hab' jetzt keine Lust, jetzt fahr ich, weißte=
Regine: =wann fährste denn eigentlich nach Belgien?
Peter: Na ja, Ende April.
Tom: Ach so (..) Ende April bis November, oder was?
Peter: Na, mmm (..) vielleicht bleib' ich auch noch da.
Tom: Eh?

This is a perfectly normal conversation amongst friends, but as a written text taken out of its original context it may seem largely incoherent. The spontaneous nature of casual speech means that there is little time for the speakers to plan what they say – hence the false starts, incomplete sentences, and repetition. There is also much hesitation, signalled for example by the use of interjections (*ja, weißte, na ja, na, mmm, eh*) and modal particles (*denn, eigentlich, auch, noch*). In addition, the speakers interrupt one another – before Peter has explained whether he is really going to give up his job, Regine asks him when he is going to Belgium. Tom then suggests the dates, even though it emerges that Peter is not really sure whether he is going at all.

When writing, there is generally much more scope to think about the presentation of a message. Writers have more time to reflect on their ideas, and to formulate these in complete sentences using complex linguistic structures. They can also organise the various ideas within a text so that they seem relevant, follow some kind of thematic progression, and therefore appear coherent to potential readers. In order to do this, writers often need to make use of the kinds of cohesive devices outlined in section 9.2.1. Furthermore, they can structure their text with the help of headings and paragraphs, lists and numbers, or emphasise certain points by using typographical features such as *italics*, **bold**, underscoring and CAPITAL LETTERS.

Perhaps it is the more 'organised' nature of the written word which leads many people to believe that writing is a superior form of communication to speech. As we shall see later in this chapter, this is partly why *formal* spoken language uses many of the linguistic forms which typify writing. Moreover, some people are very concerned about 'defending' the written language, and 'protecting' it from the corrupting influences of the spoken word (e.g. slang). But this is somewhat ironic in view of the fact that, historically, writing systems are almost always an attempt to imitate speech, and not vice versa.

Finally, it is important to note that while a fairly clear distinction has been made here between speech and writing, there are many forms of communication which blur this division. So, for example, a writer might try to imitate the speech of a dialect user in a novel or play. Alternatively, a formal spoken lecture might contain language more typical of written usage or simply consist of a written text read aloud. Modern technology has also played a significant role in breaking down the distinction between speech and writing. E-mail messages are often spontaneous forms of written communication whose structures are more akin to those of spoken language. Conversely, on the telephone, speakers cannot rely on the body language, intonation, and shared context which normally characterise face-to-face encounters.

10.2.2   Level of formality

In the previous section, we saw how people need to vary their use of language according to the medium of communication they have chosen. One of the main reasons for this lies in the *physical distance* between addressers and their addressees. When writing, for example, that distance tends to be greater than when speaking. Here, we shall be exploring a further reason why people vary their use of language, namely, **social distance**. By social distance, we mean differences in status and familiarity between participants. These are factors which, in turn, affect the level of formality which needs to be adopted.

Every time people communicate with others, they make very complex judgements about the social distance between themselves and their addressees. For example, they take into account how well they know the other person, who has the higher status, how polite they wish to appear, and what they hope to achieve from the interaction. People then use this information in order to 'position themselves' with respect to others, i.e. decide how close or distant they think they should appear. Of course, the extent to which this happens at a conscious level will vary from one situation to the next – you are likely to reflect long and hard about the impression you want to make in a job interview, though you will barely give a passing thought to a relaxed conversation with your best friend. But whatever the case, all language users draw on their perceptions of social relationships in order to gauge the level of formality which they consider appropriate in a given situation.

Because concerns about social relationships are more immediately relevant to spoken interaction, it is probably true to say that speech is more susceptible to fluctuations in levels of formality than writing. Nonetheless, it is still possible to write in ways which convey differing levels of formality – consider the earlier example of the letter to your best friend, a prospective employer, or a famous person.

In order to explore how different levels of formality work in practice, we shall now look at two telephone conversations – the first is an example of formal German usage between two people who have never met before, and takes place in a business context. The second is a private, informal chat between friends.

Formal telephone conversation

Herr Braun: Firma Meyer, guten Tag.
Herr Wolf: Ja, guten Tag. Ich hätte gern Herrn Kemmerling gesprochen.
Herr Braun: Herr Kemmerling ist heute leider nicht im Hause. Kann ich Ihnen vielleicht behilflich sein?
Herr Wolf: Nein danke, ich muss mit Herrn Kemmerling persönlich sprechen.
Herr Braun: Darf ich ihm dann etwas ausrichten?
Herr Wolf: Ja. Sagen Sie ihm bitte, er möchte morgen vor zehn Uhr bei mir anrufen.
Herr Braun: Und wie ist Ihr Name?
Herr Wolf: Mein Name ist Wolf von der Firma Großmann. Die Nummer ist 0421 – 67 98 08.
Herr Braun: 0421 – 67 98 08. Gut, Herr Wolf. Ich werde es ihm ausrichten.
Herr Wolf: Ich danke Ihnen. Aufwiederhören.
Herr Braun: Aufwiederhören, Herr Wolf.

Informal telephone conversation

Marianne: Ja, hier ist Marianne.
Sabine: Ja hallo Marianne, ist die Heike da?
Marianne: Ja, ich glaub' schon. Klein' Moment. Ich geh' mal gucken.
Heike: Hallo?
Sabine: Hi Heike. Ich bin's, Sabine.
Marianne: Ach, Sabinchen. Na? Wie geht's?
Sabine: Ach, solala. Haste Lust, heut' Abend auf'n Bier wegzugehen?
Heike: Aber immer!
Sabine: Treffen wir uns um neun in der Wunderbar?
Heike: Klaro.
Sabine: Okay, tschüss. Bis dann.
Heike: Ciao.

To begin with, there are a number of grammatical differences between the language used in these two conversations. The first draws on structures more typical of a higher register, e.g. the subjunctive *ich hätte gern/er möchte anrufen* as well as the dative suffix *-e* in *im Hause*. By contrast, the second conversation has a number of elided or contracted forms such as *ich glaub', klein' Moment, ich geh', ich bin's, wie geht's, haste, heut' Abend,* and *auf'n Bier.*

But it is in the area of vocabulary where we find the greatest number of differences. Thus, in the formal telephone conversation, a higher register is created through lexical items such as *behilflich sein* (=*helfen*) or *ausrichten* (=*weitersagen*), whereas the informal passage draws on colloquial forms such as *gucken* (=*sehen*), *solala* (=*es geht so*), *klaro* (=*klar*) and *okay*. In addition, the kinds of greetings which occur differ markedly: the first conversation has *guten Tag* and *aufwiederhören*, whereas the second uses *hallo, tschüss, bis dann,* and *ciao.*

Corresponding to these greetings are the different modes of address used by the speakers. The formal conversation requires the use of titles and surnames, e.g. *Herr Kemmerling* and *Herr Wolf.* In the informal conversation, by contrast, the speakers are on first name terms. There is also the colloquial use of the definite article, e.g. *die Heike,* as well as the addition of the suffix *-chen* to produce the term of endearment *Sabinchen.* Last but not least, German indicates formality through the different personal pronouns: *Sie* in the first extract but *du* in the second.

From these two telephone conversations, we can begin to see how different linguistic structures can be used to convey varying levels of formality in German. But it is also important to say something more about *when* and *why* people should feel the need to vary their language. How do they know, for example, when to use a more formal or informal register?

The main reason for varying language in this way relates to the social distance between the addresser and addressee – the relative **status** of each person. In general, if there is **unequal status**, then a formal register is normally used – at least by the speaker with the lower status. An example of this might be a worker speaking to the boss. In such a case, the worker's use of a more formal register would be interpreted by the boss as a mark of politeness and respect. If, by contrast, there is **equal status** between speakers, then there is generally more scope to use informal registers. For example, two friends are likely to use a lower register in conversation with one another, and this will be interpreted by both as a sign of solidarity and intimacy. Each of these examples implies, however, that speakers already know one another. What happens if they do not? In such situations, it is in fact customary to use a more formal register in order to signal politeness, the convention being that we assume a stranger to have a higher status than ourselves until we know otherwise.

Having said this, there are no hard and fast rules which account for the level of formality required in any one situation – and rules, of course, are frequently broken. Inevitably, judgements about which register to adopt will depend very much on the context of a given interaction. For example, unequal status between participants does not always guarantee that the lower status participant will adopt a formal register. Indeed, a worker might deliberately use a lower register as a way of communicating dissatisfaction with his or her boss. Similarly, equal status between participants does not always presuppose a lower register. Two teachers of the same status might consider it more appropriate to adopt a formal register at work, especially in front of their pupils. Moreover, the same two teachers might vary their use of register depending on whether they are at work or at a birthday party.

Another factor which must also be borne in mind is that the norms of politeness conveyed by different registers tend to change over time.

Traditionally, for example, many men thought it necessary to adopt more formal registers when speaking to women, and children were often taught that politeness towards all adults was of paramount importance. These are both attitudes which have shifted in the past forty years or so (though to varying extents in different families and cultures). Similarly, from the early 1970s, it became common for most young people in Germany to address one another with *du*, irrespective of whether they knew each other personally (e.g. in a bank or shop). However, this trend would appear to have been partly reversed, such that it can be very difficult to predict which personal pronoun will be appropriate. If in doubt, the best advice is always to say *Sie*, and then switch to *du* if the other person replies with *du*. This is because it is easier to rectify the over-politeness signalled by the incorrect use of *Sie*, than to put right the over-familiarity created by the inappropriate use of *du*.

Finally, given the shades of meaning which can be conveyed by these complex shifts in register, it is not difficult to see how non-native speakers of a language might sometimes appear impolite, disrespectful, or unfriendly. For example, in a situation where formality is required, it is possible to offend others by using language which is too informal – especially slang. Conversely, when dealing with friends, it is easy to appear cold and distant by speaking (or writing) in a manner which is too formal. All of this may be quite unintentional – it is simply that foreign language learners are not always sufficiently confident or competent to vary their use of the language in ways which signal the appropriate levels of formality. Being aware that language carries these additional social meanings is, of course, the first step. After that, it is a question of practice.

10.2.3   *Linguistic features of register variation in German*

The division into 'user' and 'use' has been a helpful way of organising the discussion in this chapter. But in practice the two types of variation cannot really be separated. This is because the German used in any given situation depends simultaneously on the geographical origin, social class, age, and ethnicity of the user *and* the specific uses to which the language is being put. However, if we combine the many factors affecting variation, it is possible to classify the different registers of German into three main groups as follows.

> *R1:*   This is the most casual register of everyday speech used in informal situations to discuss mundane topics. It is characterised by elided and contracted endings, grammatically incomplete sentences, and familiar vocabulary (sometimes including expletives and vulgarisms). This is

also the register where the kinds of geographical features of pronunciation, vocabulary, and grammar described in section 10.1.1 can be most frequently heard.

R2: This is a fairly neutral register typical of more formal speech and less formal styles of writing. It tends to be more complete in terms of pronunciation and grammar than R1, but still contains quite familiar vocabulary. The pronunciation, vocabulary, and grammar are also more standardised – one would be less likely to find the use of very marked regional features here than in R1. This is the register which tends to be used in elementary and intermediate teaching materials for foreign learners of German.

R3: This is the register of German which is reserved mainly for writing, though it may also be used in formal speech (e.g. lectures, radio/television news and documentaries). Since it is predominantly written, it tends to be characterised by complete grammatical structures and formal vocabulary with few, if any, regional features. R3 can also be sub-divided into the style of written German found in literary texts and that used in formal, non-literary texts such as serious newspapers, business letters, and academic writing.

(Adapted from Durrell, 1992: 6–7)

Again, it is important to emphasise that even this attempt to classify register constitutes an oversimplification. In reality, we are dealing with a continuum, along which language users will vary their usage in quite subtle ways. However, the division is still useful in terms of illustrating how and why foreign learners of German need to be aware of register variation. This is because the kind of German typically learned by students on a 'year abroad' in a German-speaking country is that of R1 – in other words, the spoken register of casual everyday, informal encounters used for discussing mundane topics. This is not, however, the register which is required of more advanced students in the later phases of a university course, for example, in written summaries and essays, or indeed more formal spoken genres such as presentations, oral examinations, and interpreting. There it is essential to be able to move along the continuum towards R3 – a register which can only really be acquired through contact with written texts (serious newspapers/news magazines, literary fiction, etc.) and the linguistically more demanding programmes on television and radio (news, documentaries, drama, etc.).

Finally, in order to provide a more specific illustration of this kind of variation, Tables 10.5, 10.6 and 10.7 summarise some of the main phonological, lexical, and morpho-syntactic features of German which vary according to register. In each case, the most formal variants (R3) are to the left of the table, with the least formal (R1) to the right.

Table 10.5 Phonological variation in register

R3	R1	Description
gehen [gehən] *eigenen* [aɪɡənən]	*gehn* [gen] *eign'n* [aɪɡŋ̩]	Assimilation/reduction of unstressed *-en* suffixes
schon mal [ʃon mɑl] *fünfzig* [fʏnft̠sɪk]	*scho ma* [ʃoma] *fuffzich* [fʊft̠sɪç]	Simplification and assimilation of consonants
haben wir [habən wiɐ] *weißt du* [vaɪst du] *wissen Sie* [vɪsən zi]	*hammer* [hamə] *weißte* [vaɪstə] *wissense* [vɪsŋ̩zə]	Reduction of pronouns
der [dɛɐ], *die* [di], *das* [das] *den, dem* *ein, eine, einen* *einem, einer*	*da* [də], *di* [dɪ], *s* *n, m* *n, ne, n'n* [nn] *nem/eim, ner*	Reduction of articles
bei den *mit dem, mit den* *mit einem, mit einer*	*bein* *mim, mitn* *minnem, minner*	Articles fused with prepositions
ich komme *ich könnt* *gehe*	*ich komm'* *ich könnt'* *geh'*	Unstressed schwa elided in verb endings
allein *fünf* *vorn*	*alleine* *fünfe* *vorne*	Unstressed schwa added to some numerals and other words
Was machst denn du hier?	*Was machs'n du hier?*	*denn* reduced and suffixed to a verb

(Adapted from Durrell, 1992: 14–16)

Table 10.6 Lexical variation in register

R3	R2	R1
die Hochschulreife	das Abitur	das Abi
sich fürchten	Angst haben	Schiß haben[a]
extrem	äußerst	unheimlich
erhalten, empfangen	bekommen	kriegen
der Treibstoff	das Benzin	der Sprit
sich beklagen	sich beschweren	meckern, maulen
speisen	essen	fressen, futtern, mampfen, naschen
das Zuchthaus	das Gefängnis	der Knast
das Antlitz das Angesicht	das Gesicht	die Fresse, die Fratze, die Visage
hervorragend	großartig	enorm, prima, klasse, toll
das Geld		die Knete, die Moneten, der Kies, der Zaster
die Hand		die Pfote
das Gesäß	der Hintern	der Arsch[a]
gelingen		klappen
der Studienrat	der Lehrer	der Pauker
lediglich	nur	bloß
die Polizei		die Polente, die Bullen
(schwer) arbeiten		schuften
entwenden	stehlen	klauen
ableben, verscheiden, entschlafen	sterben	krepieren, abkratzen, verrecken
sich erbrechen	sich übergeben brechen	kotzen[a]
(Alkohol) trinken		saufen
weshalb?	warum?	wieso?
sich entfernen	weggehen	abhauen

Note: [a]vulgar
(Adapted from Durrell, 1992: 24–8)

Table 10.7 Morpho-syntactic variation in register

R3	R1	Description
der Hut meines Vaters	*der Hut von meinem Vater*	Genitive case rare in R1
Ich haben ihn gesehen *Sie kommt heute nicht*	*Ich habe den gesehen* *Die kommt heute nicht*	Use of demonstrative instead of personal pronoun
Thomas kommt mit Angelika	*Der Thomas kommt mit der Angelika*	Definite article used with names
eine solche Farbe	*so'ne Farbe*	Replacement of *solch*
Er ist größer als ich	*Der ist größer wie ich*	Replacement of *als* with *wie*
Wir brauchen nicht so schwer zu arbeiten	*Wir brauchen nicht so schwer arbeiten*	Omission of *zu* after *brauchen*
weil er eben kein richtiges Deutsch sprechen kann	*weil der kann eben kein richtiges Deutsch (sprechen)*	*weil* followed by main clause word order + main verbs elided after some modal auxiliaries
Er hat Post von zu Hause bekommen	*Er hat Post bekommen von zu Hause*	*Ausklammerung*, i.e. elements placed after final verb (see 7.2.2)
Sie fuhr gestern	*Sie ist gestern gefahren*	Perfect tense often replaces imperfect (see also 10.1.1)
Sie sagte, sie wisse es schon	*Sie sagte, sie wüßte es schon/ Sie hat gesagt, sie weiß/ wüßte es schon*	Present subjunctive replaced by past subjunctive or present indicative

(Adapted from Durrell, 1992: 18–19)

Sources and recommended reading

- Barbour and Stevenson (1990) is a comprehensive study of variation in German, covering most of the topics presented in this chapter.
- Clyne (1995) is also very thorough, and is particularly good on the issue of German as a pluricentric language.
- Stedje (1989), Chapter 17, provides a very readable summary (in German) of geographical, social and register variation.
- Russ (1994), Chapter 2, discusses variation and contains many illustrative passages.
- Stevenson (1997) provides an accessible introduction to variation in German, covering such topics as regional variation, the differences between written and spoken language, public language, politeness, and multilingualism. All chapters contain a number of practical exercises.
- Russ (1990a) is a collection of detailed studies of the different German dialects.
- König (1978) contains many fascinating dialect maps.
- Stötzel and Wengeler (1995) is a comprehensive collection of essays (in German) on various issues relating to the German language today. See especially Wengeler on immigration debates and Hahn on youth language.
- Stevenson (1995) is a collection of essays covering many aspects of variation in German – see especially Schlobinski on youth language, Coulmas on language and nation, and Rost-Roth on intercultural communication which includes a discussion of migrant workers.
- Hoffmann (1991), Chapter 14, has a good discussion of the situation of migrant workers in the Federal Republic of Germany.
- Durrell (1992), Chapter 1, provides a summary of varieties of German and contains a number of passages illustrating different levels of register.
- Davies (1997), Chapter 6, explores the differences between styles of German from the point of view of student essay-writing, and contains many practical assignments.
- Crystal (1997) deals with many of the areas covered in this chapter (though not with specific reference to German). See especially 'Part II – Language and Identity' and Chapter 31 on the differences between speech and writing.
- Finally, if you would like to find out more about sociolinguistics in general, three good introductory textbooks are Holmes (1992), Wardhaugh (1986) and Romaine (1994a).

Exercises

1. Identify the appropriate definitions for the following terms:

TERM	DEFINITION
1. Code switching	(a) A variety of language where the pronunciation, grammar, and vocabulary signal the regional and social class background of the speaker.
2. Accent	(b) Collective term for addresser and addressee.
3. Foreigner talk	(c) Changing from one dialect or language to another, normally within the same conversation.
4. *Binnendeutsch*	(d) The social dialect of the English middle and upper classes.
5. Isogloss	(e) A socially defined variety of language, e.g. scientific, spoken, formal.
6. Participants	(f) The simplified way in which native speakers sometimes address non-native speakers.
7. Register	(g) Term used to describe any language which has more than one recognised standard variety.
8. Dialect	(h) Features of pronunciation which signal regional origin and social class identity.
9. Pluricentric	(i) The variety of German used in Germany as opposed to Switzerland, Austria, and elsewhere.
10. RP	(j) A line drawn on a map to illustrate where a particular linguistic variant/variety is used.

2. With the help of Fig. 10.1 (p. 252), say which dialect is spoken in the *area surrounding* the following towns. The first one has been done for you.

TOWN	DIALECT
1. Vienna, Austria	Mittelbairisch
2. Rostock, Germany	
3. Hamburg, Germany	
4. Cologne, Germany	
5. Leipzig, Germany	
6. Erfurt, Germany	
7. Graz, Austria	
8. Munich, Germany	
9. Bern, Switzerland	
10. Stuttgart, Germany	

3. With the help of Fig. 10.1 (p. 252), identify the groups to which the following dialects belong. The first one has been done for you.

DIALEKT	DIALEKTGRUPPE	NIEDERDEUTSCH/ MITTELDEUTSCH/ OBERDEUTSCH
1. Hessisch	Westmitteldeutsch	Mitteldeutsch
2. Märkisch		
3. Schwäbisch		
4. Holsteinisch		
5. Rheinfränkisch		
6. Hochalemannisch		
7. Westfälisch		
8. Obersächsisch		
9. Nordbairisch		
10. Ripuarisch		

4. Identify the different geographical variants in German which have roughly the same meaning in English. The first one has been done for you.

sehen   Klempner   Frühjahr   Christabend   Tischler   Erdapfel
Karotte   Tomate   Frühling   Rahm   Spengler   Gaul   gelbe Rübe
Heiligabend   Schreiner   schauen   Ross   Kartoffel   Sahne   Paradeiser
Pferd   Möhre   gucken   Obers

ENGLISH	GERMAN VARIANTS
1. to look/see	sehen/schauen/gucken
2. tomato	
3. spring (season)	
4. plumber	
5. Christmas Eve	
6. joiner/carpenter	
7. potato	
8. carrot	
9. cream	
10. horse	

Maps describing the geographical distribution of these variants can be found in König (1978) *Atlas zur deutschen Sprache*.

5. Consider the following groups of words, and then enter each item into the appropriate column in the table according to register. Note that not every column need be filled, and in some cases, more than one item can be entered into the same column. If in doubt, refer back to section 10.2.3 (p. 268) for definitions of register. The first one has been done for you.

1. übel, mies, schlecht
2. schlafen, pennen
3. sterben, krepieren, abkratzen, entschlafen, verrecken
4. hauen, schlagen
5. flink, fix, schnell
6. sehr, schwer, irre
7. still sein, schweigen, den Mund halten
8. das Pech, das Unglück
9. der Quatsch, der Nonsens, der Unsinn, der Käse
10. der Mann, der Ehemann, der Gatte, der Alte, der Gemahl
11. das Haupt, die Birne, der Kopf
12. ätzend, sehr schlecht
13. futsch, weg, verschwunden
14. schmeißen, werfen
15. sich entfernen, abhauen, gehen

	R3	R2	R1
1.	übel	schlecht	mies
2.			
3.			
4.			
5.			
6.			
7.			
8.			
9.			
10.			
11.			
12.			
13.			
14.			
15.			

Answers to exercises

Chapter 2

1.

	GERMANIC	CELTIC	ROMANCE	SLAVONIC	INDO-ARYAN
1. English	✓				
2. German	✓				
3. Italian			✓		
4. Spanish			✓		
5. Russian				✓	
6. Swedish	✓				
7. Hindi					✓
8. Welsh		✓			
9. Afrikaans	✓				
10. French			✓		

2.

	WEST GERMANIC	NORTH GERMANIC
1. Swedish		✓
2. English	✓	
3. Danish		✓
4. Icelandic		✓
5. Yiddish	✓	
6. Dutch	✓	
7. Afrikaans	✓	
8. (High) German	✓	
9. Norwegian		✓
10. Low German	✓	

3.

1b   2a   3b   4c   5b

4.

1. The Benrath Line.
2. Central and Upper German dialects.
3. AD 750–1050.
4. *Das Niebelungenlied.*
5. *Die Kanzleisprache.*
6. Hamburg, Bremen, Lübeck and Rostock.
7. He was the inventor of printing from movable type.
8. The French writer, Voltaire.
9. *Deutsches Wörterbuch.*
10. *Deutsche Bühnensprache.*

5.

1c   2a   3h   4b   5i   6e   7j   8g   9d   10f

Chapter 3

1.

1a   2b   3c   4b   5a   6b   7c   8a   9c   10b

2.

1. *Siebenbürger Sachsen.*
2. The CIS and Poland.
3. Belgium.
4. There was no referendum.
5. The Jews and the Mennonites.
6. Liechtenstein.
7. French, Italian and Romansch.
8. Namibia.
9. Commonwealth of Independent States (Former Soviet Union).
10. Prague.

3.

1e   2j   3a   4f   5b   6i   7c   8d   9h   10g

4.

Auf einem Bergchen bin/habe ich gesessen
habe die Vögel zugeschaut.
Sie haben gesungen, sie sind gesprungen,
schöne Nestchen haben sie gebaut.

I sat upon a little mountain
watching the birds.
They were singing, they were jumping,
(and) building pretty little nests.

5.

1. Three. Two brothers (Olivier and Frédéric) and one sister (Esther).
2. They are very happy: *si frou* (sind froh).
3. Saturday, 16th May 1992.
4. They are asked to make a donation to the 'Mersch Children's Village' (*Mierscher Kannerduerf*).
5. English translation:

   Olivier, Frédéric and Esther are happy to announce the birth of their little brother

   DOMINIQUE

   on Saturday 16 May 1992.

   Anyone wishing to join in our great joy may do so by sending a donation to A/C CCP 65-65 of the 'Mersch Children's Village', marked 'Donation for Dominique (XXX)'.

   (From Newton 1996: 242)

Chapter 4

1.

1. /ʃ/   Voiceless palato-alveolar fricative
2. /m/ Voiced bilabial nasal
3. /f/   Voiceless labio-dental fricative
4. /t/   Voiceless alveolar plosive
5. /x/   Voiceless velar fricative
6. /v / Voiced labio-dental fricative
7. /ç/   Voiceless palatal fricative
8. /ŋ/   Voiced velar nasal
9. /z/   Voiced alveolar fricative
10. /ʒ/ Voiced palato-alveolar fricative

2.

WORD	PHONETIC SYMBOL	VOWEL NUMBER	VOWEL LENGTH	DESCRIPTION	POSITION OF LIPS
1. L*ie*be	/i/	1	Long	High front	Spread
2. R*e*cht	/ɛ/	4	Short	Mid-low front	Slightly spread
3. M*a*ß	/ɑ/	5	Long	Low, central	Neutral
4. gr*ü*n	/y/	11	Long	High, front	Strongly rounded
5. bess*e*r	/ɐ/	16	Short	Mid-low, central	Neutral
6. B*oo*t	/o/	7	Long	Mid-high, back	Rounded
7. g*u*t	/u/	9	Long	High, back	Strongly rounded
8. m*ü*ssen	/ʏ/	12	Short	High, front	Strongly rounded
9. K*ö*nig	/ø/	13	Long	Mid-high, front	Strongly rounded
10. m*ü*de	/ə/	15	Short	Mid, central	Neutral

3.

1. /m/ and /n/
2. /ø/ and /o/
3. /i/ and/ʏ/
4. /ɐ/ and /ə/
5. /y/ and /ɑ/

6. /ʊ/ and /ʏ/
7. /ç/ and /ʃ/
8. /ɑ/ and /a/
9. /ŋ/ and /n/
10. /y/ and/u/

4.

Mein Name ist Maria Schmidt. Ich bin fünfundzwanzig Jahre alt und wohne in Mannheim. Ich habe eine Zweizimmerwohnung in der Stadtmitte. Ich habe drei Katzen, die Mitzi, Schnucki und Pinko heißen. Im Juli fahre ich in Urlaub. Ich werde zwei Wochen auf Kreta verbringen. Ich freue mich schon sehr darauf.

5.

1. /mʊs/
2. /dɑbaɪ/

3. /dɔɪtʃ/
4. /gəbʀaʊxt/

5. /østəraɪç/
6. /ʃulə/
7. /ʃlisɪç/

8. /gʀʏndə/
9. /hantfɛst/
10. /temən/

6.

1. Fricatives
2. Short vowels
3. Plosives
4. Front vowels
5. Velars

6. Voiceless consonants
7. (Voiceless) glottals
8. Diphthongs
9. Alveolars
10. Lip-rounding

7.

Group A
1. Voiceless bilabial plosive /p/ shifts to voiceless labio-dental fricative /f/
   (e.g. *pater* → father/*Vater*).
2. Voiceless alveolar plosive /t/ shifts to voiceless dental fricative /θ/
   (e.g. *tres* → three, later *drei*).
3. Voiceless velar plosive /k/ shifts to voiceless glottal fricative /h/
   (e.g. *canis* → hound/*Hund*).

   → Voiceless plosives have all shifted to voiceless fricatives.

Group B
1. Voiced bilabial plosive /b/ shifts to voiceless bilabial plosive /p/
   (e.g. *labium* → lip/*Lippe*).
2. Voiced alveolar plosive /d/ shifts to voiceless alveolar plosive /t/
   (e.g. *duo* → two, later *zwei*).
3. Voiced velar plosive /g/ shifts to voiceless velar plosive /k/
   (e.g. *genu* → knee/*Knie*).

   → Voiced plosives have all shifted to voiceless plosives.

8.

Group A
1. Voiceless bilabial plosive /p/ shifts to voiceless affricate /p͡f/
   (e.g. apple/*Apfel*).
2. Voiceless alveolar plosive /t/ shifts to voiceless affricate /t͡s/
   (e.g. time/*Zeit*).

3. Voiceless velar plosive /k/ shifts to voiceless affricate /k͡x/ (e.g. cow/*Kuh*)
   (Upper German dialects only – remains unchanged in other dialect groups.)

   → Voiceless plosives have all shifted to (voiceless) affricates.

Group B

1. Voiceless bilabial plosive /p/ shifts to voiceless labio-dental fricative /f/
   (e.g. sharp/*scharf*).
2. Voiceless alveolar plosive /t/ shifts to voiceless alveolar fricative /s/
   (e.g. that/*dass*).
3. Voiceless velar plosive /k/ shifts to voiceless velar fricative /x/ after back
   vowel, e.g. 'book' to *Buch*. After front vowels the shift is to voiceless
   palatal fricative /ç/, e.g. 'oak' to *Eiche*.

   → Voiceless plosives have all shifted to voiceless fricatives.

9.

1. thick/*dick*
English:	/θ/	voiceless dental fricative
German:	/d/	voiced alveolar plosive

2. book/*Buch*
English:	/k/	voiceless velar plosive
German:	/x/	voiceless velar fricative

3. hand/*Hand*
English:	/d/	voiced alveolar plosive
German:	/t/	voiceless alveolar plosive

4. father/*Vater*
English:	/ð/	voiced dental fricative
German:	/t/	voiceless alveolar plosive

5. milk/*Milch*
English:	/k/	voiceless velar plosive
German:	/ç/	voiceless palatal fricative

6. apple/*Apfel*
English:	/p/	voiceless bilabial plosive
German:	/p͡f/	voiceless affricate (bilabial plosive + labio-dental fricative)

7. out/*aus*
   English: /t/   voiceless alveolar plosive
   German: /s/   voiceless alveolar fricative

8. ten/*zehn*
   English: /t/   voiceless alveolar plosive
   German: /ts̪/   voiceless affricate (alveolar plosive + alveolar fricative)

9. love/*Liebe*
   English: /v/   voiced labio-dental fricative
   German: /b/   voiced bilabial plosive

10. open/*offen*
    English: /p/   voiceless bilabial plosive
    German: /f/   voiceless labio-dental fricative

Chapter 5

1.

1. näm.lich
2. halb.tags
3. ei.ni.ge
4. ge.macht
5. ha.tte

6. Schme.tter.ling.e
7. auf.re.gend
8. Ma.ri.a.nne
9. ge.ra.de
10. aus.at.men

2.

1. Systemic. Short vowels cannot normally occur in *open* syllables.
2. Systemic. /ŋ/ cannot occur in *initial* position.
3. Accidental.
4. Systemic. Syllables cannot end in *voiced* obstruents such as /g/.
5. Accidental.
6. Systemic. Schwa cannot occur in *stressed* syllables.
7. Accidental.
8. Accidental.
9. Systemic. German syllables cannot begin with more than *three* consonants.
10. Accidental.

3.

	[t]	[d]
1. Länder		×
2. Land	×	
3. Landkarte	×	
4. Rind	×	
5. Rinder		×
6. Rindlein	×	

	[p]	[b]
1. halb	×	
2. halbtags	×	
3. halbieren		×
4. Dieb	×	
5. Diebstahl	×	
6. Diebe		×

	[k]	[g]
1. Tag	×	
2. Tage		×
3. täglich	×	
4. fliegen		×
5. flog	×	
6. Flüge		×

4.

1. Auflage [aʊfl̥aɡə] /l/ → [l̥]
   Devoicing. The *voiced* alveolar lateral /l/ has become the *voiceless* alveolar lateral [l̥] following the *voiceless* labio-dental fricative /f/.

2. Einkauf [aɪŋkaʊf] /n/ → [ŋ]
   Assimilation of place. The voiced *alveolar* nasal /n/ has become the voiced *velar* nasal [ŋ] before the voiceless *velar* plosive /k/.

3. weit besser [vaɪp bɛsɐ] /t/ → [p]
   Assimilation of place. The voiceless *alveolar* plosive /t/ has changed to the voiceless *bilabial* plosive [p] before the voiced *bilabial* plosive /b/.

4. maßgeblich [mɑsɡ̊eplɪç] /g/ → [ɡ̊]
   Devoicing. The *voiced* velar plosive /g/ has become the *voiceless* velar plosive [ɡ̊] following the *voiceless* alveolar fricative /s/.

5. hat sein [hat z̥aɪn] /z/ → [z̥]
   Devoicing. The *voiced* alveolar fricative /z/ has become the *voiceless* alveolar fricative [z̥] following the *voiceless* alveolar plosive /t/.

6. hoff' ich [hɔvɪç] /f/ → [v]
   Voicing. The *voiceless* labio-dental fricative /f/ has become the *voiced* labio-dental fricative [v] between two *voiced* vowels (i.e. intervocalically).

7. Kravatte [kʀ̥avatə] /ʀ/ → [ʀ̥]
   Devoicing. The *voiced* uvular roll /ʀ/ has become the *voiceless* uvular roll [ʀ̥] following the *voiceless* velar plosive /k/.

8. Magnet [maŋnet] /g/ → [ŋ]
   Assimilation of manner. The voiced velar *plosive* /g/ has become the voiced velar *nasal* [ŋ] before the voiced alveolar *nasal* /n/.

9. schönes Stück [ʃønəʃʃtʏk]
   Assimilation of place. The voiceless *alveolar* fricative /s/ has become the voiceless *palato-alveolar* fricative [ʃ] before the voiceless *palato-alveolar* fricative /ʃ/.

10. Bundesrepublik [bʊnnəsʀepublik]
    Assimilation of manner. The voiced alveolar *plosive* /d/ has become the voiced alveolar *nasal* [n] after the voiced alveolar *nasal* /n/.

Note how in the final two examples, the double consonants which are produced, e.g. [ʃʃ] and [nn], might then be reduced to one consonant only, e.g. [ʃ] and [n].

5.

1. [habm̩]   [m̩] occurs after bilabial plosive /b/
2. [mʏsn̩]   [n̩] occurs after alveolar fricative /s/
3. [ʃɪŋkŋ̍]   [ŋ̍] occurs after velar plosive /k/ (and before)
4. [gabm̩]   [m̩] occurs after bilabial plosive /b/
5. [zagŋ̍]   [ŋ̍] occurs after velar plosive /g/
6. [faln̩]   [n̩] occurs after alveolar lateral /l/
7. [bɔmbm̩]   [m̩] occurs after bilabial plosive /b/
8. [lezn̩]   [n̩] occurs after alveolar fricative /z/
9. [zaxŋ̍]   [ŋ̍] occurs after velar fricative /x/
10. [zɪtn̩]   [n̩] occurs after alveolar plosive /t/

6.

1. 'Erzbischof
2. 'Eisenbahn
3. Offi'zier
4. zwischen'durch

5. musi'kalisch
6. 'barfuß
7. ge'währleisten
8. Gra'mmatik

9. Ma'schine
10. 'Fahrkarte
11. Litera'tur
12. Poli'tik
13. Pro'test
14. Demokra'tie

7.

1. Das 'kannst du nicht 'machen.
2. Wir 'fahren 'übermorgen nach 'London.
3. Wie 'weit von Ihrem 'Haus ist die neue 'Schule?
4. Das 'kann ich mir über'haupt nicht 'vorstellen.
5. 'Heidelberg ist eine 'wunderschöne 'Stadt aber 'Wien gefällt mir 'besser.
6. Mein 'Bruder studiert Germa'nistik und Ang'listik an der Universität 'Hamburg.
7. Ich 'reite und 'schwimme sehr 'gern.
8. Was 'halten Sie da'von, wenn wir das erst 'morgen be'sprechen?
9. Ich 'habe schon 'gar keine 'Lust mehr, in 'Urlaub zu 'fahren.
10. Die deutsche 'Satzbetonung zu be'schreiben ist nicht 'einfach.

Chapter 6

1.

1. Bahn+hof
2. ver+gess+en
3. Spion+age
4. gelb (one morpheme only)
5. Demo+krat+isier+ung
6. grau+sam
7. un+be+ein+druck+t
8. gestern (one morpheme only)
9. Be+deut+ung
10. bleib+en

2.

Auf	d+	em	Schreib+	tisch	lieg+	t
lexical free	grammatical bound	grammatical bound	lexical free	lexical free	lexical free	grammatical bound

ein	grün+	lich+	es	Büch+	lein
grammatical free	lexical free	lexical bound	grammatical bound	lexical free	lexical bound

3.

WORD	WORD FORM	LEXEME
1. Bücher	✓	
2. lachen		✓
3. gebacken	✓	
4. saß	✓	
5. Bleistift		✓
6. Grammatik		✓
7. Tisch		✓
8. schlief	✓	
9. Deutschland		✓
10. gesprochen	✓	
11. Wörter	✓	
12. laufen		✓
13. Geschäfte	✓	
14. Feuer		✓
15. springen		✓
16. Mütter	✓	
17. Risiken	✓	
18. hätte	✓	
19. Funde	✓	
20. offen		✓

4.

Marion (N) **Gräfin** (N) **Dönhoff** (N) – **Dame** (N)
am (Prep + Det) **Puls** (N) **der** (Det) **'Zeit'** (N)

Liberaler (Adj) Journalismus (N) und (Conj) preußische (Adj) Prägung (N), Fortschritt (N) und (Conj) die (Det) notwendige (Adj) Selbstbeschränkung (N) in (Prep) der (Det) Freiheit (N): Themen (N), die (Pro) Marion (N) Gräfin (N) Dönhoff (N) (86) (Adj), die (Det) große (Adj) alte (Adj) Dame (N) des (Det) politischen (Adj) Journalismus (N), bewegen (V). Sie (Pro) war (V) im (Prep + Det) Widerstand (N) gegen (Prep) Hitler (N); 1946 (Adv) ging (V) sie (Pro) in (Prep) die (Det) neugegründete (Adj) Redaktion (N) der (Det) Hamburger (Adj) Wochenzeitung (N) 'DIE (Det) ZEIT' (N). 22 (Det) Jahre (N) später (Adv) wurde (V) sie (Pro) Chefredakteurin (N) – 1973 (Adv) wechselte (V) sie (Pro) in (Prep) die (Det) Position (N) der (Det) Herausgeberin (N). Kürzlich (Adv) feierte (V) ihre (Det) 'ZEIT' (N) (Auflage (N) 484 000 (Adj)) 50. (Adj) Geburtstag (N). Das (Det) Motto (N) der (Det) Gräfin (N): 'Ohne (Prep) Schreiben (N) könnte (V) ich (Pro) nicht (Adv) leben (V).'

5.

1. Wir gehen in ein neuES Theaterstück.
   (no strong ending on *ein*, hence strong ending on *neues*)
2. Es stand in der heutigEN Zeitung.
   (strong ending on *der*, hence weak ending on *heutigen*)
3. Es ist ein lustigES Buch.
   (no strong ending on *ein*, hence strong ending on *lustiges*)
4. Wir lesen gern die klassischEN Dichter.
   (strong ending on *die*, hence weak ending on *klassischen*)
5. Ich sah es in einER Zeitschrift.
   (strong ending on *einer*)
6. Ich lese gerade einen neuEN Roman.
   (strong ending on *einen*, hence weak ending on *neuen*)
7. Es ist das bestE aber auch das teuerstE Wörterbuch.
   (strong ending on *das*, hence weak ending on *beste* and *teuerste*)
8. Es war eine sehr romantischE Geschichte.
   (no strong ending on *eine*, hence strong ending on *romantische* –
   however, strong and weak endings are the same e.g. *-e*)
9. Steht es vor deinem großEN Bücherregal?
   (strong ending on *deinem*, hence weak ending on *großen*)
10. Hast du das kleinE schwarzE Heft?
    (strong ending on *das*, hence weak endings on *kleine* and *schwarze*)

6.

1 Sport → Sportler
  noun → noun
  suffix *-er*
  explicit

2. leiden → Leidenschaft
   verb → noun (deverbal nominalisation)
   suffix *-schaft*
   explicit

3. essen → Essen
   verb → noun (deverbal nominalisation)
   zero derivation or conversion
   implicit

4. brauchen → brauchbar
   verb → adjective (deverbal adjectivalisation)
   suffix *-bar*
   explicit

5. krank → kränklich
   adjective → adjective
   umlaut + suffix -*lich*
   explicit + implicit

6. Haus → hausieren
   noun → verb (denominal verbalisation)
   suffix -*ieren*
   explicit

7. treiben → Getriebe
   verb → noun (deverbal nominalisation)
   ablaut + circumfix (discontinuous affix/morpheme) *Ge-/-e*
   explicit + implicit

8. Mode → modisch
   noun → adjective (denominal adjectivalisation)
   suffix -*isch*
   explicit

9. beißen → bissig
   verb → adjective (deverbal adjectivalisation)
   ablaut + suffix -*ig*
   explicit + implicit

10. lang → langsam
    adjective → adjective
    suffix -*sam*
    explicit

7.

1. das Schema (suffix -*ma*)
2. das Dynamit (suffix -*it*)
3. die Panik (suffix -*ik*)
4. die Natur (suffix -*ur*)
5. der Wurf (ablaut - from *werfen*)
6. die Basis (suffix -*sis*)
7. der Teppich (suffix -*ich*)
8. der Betrieb (ablaut – from *betreiben*)
9. die Flucht (suffix -*t*)
10. das Machen (zero derivation or conversion, verb to noun)

Chapter 7

1.

1b 2j 3g 4h 5d 6c 7e 8f 9a 10i

2.

1. Ich finde *es* (AO) nicht gut.
2. Er wollte immer *Lehrer* (C) werden.
3. Hast du *Lust* (AO)?
4. Können Sie *die Arbeit* (AO) morgen machen?
5. Seid Ihr *Engländer* (C)?
6. Sie wurden *sehr unglücklich* (C).
7. Sie bekamen *viel Geld* (AO) dafür.
8. Wir haben *ihr* (DO) *einen Brief* (AO) geschrieben.
9. Wir waren *ziemlich enttäuscht* (C).
10. *Mir* (DO) waren sie *sehr unsympathisch* (C).

3.

1.

Es	ist	neu.
Subject	Verb	Complement
(Pro)	(V)	(Adj)

2.

Wo	wohnen	Sie?
Adverbial	Verb	Subject
(Adv)	(V)	(Pro)

3.

Ich	mache	es	jetzt.
Subject	Verb	Accusative Object	Adverbial
(Pro)	(V)	(Pro)	(Adv)

4.

Sie	ist	eine sehr gute Schauspielerin.
Subject	Verb	Complement
(Pro)	(V)	(Det+Adv+Adj+N)

5.

Ich	fahre	Auto.
Subject	Verb	Accusative Object
(Pro)	(V)	(N)

6.

Sie	hat	dir	das Buch	vor zwei Wochen	gekauft.
Subject	Verb 1	Dative Object	Accusative Object	Adverbial	Verb 2
(Pro)	(V)	(Pro)	(Det+N)	(Prep+Det+N)	(V)

7.

Hat	sie	es	dir	geschenkt?
Verb 1	Subject	Accusative Object	Dative Object	Verb 2
(V)	(Pro)	(Pro)	(Pro)	(V)

8.

Ich	kann	diese Frage	nicht	beantworten.
Subject	Verb	Accusative Object	Adverbial	Verb 2
(Pro)	(V)	(Det+N)	(Adv)	(V)

9.

Diese Frage	kann	ich	beantworten.
Accusative Object	Verb 1	Subject	Verb 2
(Det+N)	(V)	(Pro)	(V)

10.

Mir	gefällt	das Buch.
Dative Object	Verb	Subject
(Pro)	(V)	(Det+N)

4.

Wir [S] haben *schon im Sommer* [A] *einen Brief* [AO] *an das Wohnungsvermittlungsbüro Wippel und Co.* [APO] geschrieben: 'Sehr geehrte Herren! *Wir* [S] sind *zwei Studentinnen* [C], achtzehn und einundzwanzig Jahre alt, und *wir* [S] werden *ab 1. Oktober dieses Jahres* [A] *in Wien* [A] leben. *Wir* [S] bitten *Sie* [AO], *uns* [DO] mitzuteilen, ob *Sie* [S] *uns* [DO] beim Finden einer passenden Wohngelegenheit behilflich sein wollen. *Es* [S] handelt sich *um zwei große, helle Zimmer* [APO], zentralgeheizt, evtl. Balkon, mit Telefon, in verkehrsgünstiger Grünlage, Bad und Küche, in Untermiete zu studentischem Preis. *In Erwartung Ihrer Nachricht* [A] grüßen *wir* [S] *Sie* [AO] *mit vorzüglicher Hochachtung* [A].' Und *wir* [S] haben *das Briefpapier* [AO] aus dem Geschäft von Lores Vater verwendet, damit *sie* [S] sehen, daß *wir* [S] *aus gutem Haus* [C] sind. Aber *das Vermittlungsbüro* [S] hat *nicht* [A] geantwortet, und *jetzt* [A] sitzen *wir* [S] *bei der Familie Krebich* [A].

5.

1. Complex sentence. Main clause, followed by subordinating conjunction *dass*, and a subordinate clause.
2. Complex sentence. Relative clause embedded within main clause.
3. Three simple sentences.
4. Complex sentence. Two main clauses connected by coordinating conjunction *und*.
5. Simple sentence.

Chapter 8

1.

1d   2f   3h   4i   5c   6j   7a   8e   9g   10b

2.

1. schreiten, <u>sich bewegen</u>, schlendern, spazieren
2. Rock, Hose, <u>Kleidung</u>, Krawatte, Schuh
3. Tropfen, Pillen, Tabletten, <u>Arzneimittel</u>
4. Hund, <u>Haustier</u>, Katze, Hamster, Kaninchen
5. Schach, Damen, <u>Spiel</u>, Mensch ärgere Dich nicht, Karten
6. Bruder, Onkel, Großvater, Vetter, <u>Verwandter</u>
7. Finger, <u>Körperteil</u>, Arm, Bein, Auge
8. Tisch, <u>Möbelstück</u>, Sessel, Lampe, Schrank
9. Blumenkohl, <u>Gemüse</u>, Bohnen, Kartoffeln, Erbsen
10. hinrichten, <u>töten</u>, ermordern, erschießen

3.

1.

2.

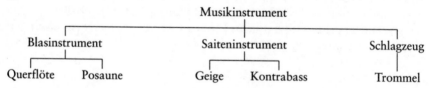

3.

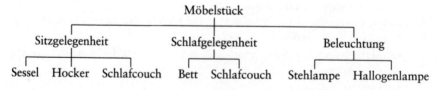

4.

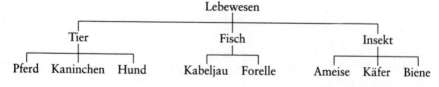

5.

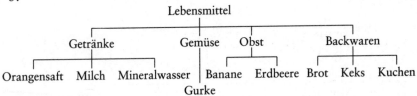

4.

1. Gradable antonyms.
2. Gradable antonyms.
3. Complementaries or gradable antonyms? If you see masculinity and femininity as biological categories, then they are probably (although not necessarily) complementaries. If you see them as social characteristics, then they are gradable. For example, it is possible to describe someone as 'more feminine' or 'less masculine'.
4. Relational opposites.
5. Gradable antonyms.
6. Complementaries or gradable antonyms? Probably complementaries although people do talk in terms of states between life and death.
7. Complementaries or gradable antonyms? Probably complementaries although it is not uncommon to hear people say that something more or less makes sense, e.g. *etwas ist sinnvoller/weniger sinnvoll.*
8. Relational opposites.
9. Complementaries or gradable antonyms? This depends on how you view the act of waking and sleeping. Technically, they are complementaries, but it is possible to think in terms of states somewhere between being awake and being asleep.
10. Relational opposites.

5.

	WORD A	WORD B	SENSE RELATION
1.	Rock (Kleidung)	Rock (Musik)	Homophones and homographs
2.	Montage (erste Tage der Woche)	Montage (das Montieren)	Homographs
3.	Birne (Frucht)	Birne (Leuchtkörper)	Homophones and homographs
4.	umfahren (zu Fall bringen)	umfahren (um . . . herumfahren)	Homographs
5.	arm (finanziell)	Arm (Körperteil)	Homophones
6.	Bank (Sitzgelegenheit)	Bank (Geldinstitut)	Homophones and homographs
7.	Pferd (Tier)	Pferd (Schachfigur)	Homophones and homographs
8.	Bremse (beim Auto)	Bremse (Stechfliege)	Homophones and homographs
9.	kosten (wert sein)	kosten (probieren)	Homophones and homographs
10.	Beete (Blumenbeete)	Bete (rote Bete)	Homophones

Chapter 9

1.

1P   2P   3C   4C   5P   6C   7C   8P   9P   10P

2.

VERB	REPRESENTATIVE	DIRECTIVE	COMMISSIVE	EXPRESSIVE	DECLARATIVE
1. schwören			✓		
2. vermuten	✓				
3. glauben	✓				
4. befehlen		✓			
5. gratulieren				✓	
6. versprechen			✓		
7. fragen		✓			
8. taufen					✓
9. bitten		✓			
10. danken				✓	

3.

1. Jürgen was sad.
2. Last time he arrived late.
3. Travelling abroad used to be difficult.
4. The Spaniards were already dissatisfied.
5. Something was said.
6. Germany was divided.
7. Your bicycle is outside.
8. Someone else is also an only child.
9. He has been married three times before.
10. Your things are on the table (and they are in the way).

4.

Es war einmal ein fröhlicher Müllersbursch. Der hatte in den ersten milden Frühlingstagen sein Ränzlein geschnürt und sich auf Wanderschaft begeben, nachdem er von Vater und Mutter recht herzlich Abschied genommen hatte. Am Abend des ersten Tages seiner Wanderschaft kam er in einen tiefen, dunklen Wald. Er fühlte sich sehr alleine und sehnte sich nach Gesellschaft. Traurig dachte er an seine Eltern. Plötzlich aber hörte er von weitem ein lustiges Singen . . .

(Source: Linke *et al.,* 1994: 240)

5.

Model answer: BPBS(E)

> *Background:*
> Um der Forderung nach einer Gehaltsvorauszahlung Nachdruck zu verleihen, hat der Copilot eines Airbusses den Bordcomputer ausgebaut.

The first sentence describes how the co-pilot of an airbus stole the on-board computer. He did this in an attempt to try to persuade his employers to pay his salary in advance.

> *Problem:*
> 323 Passagiere saßen deshalb am Sonntag acht Stunden auf dem Flughafen Berlin-Tegel fest.

As a result of the co-pilot's actions, 323 passengers were stranded at Tegel airport in Berlin for eight hours on the Sunday in question.

> *Background:*
> Nach Angaben der 'Holiday Airlines' wollten sie in den türkischen Ferienort Antalya fliegen. Eine Sprecherin der türkischen Fluggesellschaft sagt, der 33jährige Copilot habe gefordert, sein Arbeitgeber möge ihm sein Gehalt bis Ende der Saison im voraus zahlen. Als er dies nicht erhielt, baute er den Bordcomputer aus und steckte ihn in seine Tasche.

The tourists were hoping to fly to the Turkish holiday resort of Antalya. A representative of the Turkish airline explained that the 33-year-old co-pilot had requested that his employers provide advance payment of his salary until the end of the season. When they refused, the co-pilot dismantled the on-board computer and put it in his pocket.

> *Solution:*
> Erst Stunden später wurde der geklaute Bordcomputer bei ihm entdeckt und wieder in den Airbus eingebaut. Der Copilot wurde entlassen.

The problem was not solved for several hours until the co-pilot was found to be carrying the on-board computer, which was then refitted into the aeroplane. The co-pilot was dismissed.

The evaluation of the solution is not explicitly stated. However, the *implication* is that the pilot's dismissal is an effective way of preventing the problem from occurring again.

6.

1. The use of *der* is anaphoric and refers back to *Der 30jährige Insektenforscher Mel.*
2. *Eltern* = superordinate term.
   Adoptiveltern/leibliche Eltern = hyponyms of *Eltern*. Co-hyponyms and (possibly) opposites in relation to one another.
   Mutter/Vater = hyponyms of *Eltern*. Co-hyponyms and antonyms in relation to one another.
3. The use of *die* is anaphoric. It refers back to *Nancy.*
4. *Die beiden ersten Adressen.*
5. Deictic. You need to know when exactly Lonnie found out that his father had been in prison in order to know what is meant by '20 years ago'.
6. It is elliptical in the sense that there is no verb. This is often a neater way of ending a text.
7. Terms relating to the 'family', in general, and Mel's family, in particular, e.g. *Adoptiveltern, leibliche Eltern, Eltern, Mutter, Vater, Sohn, Ehefrau, Bruder, Mel, Nancy, Mary, Richard, Lonnie, Familie.* Note how, with the exception of sentence 5, every sentence contains at least one of these words.

Chapter 10

1.

1c   2h   3f   4i   5j   6b   7e   8a   9g   10d

2.

TOWN	DIALECT
1. Vienna, Austria	Mittelbairisch
2. Rostock, Germany	Mecklenburgisch
3. Hamburg, Germany	Nordniedersächsisch
4. Cologne, Germany	Ripuarisch
5. Leipzig, Germany	Obersächsisch
6. Erfurt, Germany	Thüringsch
7. Graz, Austria	Südbairisch
8. Munich, Germany	Mittelbairisch
9. Bern, Switzerland	Hochalemannisch
10. Stuttgart, Germany	Südfränkisch

3.

DIALEKT	DIALEKTGRUPPE	NIEDERDEUTSCH/ MITTELDEUTSCH/ OBERDEUTSCH
1. Hessisch	Westmitteldeutsch	Mitteldeutsch
2. Märkisch	Ostniederdeutsch	Niederdeutsch
3. Schwäbisch	Alemannisch	Oberdeutsch
4. Holsteinisch	Westniederdeutsch	Niederdeutsch
5. Rheinfränkisch	Westmitteldeutsch	Mitteldeutsch
6. Hochalemannisch	Alemannisch	Oberdeutsch
7. Westfälisch	Westniederdeutsch	Niederdeutsch
8. Obersächsisch	Ostmitteldeutsch	Mitteldeutsch
9. Nordbairisch	Bairisch	Oberdeutsch
10. Ripuarisch	Westmitteldeutsch	Mitteldeutsch

4.

ENGLISH	GERMAN VARIANTS
1. to look/see	sehen/schauen/gucken
2. tomato	Tomate/Paradeiser
3. spring (season)	Frühjahr/Frühling
4. plumber	Klempner/Spengler
5. Christmas Eve	Christabend/Heiligabend
6. joiner/carpenter	Tischler/Schreiner
7. potato	Kartoffel/Erdapfel
8. carrot	Karotte/Möhre/gelbe Rübe
9. cream	Sahne/Rahm/Obers
10. horse	Pferd/Gaul/Ross

5.

	R3	R2	R1
1.	übel	schlecht	mies
2.	schlafen		pennen
3.	entschlafen	sterben	krepieren, abkratzen, verrecken
4.	schlagen		hauen
5.	flink	schnell	fix
6.	sehr		irre, schwer
7.	schweigen	still sein	den Mund halten
8.	das Unglück		das Pech
9.	der Nonsens	der Unsinn	der Quatsch, der Käse
10.	der Ehemann, der Gatte, der Gemahl	der Mann	der Alte
11.	das Haupt	der Kopf	die Birne
12.	sehr schlecht		ätzend
13.	verschwunden	weg	futsch
14.	werfen		schmeißen
15.	sich entfernen	gehen	abhauen

Bibliography

Ager, Dennis 1990: *Sociolinguistics and Contemporary French*. Cambridge: CUP.

Ager, Dennis, Muskens, George and Wright, Sue (eds) 1993: *Language Education for Intercultural Communication*. Clevedon: Multilingual Matters.

Ahlzweig, Claus 1994: *Muttersprache – Vaterland. Die deutsche Nation und ihre Sprache*. Opladen: Westdeutscher Verlag.

Ammon, Ulrich 1991: *Die internationale Stellung der deutschen Sprache*. Berlin: de Gruyter.

Ammon, Ulrich 1995a: *Die deutsche Sprache in Deutschland, Österreich und der Schweiz. Das Problem der nationalen Varietäten*. Berlin: de Gruyter.

Ammon, Ulrich 1995b: To what extent is German an international language? In P. Stevenson (ed.), *The German Language and the Real World*, pp. 25–54.

Baetens Beardsmore, Hugo (ed.) 1993: *European Models of Bilingual Education*. Clevedon: Multilingual Matters.

Barbour, Stephen and Stevenson, Patrick 1990: *Variation in German*. Cambridge: CUP.

Baur, Arthur 1988: *Schwyzertüütsch. 'Grüezi mitenand'* (9th edition). Winterthur: Gemsberg Verlag.

Berend, Nina and Mattheier, Klaus J. (eds) 1994: *Sprachinselforschung*. Frankfurt: Peter Lang.

Berg, Guy 1993: *'Mir wëlle bleiwe, wat mir sin.' Soziolinguistische und sprachtypologische Betrachtungen zur luxemburgischen Mehrsprachigkeit*. Tübingen: Niemeyer.

Bergmann, Rolf and Pauly, Peter 1975: *Neuhochdeutsch. Arbeitsbuch zum linguistischen Unterricht*. Vandenhoeck & Ruprecht: Göttingen.

Bertelsmann 1996: *Die neue deutsche Rechtschreibung*. München: Bertelsmann Lexikon Verlag.

Böll, Heinrich 1978: *Frankfurter Vorlesungen*. In B. Balzer (ed.), *Heinrich Böll. Werke. Essayistische Schriften und Reden*. vol. II. Köln: Kiepenheuer & Witsch.

Born, J. and Dickgießer, S. 1989: *Deutschsprachige Minderheiten. Ein Überblick über den Stand der Forschung für 27 Länder*. Mannheim: Institut für Deutsche Sprache.

Born, J. and Jakob, G. 1990: *Deutschsprachige Gruppen am Rande und außerhalb des geschlossenen deutschen Sprachgebiets* (2nd edition). Mannheim: Institut für Deutsche Sprache.

Born, J. and Stickel, G. (eds) 1993: *Deutsch als Verkehrssprache in Europa*. Berlin: de Gruyter.

Braun, Peter 1979: *Tendenzen in der deutschen Gegenwartssprache*. Stuttgart: Urban-Taschenbücher.

Burkhardt, Armin and Fritzsche, K. Peter 1995: *Sprache im Umbruch – Politischer Sprachwandel im Zeichen von 'Wende' und 'Vereinigung'*. Berlin: de Gruyter.

Byram, Michael 1986: *Minority Education and Ethnic Survival. Case Study of a German School in Denmark*. Clevedon: Multilingual Matters.

Byram, Michael 1993: Bilingual or Bicultural Education and the Case of the German Minority in Denmark. In H. Baetens Beardsmore (ed.), *European Models of Bilingual Education*. Clevedon: Multilingual Matters, pp. 54–65.

Chambers, W. Walker and Wilkie, John 1970: *A Short History of the German Language*. London: Methuen and Co.

Clyne, Michael 1984: *Language and Society in the German-speaking Countries*. Cambridge: CUP.

Clyne, Michael 1992: *Pluricentric Languages: Differing Norms in Different Nations*. Berlin: de Gruyter.

Clyne, Michael 1995: *The German Language in a Changing Europe*. Cambridge: CUP.

Collins 1981: *German–English, English–German Dictionary*. London: Collins.

Cook, Guy 1989: *Discourse*. Oxford: OUP.

Coulmas, Florian 1995: Germanness: Language and Nation. In P. Stevenson (ed.), *The German Language and the Real World*. Oxford: OUP, pp. 55–68.

Crystal, David 1997: *The Cambridge Encyclopedia of Language*. Second edition. Cambridge: CUP.

Davies, Winifred V. 1997: *Essay-writing in German: A Student's Guide*. Manchester: MUP.

Daweke, Klaus (ed.) 1995: Auf der Reservebank? Die Kulturbeziehungen zwischen Deutschland und Kanada. *Zeitschrift für Kulturaustausch*. Nr 2. Stuttgart: Institut für Auslandsbeziehungen.

Dittmar, Norbert 1995: Theories of sociolinguistic variation in the German context. In P. Stevenson (ed.) *The German Language and the Real World*. Oxford: OUP, pp. 135–68.

Domaschnew, Anatolij I. 1993: Deutsch als eine der Verkehrssprachen in Osteuropa – am Beispiel der UdSSR (Russische Föderation). In J. Born and G. Stickel (eds), *Deutsch als Verkehrssprache in Europa*. Berlin: de Gruyter, pp. 251–61.

Duden 1963: *Das Herkunftswörterbuch. Eine Etymologie der deutschen Sprache*. Mannheim/Wien/Zürich: Dudenverlag.

Duden 1970: *Das Stilwörterbuch. Grundlegend für gutes Deutsch*. Mannheim/Wien/Zürich: Dudenverlag.

Duden 1980: *Wie sagt man in Österreich?* Mannheim/Wien/Zürich: Dudenverlag.

Duden 1989: *Wie sagt man in der Schweiz?* Mannheim/Wien/Zürich: Dudenverlag.

Durrell, Martin 1990: Westphalian and Eastphalian. In C. Russ (ed.), *The Dialects of Modern German*. London: Routledge, pp. 59–90.

Durrell, Martin 1991: *Hammer's German Grammar and Usage*. London: Edward Arnold.

Durrell, Martin 1992: *Using German: A Contemporary Guide*. Cambridge: CUP.

Durrell, Martin and Davies, Winifred 1990: Hessian. In C. Russ (ed.), *The Dialects of Modern German*. London: Routledge, pp. 210–40.

Durrell, Martin, Kohl, Katrin and Loftus, Gudrun 1993: *Practising German Grammar: A Workbook*. London: Edward Arnold.

Ebner, Jakob 1992: Österreichisches Deutsch. In R. Ulshöfer (ed.) *Der Deutschunterricht*, 44, 6, 44–55.

Ehmann, Hermann 1993: *Affengeil. Ein Lexikon der Jugendsprache*. Munich: Beck.

Eichinger, Ludwig M. 1992: Das Deutsch als Minderheitensprache. Zur Lage des Deutschen in einer Zeit politischen Wandels. In R. Ulshöfer (ed.), *Der Deutschunterricht*, 44, 6, 56–69.

Eisenberg, Peter 1994: German. In E. König and J. van der Auwera (eds), *The Germanic Languages*. London: Routledge, pp. 349–87.

Extra, Guns and Verhoeven, Ludo (eds) 1992: *Immigrant Languages in Europe*. Clevedon: Multilingual Matters.

Fleischer, Wolfgang, Michel, Georg and Starke, Günter 1993: *Stilistik der deutschen Gegenwartssprache*. Frankfurt: Peter Lang.

Földes, Csaba 1993: Deutsch als Verkehrssprache in Ostmitteleuropa – am Beispiel Ungarns. In J. Born and G. Stickel (eds), *Deutsch als Verkehrssprache in Europa*. Berlin: de Gruyter, pp. 217–35.

Fox, Anthony 1990: *The Structure of German*. Oxford: Clarendon Press.

Frank, Helene 1995: *Zur sprachlichen Entwicklung der deutschen Minderheit in Rußland und in der Sowjetunion*. Frankfurt: Peter Lang.

Fromkin, Victoria and Rodman, Robert 1993: *An Introduction to Language*. 5th edition. New York: Harcourt Brace.

Gardner-Chloros, Penelope 1991: *Language Selection and Switching in Strasbourg*. Oxford: Clarendon Press.

Girtler, Roland 1992: *Verbannt und vergessen. Eine untergehende deutschsprachige Kultur in Rumänien*. Linz: Veritas.

Glück, Helmut and Sauer, Wolfgang Werner 1990: *Gegenwartsdeutsch*. Stuttgart: Metzler.

Glück, Helmut and Sauer, Wolfgang Werner 1992: Man spricht Deutsch. German spoken. On parle allemand. Die deutsche Spracheinheit, von außen gesehen durch die inländische Brille. In R. Ulshöfer (ed.), *Der Deutschunterricht*, 44, 6, 16–27.

Glück, Helmut and Sauer, Wolfgang Werner 1995: Directions of change in contemporary German. In P. Stevenson (ed.), *The German Language and the Real World*. Oxford: OUP, pp. 95–117.

Green, W.A.I. 1990: The dialects of the Palatinate (*Das Pfälzische*). In C. Russ (ed.), *The Dialects of Modern German*. London: Routledge, pp. 241–64.

Hahn, Silke 1995a: 'Halbstarke', 'Hippies' und 'Hausbesetzer'. Die Sprache und das Bild der Jugend in der öffentlichen Betrachtung. In G. Stötzel and M. Wengeler (eds), *Kontroverse Begriffe*. Berlin: de Gruyter, pp. 211–44.

Hahn, Silke 1995b: Vom 'zerissenen Deutschland' zur 'vereinigten Republik'. Zur Sprachgeschichte der 'deutschen Frage'. In G. Stötzel and M. Wengeler (eds), *Kontroverse Begriffe*. Berlin: de Gruyter, pp. 285–354.

Hall, Christopher 1992: *Modern German Pronunciation*. Manchester: MUP.

Hauck, Werner 1993: Die Amtssprachen der Schweiz – Anspruch und Wirklichkeit. In J. Born and G. Stickel (eds), *Deutsch als Verkehrssprache in Europa*. Berlin: de Gruyter, pp. 147–63.

Henriksen, Carol and van der Auwera, Johan 1994: The Germanic languages. In E. König and J. van der Auwera (eds), *The Germanic Languages*. London: Routledge, pp. 1–18.

Hoffmann, Charlotte 1991: *An Introduction to Bilingualism*. London: Longman.

Hoffmann, Fernand 1996: Textual varieties of Lëtzebuergesch. In G. Newton (ed.), *Luxembourg and Lëtzebuergesch: Language and Communication at the Crossroads of Europe*. Oxford: OUP, pp. 217–50.

Holmes, Janet 1992: *An Introduction to Sociolinguistics*. London: Longman.

Hurford, James R. 1994: *Grammar: A Student's Guide*. Cambridge: CUP.

Jäger, Siegfried 1995: Political discourse: the language of Right and Left in Germany. In P. Stevenson (ed.), *The German Language and the Real World*. Oxford: OUP, pp. 231–57.

Jung, Matthias 1995: Amerikanismen, ausländische Wörter, Deutsch in der Welt. Sprachdiskussionen als Bewältigung der Vergangenheit und Gegenwart. In G. Stötzel and M. Wengeler (eds), *Kontroverse Begriffe*. Berlin: de Gruyter, pp. 245–84.

Keller, R.E. 1961: *German Dialects*. Manchester: MUP.

Keller, R.E. 1978: *The German Language*. London: Faber and Faber.

König, Christoph (ed.) 1995: *Germanistik in Mittel- und Osteuropa*. Berlin: de Gruyter.

König, Ekkehard and van der Auwera, Johan (eds) 1994: *The Germanic Languages*. London: Routledge.

König, Werner 1978: *Atlas der deutschen Sprache*. Munich: dtv.

Kürschner, Wilfried 1993: *Grammatisches Kompendium*. Tübingen/Basel: Francke.

Lebrun, Nathalie and Baetens Beardsmore, Hugo 1993: Trilingual education in the Grand Duchy of Luxembourg. In H. Baetens Beardsmore (ed.), *European Models of Bilingual Education*. Clevedon: Multilingual Matters, pp. 101–20.

Liddell, Peter 1995: *Germans in British Columbia*. University of British Columbia: IVG.

Linke, Angelika, Nussbaumer, Markus and Portmann, Paul R. 1994: *Studienbuch Linguistik*. Tübingen: Niemeyer.

Lodge, R. Anthony, Armstrong, Nigel, Ellis, Yvette and Shelton, Jane F. 1997: *Exploring the French Language*. Edward Arnold: London.

Löffler, Heinrich 1985: *Germanistische Soziolinguistik*. Berlin: Erich Schmidt Verlag.

MacCarthy, Peter 1975: *The Pronunciation of German*. Oxford: OUP.

Mackensen, Lutz 1971: *Die deutsche Sprache in unserer Zeit*. Heidelberg: Quelle & Meyer.

Mattheier, Klaus J. 1980: *Pragmatik und Soziologie der Dialekte*. Heidelberg: Quelle & Meyer.

Moelleken, Wolfgang W. 1983: Language maintenance and language shift in Pennsylvania German: a comparative investigation. *Monatshefte* 75, 2, 172–86.

Moosmüller, Sylvia 1995: Evaluation of language use in public discourse: language attitudes in Austria. In P. Stevenson (ed.), *The German Language and the Real World*. Oxford: OUP, pp. 257–78.

Muhr, Rudolf (ed.) 1993: *Internationale Arbeiten zum österreichischen Deutsch und seinen nachbarsprachlichen Bezügen*. Wien: Hölder-Pichler-Tempsky.

Muhr, Rudolf, Schrodt, Richard and Wiesinger, Peter (eds) 1995: *Österreichisches Deutsch. Linguistische, sozialpsychologische und sprachpolitische Aspekte einer nationalen Variante des Deutschen*. Wien: Hölder-Pichler-Tempsky.

Müller, Martin and Wertenschlag, Lukas 1994: *'Los emol'. Schweizerdeutsch verstehen*. Zürich: Langenscheidt.

Newton, Gerald 1987: The German language in Luxembourg. In C. Russ and C. Volkmar (eds), *Sprache und Gesellschaft in den deutschsprachigen Ländern.* Munich: Goethe Institut, pp. 153–79.

Newton, Gerald 1990: Central Franconian. In C. Russ (ed.), *The Dialects of Modern German.* London: Routledge, pp. 136–209.

Newton, Gerald (ed.) 1996: *Luxembourg and Lëtzebuergesch: Language and Communication at the Crossroads of Europe.* Oxford: OUP.

Oxford-Duden 1995: *German–English, English–German Dictionary.* Oxford: Clarendon Press.

Parkes, Stuart 1997: *Understanding Contemporary Germany.* London: Routledge.

Philipp, Marthe and Bothorel-Witz, Arlette 1990: Low Alemannic. In C. Russ (ed.), *The Dialects of Modern German.* London: Routledge, pp. 313–36.

Polenz, Peter von 1978: *Geschichte der deutschen Sprache.* Berlin: de Gruyter.

Pollak, Wolfgang 1992: *Was halten die Österreicher von ihrem Deutsch?* Wien: OGS.

Reiher, Ruth and Läzer, Rüdiger (eds) 1993: *Wer spricht das wahre Deutsch? Erkundungen zur Sprache im vereinigten Deutschland.* Berlin: Aufbau Taschenbuch Verlag.

Romaine, Suzanne 1994a: *Language in Society: An Introduction to Sociolinguistics.* Oxford: OUP.

Romaine, Suzanne 1994b: Germanic creoles. In E. König and J. van der Auwera (eds), *The Germanic Languages.* London: Routledge, pp. 566–603.

Rost-Roth, Martina 1995: Language in intercultural communication. In P. Stevenson (ed.), *The German Language and the Real World.* Oxford: OUP, pp. 169–204.

Rowley, A.R. 1987: Linguistic minorities in Central Europe – the South Tyroleans and the Burgenland Croats: a report on some recent comparative research. In C. Russ and C. Volkmar (eds), *Sprache und Gesellschaft in deutschsprachigen Ländern.* Munich: Goethe Institut, pp. 122–35.

Rowley, Anthony 1990: North Bavarian. In C. Russ (ed.), *The Dialects of Modern German.* London: Routledge, pp. 417–37.

Russ, Charles V.J. 1978: *Historical German Phonology and Morphology.* Oxford: OUP.

Russ, Charles V.J. 1987: Language and society in German Switzerland. Multilingualism, diglossia and variation. In C. Russ and C. Volkmar (eds), *Sprache und Gesellschaft in deutschsprachigen Ländern.* Munich: Goethe Institut, pp. 94–121.

Russ, Charles V.J. 1990a: *The Dialects of Modern German.* London: Routledge.

Russ, Charles V.J. 1990b: High Alemannic. In C. Russ (ed.), *The Dialects of Modern German.* London: Routledge, pp. 364–93.

Russ, Charles V.J. 1994: *The German Language Today.* London: Routledge.

Russ, Charles V.J. and Volkmar, Claudia (eds) 1987: *Sprache und Gesellschaft in deutschsprachigen Ländern.* Munich: Goethe Institut.

Salkie, Raphael 1995: *Text and Discourse Analysis.* London: Routledge.

Sauer, Wolfgang Werner and Glück, Helmut 1995: Norms and reforms: fixing the form of the language. In P. Stevenson (ed.), *The German Language and the Real World.* Oxford: OUP, pp. 69–94.

Saxalber, Annemarie and Lanthaler, Franz 1992: Zwischen innerer und äußerer Mehrsprachigkeit. Zum muttersprachlichen Unterricht in Südtirol. In R. Ulshöfer (eds), *Der Deutschunterricht*, 44, 6, 70–83.

Schlobinski, Peter 1995: 'Jugendsprachen': speech styles of youth subcultures. In P. Stevenson (ed.), *The German Language and the Real World*. Oxford: OUP, pp. 315–38.

Schmidt-Veitner, Claudia and Wieland, Regina 1995: *Grammatik aus Texten 1. Übungen zu Adjektiven, Nomen und Verben für die Mittelstufe*. Ismaning: Max Hueber Verlag.

Schönfeld, Helmut and Schlobinski, Peter 1995: After the Wall: social change and linguistic variation in Berlin. In P. Stevenson (ed.), *The German Language and the Real World*. Oxford: OUP, pp. 117–34.

Sieber, Peter 1992: Hochdeutsch in der Schweiz. In R. Ulshöfer (ed.), *Der Deutschunterricht*, 44, 6, 28–43.

Søndergaard, Bent 1993: The problem of pedagogy versus ideology: the case of a Danish–German bilingual school-type. In H. Baetens Beardsmore (ed.), *European Models of Bilingual Education*. Clevedon: Multilingual Matters, pp. 66–85.

Stedje, Astrid 1989: *Deutsche Sprache gestern und heute*. Munich: W. Fink Verlag.

Stevenson, Patrick (ed.) 1995: *The German Language and the Real World*. Oxford: OUP.

Stevenson, Patrick 1997: *The German-speaking World: A Practical Introduction to Sociolinguistic Issues*. London: Routledge.

Stötzel, Georg 1995: Der Nazi-Komplex. In G. Stötzel and M. Wengeler (eds), *Kontroverse Begriffe*. Berlin: de Gruyter, pp. 355–82.

Stötzel, Georg and Wengeler, Martin (eds) 1995: *Kontroverse Begriffe. Geschichte des öffentlichen Sprachgebrauchs in der Bundesrepublik Deutschland*. Berlin: de Gruyter.

Teubert, Wolfgang 1993: Sprachwandel und das Ende der DDR. In R. Reiher and R. Läzer (eds), *Wer spricht das wahre Deutsch?* Berlin: Aufbau Taschenbuch Verlag, pp. 28–54.

Thierse, Wolfgang 1993: 'Sprich, damit ich dich sehe' – Beobachtungen zum Verhältnis von Sprache und Politik in der DDR-Vergangenheit. In J. Born and G. Stickel (eds), *Deutsch als Verkehrssprache in Europa*. Berlin: de Gruyter, pp. 114–26.

Thomson, David 1966: *Europe since Napoleon*. Harmondsworth: Penguin.

Townson, Michael 1987: Language and politics – a case study of German fascism 1933–45. In C. Russ and C. Volkmar (eds), *Sprache und Gesellschaft in deutschsprachigen Ländern*. Munich: Goethe Institut, pp. 275–94.

Trask, R.L. 1994: *Language Change*. London: Routledge.

Trask, R.L. 1996: *A Dictionary of Phonetics and Phonology*. London: Routledge.

Ulshöfer, Robert (ed.) 1992: Deutsche Sprache – Einheit und Vielfalt. *Der Deutschunterricht* Jahrgang 44, Nr 6.

Van Ness, Silke 1994: Pennsylvania German. In König, E. and van der Auwera, J. (eds), *The Germanic Languages*. London: Routledge, pp. 420–38.

Vassberg, Liliane M. 1993: *Alsatian Acts of Identity*. Clevedon: Multilingual Matters.

Wahrig, Gerhard 1980: *Deutsches Wörterbuch*. Gütersloh: Mosaik Verlag.

Walker, Alastair 1987: Language and Society in Schleswig. In C. Russ and C. Volkmar (eds), *Sprache und Gesellschaft in deutschsprachigen Ländern*. Munich: Goethe Institut, pp. 136–52.

Walsh, M. O'C. 1974: *A Middle High German Reader*. Oxford: OUP.

Wardhaugh, Ronald 1986: *An Introduction to Sociolinguistics*. Oxford: Blackwell.

Wells, C.J. 1985: *German: A Linguistic History to 1945*. Oxford: Clarendon Press.

Wengeler, Martin 1995: Multikulturelle Gesellschaft oder Ausländer raus? Der sprachliche Umgang mit der Einwanderung seit 1945. In G. Stötzel and M. Wengeler (eds), *Kontroverse Begriffe*. Berlin: de Gruyter, pp. 711–46.

Wiesinger, Peter 1990: The Central and Southern Bavarian dialects in Bavaria and Austria. In C. Russ (ed.), *The Dialects of Modern German*. London: Routledge, pp. 438–519.

Wright, Laura and Hope, Jonathan 1996: *Stylistics: A Practical Coursebook*. London: Routledge.

Index

Terms are listed in English unless there is no suitable translation, e.g. for *Althochdeutsch*, see Old High German, but for *Auslautverhärtung* see *Auslautverhärtung*. Numbers in **bold** denote page numbers on which key terms are discussed.